APRIL AS

Duncan F
1948. He
lived in Ber
for a time e *Boulevard*
magazines. T ull-length book.

In order to survive the kind of hypocrisy sometimes displayed by otherwise tolerant people when faced with the subject of a sex change, a very resilient sense of humour is called for. This April Ashley has in abundance. This, her story, tells of a marvellous, joyful life, despite its harrowing obstacles – dashing and hilarious by turns, full of not just notable, but interesting people. Her book reflects tremendous wit and warmth, a great deal of wisdom and, most of all, generosity of spirit.

ARENA

Duncan Fallowell & April Ashley

APRIL ASHLEY'S ODYSSEY

ARENA

An Arena Book
Published by Arrow Books
17–21 Conway Street, London W1P 6JD

An imprint of the Hutchinson Publishing Group

London Melbourne Sydney Auckland
Johannesburg and agencies throughout
the world

First published Jonathan Cape 1982

Arena edition 1983

Photoset by Rowland Phototypesetting Ltd
Bury St Edmunds, Suffolk

Made and printed in Great Britain
by Guernsey Printing Company Ltd
Guernsey, Channel Islands

ISBN 0 09 931510 6

This book is dedicated to Rita Wallace and her children, David, Paul, Mandy and Phillip, and to the loving memories of Edward Madok and my father

A.A.

Contents

	Acknowledgments	viii
1	Liverpool	1
2	Sea	13
3	Madness	27
4	Paris	51
5	To the Wizard of Casablanca	73
6	Scandal	97
7	Spain	123
8	Rome	151
9	In Which I Meet Just About Everybody	175
10	Divorce	206
11	AD8	232
12	A Woman of Property	261
	Index	279

Acknowledgments

For their help and encouragement we should like to thank Mr Leo Abse, M.P.; Dr C. N. Armstrong; Sir John Dewhurst; Miss Wendy Fallowell; the directors of Furness Withy Ltd; Ms Jane Hill; the editor of the *Lancet*; Professor Ivor Mills; Miss Sarah Moffett; Mr Christopher Richardson; Mr Terry Walton; Miss Von Whiteman; and especially Mrs Pat Wigington.

For permission to reproduce photographs we are grateful to the following: David Bailey, 26; *Bristol Evening Post*, 6; *Daily Mail*, London, 21; Richard Dormer, 29; Roger Foucher-Créteau, 12; Granada Television Ltd, 1; Jean Kerby, 11; London Express News and Feature Services, 20, 28; Peter Ward, 27. In spite of every effort, it has proved impossible to trace Ken Walker (25 and front flap of jacket).

D. F. and A. A.

1 Liverpool

'And, darling . . . '

It was dear old Prince Max von Hohenlohe-Langenburg, fat and twinkly in his decorations, sitting on my left at a gala dinner in the south of Spain. The room glittered with crystal and silver, pineapples, lobsters and champagne. And the smart talk – what a row! One side of the room was a semi-circle of colonnaded windows through which jewelled figures slid out to the candlelit terrace and the beating of a band. I gave up toying with my truffles and let my gaze move across the breathless midnight Mediterranean lit up with yachts and beyond, way beyond, to the lights of Africa.

Max was leaning over me and looking downwards. 'And, darling, what colour – ?'

The Princess Bismarck came past our table on her sticks. Click-swoosh, click-swoosh, on her way to the lavatory. He managed to stand, sway, and bow. I laughed. She nodded from the crow's nest of her great height and proceeded fitfully through the wrong door.

'Darling, what – ?'

'Max, do spit it out!'

'Well, dear, I was wondering what colour your nipples are. Brown or pink?'

I smoothed my delicate bosom held by a band of ice-pink shantung and said, 'The palest, Max, pink.'

He took out a Corona and began to tremble, so violently that he set fire to one of his fingers, which was wet with brandy, and I had to light the cigar for him.

'Young cherries, sweet rosebuds, ah – you see that woman over there?' He indicated an American acquaintance who had inherited a large piece of Ohio and fled with it to Europe. 'Dried figs! Chewed up . . . but you, mmm, pink pips, my treasure, you are high-born I think.'

Angelic Max. Perfect manners. And quite wrong about my origins. Don Pedro tapped me on the shoulder from behind. 'May I have the pleasure?' he said. Don Pedro squeaked at the waist when he danced. But such a noble head. And we went off to Watutsi on the terrace.

High-born! How funny. I didn't know what a present was until my eleventh birthday.

'I've got a present for you,' Mother said. I gripped the table to steady myself and broke out in goose-pimples. 'But you can't have it until you get home from school.'

The bell clanged, I ran out of the gates, made a quick sign of the cross as I flew past the church. At home Mother was holding a brown-paper parcel. I took it breathing heavily. Out rolled a pair of grey socks.

Conceived one summer at the Fort Hotel (where my mother was a chambermaid) on the Isle of Man, I was born a boy in the Smithdown Road Hospital, Liverpool, on 29 April 1935. This birthday I share with Emperor Hirohito of Japan, which makes us Taureans like Fred Astaire, Catharine the Great, Shirley Temple and Hitler.

Next, Mother brought me home to a black dockland slum called Pitt Street and christened me George. You didn't get lower than Pitt Street. Even in those days the police patrolled it in pairs. If you moved at all it could only be up. And we did, very slightly. When I was a couple of years old the family was rehoused on a new council estate in Norris Green on the edge of town. Since the rest of Pitt Street moved with us, along with the equally notorious Scotland Road, the atmosphere continued to be full of fists.

51 Teynham Crescent had an outside lavatory and a bath full of coal. Families like ours stored coal in the bath to stop it being stolen. But we had the luxury of three bedrooms. The smallest was reserved for me alone because for the first fourteen years of my life I nervously wet the bed. As a punishment I would be locked in there without heat or light and told there were ghosts.

My parents were both Liverpudlians. Mother was born Ada Brown, a name I now use when attempting to travel incognito.

She, a Protestant, married my father, Frederick Jamieson, when she was sixteen. He was a Roman Catholic and so virtually she dropped one child a year: Roddy, Theresa, Freddie, Me, Ivor, Marjorie. Apart from us there were several who died at birth.

Being a middle child I never had new clothes. Just grey hand-me-downs, patched, darned, frayed, hanging off my scrawny frame. Even my clogs – then *de rigueur* among poor scouse kids – even these were hand-me-downs. I thought I should never see the end of those clogs coming down to me, hard wooden shells with a steel rim nailed on to the undersides. These rims were always falling off and had to be hammered back on, so one felt like a horse.

In her youth Mother was pretty and flirtatious, with fine brown hair and eyes and good teeth. She adored to go out dancing or 'jigging' as she called it. This was hardly ever since she was always pregnant. My first impression of her was that she didn't like me. There was so little between us that was physical. But she had a large heart for taking in strangers. Big blue-eyed Roddy, who went to sea when I was very young, was constantly bringing back strays. One was called Reggie Endicott, half-Indian, always laughing, fabulous-looking, who stayed with us for a long time and shook up the house by buying a gramophone and playing Frankie Lane records until the plaster cracked. An Australian, Bernie Cartmell, followed Roddy in through the door one day. He was skinny and floppy, all hands and feet. We called him 'the long streak of piss' and wondered when he would leave. And there was a Mexican girl, Beautiful Phyllis. Mother had gone out to the lavatory in the morning and found Phyllis in there asleep. In her arms was a baby covered with sores. Of course Mother took them both in. There were always processions through the house. Usually they slept where they fell.

Father was a cook in the Royal Navy and not often home. When he was, he would hand out bars of chocolate white with age and while we munched he would describe exotic seaports or indulge his passion for oysters washed down with Guinness. Father was as short as Mother, slightly built but good-looking, with strong dark eyes which I inherited and a heavenly, puckish smile. He was also a scoundrel, a heavy drinker and spent every penny on the booze. I was mad about him.

The house was always active, but I don't recall many other relations. My only living grandparent, Mother's mother, was so taken aback by the sound of the first air-raid siren that she had a heart attack and died on the spot. One of Father's brothers was said to own a Stradivarius, but we never saw it.

Father's irresponsibility meant that Mother had to work very hard to keep us alive. She heaved sacks of potatoes and boxes of oranges at a grocery shop and during the Second World War made bombs at the Fazakerly bomb factory. Because of the daily proximity of TNT, she lost much hair and all her teeth. Doris Paper, Mother's best friend from across the road, worked in the same establishment. They would go off together every day in their slacks and overalls, their hair knotted up in turbans. One morning in the factory Doris said, 'I feel all queer.' In fact she was burning up. TNT can do that to you. She and Mother were brought home in an ambulance. Mother made a pot of tea and Doris started yelling, 'I've got to go to the lav! I've got to go to the lav!' Ripping off all her clothes she ran out of the back door. Mother found her dead on the toilet seat.

I was a problem child. Apart from the bed-wetting, I was born with a severe calcium deficiency. This led to frequent accidents which left me unable to walk. On a poaching trip I fell off a twenty-foot wall on Lord Derby's estate, escaping from the gamekeepers who were trying to shoot me. The fall immobilised my legs for three months. Roddy and Freddie constructed a go-cart from an orange-box and old perambulator wheels so that I could be pulled around the neighbouring streets. It was always breaking down, or smashing into walls when they raced it. People kept finding me lying in roads, which irritated them after a while.

There were weekly calcium injections at the Alder Hay Children's Hospital. If I were out of action, Mother would have to carry me piggy-back. She could rest on the tram, then pick me up again and carry me to the hospital. These journeys were made in complete silence, with Mother's mouth set in an unnerving way.

Eating was another problem. I didn't take to it at all. We lived on a basic diet of brown-sauce sandwiches but Mother would bribe me to eat with chip butties, which I did like. Sometimes I stole beetroots from allotments and ate them raw, or carrots which I would clean by scraping them on a wall and share with my mongrel pointer Prince.

Roddy didn't bring back only people. He brought back the first bottle of Heinz Tomato Ketchup I ever saw. And the first post-war banana. It was cut into six pieces, one each. Such a bizarre taste. I spat mine out and haven't touched them since. And when I was seven years old, he brought back Prince. We adopted each other immediately. He would follow me to school and wait outside the gates until I reappeared. He followed me to the Saturday Morning Pictures at the Broadway Regal, running along behind the tramcar, and while I was inside enjoying my favourite series, *The Perils of Pauline*, he would sit patiently outside surveying the street. As the one whom nobody wanted in their gang, I always felt safe with Prince. His only vice was killing cats. He murdered about twenty of them before a great tom cured him with several nasty blows in the face.

Liverpool had twenty-three miles of docks, the largest dockland in the world at that time, and was bombed heavily during the war. When the siren blew at night, everyone was supposed to run into the Anderson shelter. These were made of corrugated iron and were to be buried in the garden and covered with earth. Ours wasn't. It was stuck out the back at a lopsided angle in a few inches of soil. There were three bunks on either side full of fleas and bugs. I detested going in there even more than into the single bedroom and if Father were home he would allow me to crouch close to him under the hedge while explosions shook the house and the sky over Liverpool turned red. But what I most remember is the smell of salt in his uniform.

My schooldays – such torture. Those nuns, those priests, those hopeless teachers, those disgusting children! Although he never went to church himself, Father insisted we were brought up as strict Catholics. I was sent to St Theresa's Primary School, a vicious and backward institution run by the clergy where one was forced to one's knees four times a day in prayer. It was very rough. We spent a great deal of time cleaning the floors with dusters tied to our clogs and if we were slow the nuns would rattle rulers between our knees. Knees were the big thing at St Theresa's.

On the whole my education consisted of learning how to run fast. I was the ultimate weed. My head looked far too large and this was emphasised by Mother's penchant for cutting my hair into a Henry V pudding bowl. If they weren't calling me Sissy they called me Chinky, and I was the target of school bullies. It was fortunate that after school the staff would inspect all the air-raid shelters because often they would discover me inside one, tied down to a bunk. It wasn't so dreadful being tied on one's back. But being tied face downwards left ugly red marks across one's cheeks from the bare bunk springs. Once a gang held me to the ground while several more jumped rapidly up and down on my feet. This meant another term missed, more piggy-back rides to hospital, and Roddy and Freddie wheeling me about in a box.

In an attempt to freshen up my life, Miss Filben – an eager young Canadian teacher with large expensive teeth – decided to make me class monitor with responsibility for distributing books. As I came by with the decomposing red textbooks (I can't remember what they were, Miss Filben never managed to get very far into instruction), the urchins lashed out with their iron-clad clogs. After a fortnight of being rendered black and blue by my privilege, I had had enough and the next time that breezy Canadian accent came lilting over the desks – 'The books please, Jamieson' – I froze. Miss Filben tried again. Nothing happened.

'Jamieson, will you *please hand out those* goddam *books*!' By now she was standing in front of me and sweating in a bright-yellow blouse. I was paralysed and she slapped me in the face. I slapped her back. We were all flabbergasted. Her pretty eyes filled with tears but I lost the job.

Anything else in the academic line? An essay: *What do you want to be when you grow up?* I wrote: 'I want to be a Film Star and live a lovely life.' It got me hooted to the back of the class. One was supposed to say 'train driver' or 'priest'.

Sport. 'Can you swim, boy?'

I'd never tried, so I said, 'Yes, sir.'

'Dive in then.'

I came up blue in the face and frantic but from that moment I swam. Eventually they awarded me a bronze medal for life-saving.

Vincent Patterson was my only friend at school. He was dark and pale like me but bigger. He didn't enjoy fighting but was good at it if somebody insisted. We were very religious together and decided not to swear. For such a place Vincent was exceptionally ethereal and he might well have become a priest. One day he went on an outing to Bromborough in Cheshire and drank from a polluted stream. Three days later he was dead.

I was thirteen years old, very shaken, and committed the mortal sin of missing Sunday Mass. During Confession the priest said, 'Why weren't you in church on Sunday?'

'I want to think about it, Father.'

'If you have to think about God you're damned for ever! Get out of this church!'

He had been among a group of priests I had seen drunk and cursing in their garden several weeks before, so I didn't feel unduly deprived. A by-product of my loss of faith was a loss of guilt over poaching. Thus cleansed, Prince and I caught rabbits with renewed zeal on the estates of Lord Sefton and Lord Derby. These were about half-an-hour's walk into the countryside from Norris Green, dreamy spots on a sunny afternoon, but the arrival of myxomatosis put an end to it.

Not long after Vincent's death, Mother had Father evicted from the house, which therefore ceased to be home for me too. Long voyages at sea, and when he was home getting plastered in pubs on rum with beer chasers, he would go Absent Without Leave. There would be fights, Father coming off worse. 'But, Ada love – .' Slap, slap, she'd go at him, then he would sit groggily in a corner waiting for the Military Police to come and take him away.

Besides, Mother was now getting on very well with Bernie Cartmell. After Father's eviction, she and Bernie lived as man and wife. Father was eventually invalided out of the Royal Navy with shrapnel wounds in his stomach and legs which refused to heal. He worked briefly as a bus driver, then tramped round Liverpool on a tiny pension.

Just before my fourteenth birthday I had another terrible shock. The school leaving age went up to fifteen. The most intelligent course of action was to ignore it – until the authorities threatened Mother with prosecution. One day the Headmaster came into the classroom. We stood up in uneasy silence. While talking to the teacher, he suddenly span round. 'Who was that whispering? It came from over there.' His long bony finger stretched towards me and I cowered.

'You! Come up here! You were whispering!'

'I wasn't, sir.'

'Don't lie!'

'I'm not lying, sir.'

'Don't argue!' And he began to strike me in the chest so hard that I fell over.

Hurt and angry, I yelled, 'You horrible man, I told you it wasn't me!' and ran home sobbing.

Mother was furious. 'Come along,' she said, 'I'll deal with him.'

When we arrived back at the classroom the Headmaster was in full flood on the evils of insubordination. Mother barged straight in. 'Did you knock my child to the ground?' She was puce, clenching her fists so hard that the knuckles were white. The Headmaster made the mistake of trying to patronise her.

'Don't you "My Good Woman" me! You bloody Roman Catholic, I'll kill you if you touch one of my kids again!'

'How dare you swear in my school!'

Mother decided to smack his face but since it was about two feet above her she was forced to jump. 'Swear'? She was jumping up and down, hitting him. 'I'll bloody well say what I damn well like, you silly bugger! I'm Protestant. I didn't want my kids brought up bloody Catholics anyway, I'm sick to death of them spendin' half their bloody life on their knees prayin'!' She slapped him again, grabbed my arm, and we left. The word went round about Raving Ada of Teynham Crescent and my final months at school were largely untroubled. What a hard life it is for mothers and headmasters in the slums.

If I have given the impression that home life and school life, though brutish, were continuous, I shall correct that now. From the age of ten I started moving out.

John and Edna Lundy ran a grocery shop in the old iron St John's Market (now demolished). John's brother was briefly engaged to my sister Theresa (goodness, the times Tess was 'engaged' as she called it). When I began to drift away from home it was towards them. They employed me as errand boy at their shop, which was famous for bacon. I hauled sides of it which were much larger than myself. Half-a-crown a day plus tips, 8 a.m. to 10 p.m., astonishing wealth for a ten-year-old. This was at weekends and during the holidays. Later, whenever I chose to ditch school, which was often every other day.

John was large, fair and given to mirth. 'Hullo, Nugget.' This was their special nickname for me. 'Another religious holiday? O.K., the bike's round the back, here's a list of deliveries.' Edna was dark, with buck teeth and a rich Devonshire accent which fascinated me. I tried to imitate it and in doing so fell between two stools, as far as accents go, so that later when I moved to London it became easy for me to speak with no accent at all. John and Edna turned into surrogate parents and I lived for long periods in their warm flat. For the first time I encountered wine and uncracked crockery and could sneak slugs of whisky from the bulbous cocktail cabinet with a musical cigarette-box on top.

Edna became pregnant, a business one vaguely understood in a creepy way. Something about it had been indicated to us at school via readings from the Bible, but on the whole the nuns and priests, celibate themselves, circumnavigated the problem by filing it *en bloc* under 'Sin' and trying to pass their sense of revulsion on to us. At home, where we were frightened even to put our arms round each other, the entire subject was taboo.

But one cannot live long in a town like Liverpool and remain ignorant of the facts of life. The red-light district in the port was Sodom and Gomorrah with flick-knives. From one's earliest memory the prostitutes were a city sight. It was said that if ever a virgin walked down Lime Street the lions outside St George's Hall would roar. Each Friday evening the girls would gather on Lime Street Station, wearing red lips and red shoes, to meet trains bringing in the G.I.s from Warrington for a dirty weekend. We would follow, making grabs at the sprays of chewing gum which went flying across the platform as the carriage doors crashed open. If any girlfriends were there to greet their beaux, the tarts would flay them with handbags: 'Piss off, ya lousy free fuck!'

When Edna became pregnant again and gave birth to a second daughter, I had to return to sleep at Teynham Crescent, obliged to run a gauntlet of catcalls and kicks from the tramstop to the front door. If this sounds melodramatic, be assured that scarcely a day passed when I was not subjected to some barbarism by the local tough boys, so that early on there was forced upon me a sense of my own uniqueness.

Thank God, through cutting so much school to work in the Market, I was rich. As a bonus John would push a bunch of tea coupons into my hand (rationing still prevailed). Everyone was mad for the thrill of an extra ¼lb. of tea and I sold them on the black market for a shilling each. With my wealth I bought Mother presents – scarves, stockings, cheap jewellery. 'I'll put them in my Bottom Drawer for a rainy day,' she would say. Weird.

After he was turned out of the house, Father would hang around the Market or the school gates and ask me for a few bob. I gave him what I had, knowing he would make for the nearest pub. When at the age of fourteen I made my first court appearance – Prince had returned to his old ways, been caught biting the head off a cat, and the outraged owners prosecuted me – I was able to pay the fine of ten shillings. Funnily enough, I hardly ever bought anything for myself.

Except shoes. The bliss of those first shoes. It was like walking in bed.

On leaving school I went to work for the Lundys full-time, one of the fortunate ones with a job to go to. My hair gew out of its embarrassing pudding bowl and, with all the bicycling, I developed slight roses in my cheeks. I came to work one morning, put on my white coat and was about to nip under the counter to collect the orders, when Edna said, 'Why, Nugget, you're quite beautiful.' A momentary dizziness. Physical references to myself always made me feel ill. I assumed I was ugly, a belief most others seemed happy to confirm.

Later I checked up in the mirror. Thin and stunted for my age. Teeth crooked. Eyes dark, greenish brown, eyelashes very long and eyebrows finely arched. This part of my face was always held in a deep frown, except when it lifted into bewilderment. No spots – I never went through that ordeal. A bit of red in an otherwise gruesome pallor. Thick black hair. So what was new?

Soon after, returning from the Pierhead on the No. 14 tram with Jo, a neighbour from Norris Green, I dozed off. Unexpectedly he knocked me in the ribs. 'Are we there?' I asked.

'No, but you fockin' wake up, you look like a fockin' woman when you're asleep.'

At fifteen I had no facial or pubic hair, my voice hadn't broken, I was not overwhelmed by sexual desire, and I hadn't shot up. In comparison many of my contemporaries were hulking brutes covered with fluff. Although I neither wanted to play with dolls nor dress up in Mother's clothes, I was constantly taunted for being like a girl and yes, I wanted to be one. Until my loss of faith I would have long conversations with God each night, asking Him to make me wake up normal, wake up a girl, wake up whatever it was proper for me to be. Instinctively, without knowing why, we all knew me to be a misfit.

Therefore I decided to take myself in hand. It was no longer any good wanting to be a girl. I wanted to be a man. When nobody was around I croaked away in the lower registers until my voice was forcibly broken or at least roughened up. I couldn't speak for five days and the Indian doctor told Mother I had 'done something mental' to my voice. Far more important, I privately determined to go to sea. All the other men in my family did, even little Ivor in the end. It seemed to be one of the things that made you a man.

My grocery deliveries took me to the smartest districts of Liverpool. Since these were a long way from the town centre, I would be given cups of tea when I arrived. One of my favourite destinations was the house of Mrs Rossiter. To me she was a creature from outer space, with her hair-dos and long fingernails, her Tradesmen's Entrance and sprinkler on the lawn. Mr Rossiter was an important man with Cunard and when I confided in his wife she arranged for him to interview me in the Cunard Building itself.

'But you are much too young to go to sea,' he said.

I was fifteen and looked about eleven years old. 'But I'm not too young to go to training school, am I?'

He gave me a magnificent letter of introduction on embossed Cunard paper. It cut through all the red tape such as medical tests and parental consent, which was a boon because I had told none of my family or friends about this – not even John and Edna who were more important than anyone – in case they raised obstructions.

The night before departure I came home from work and said, 'Mum, I'm leaving tomorrow to join a cadet ship.'

'Well, isn't that somethin',' she said and carried on cooking Bernie's chips.

On a damp November morning I found myself at Lime Street Station with a small brown cardboard suitcase, waiting for the train to Bristol and the cadet ship S.S. *Vindicatrix*. My only personal memento – rosary beads. How superstition sticks!

The course was very intense – six weeks long.

'What are these, sir?'

'Knots!'

'What the bloody hell,' I thought. Knots. I never could do them. I did bows instead.

The first three weeks were spent in nissen huts. There were about two dozen of us. We were issued with blue serge trousers and a boiler jacket, thick woolly socks, square-bashing boots and a beret to be worn at a jaunty angle. There were no fittings. Everything simply came at you out of a big cupboard. All mine were far too large. I looked like a vaudeville act.

Up before dawn, ablutions, tidy the bed and locker, polish buttons and boots, clean the washroom, marching, breakfast, formal classes, lunch, potato-peeling and floor-scrubbing, physical jerks, dinner, lights out at 9 p.m. There was no time for conversation.

The second three weeks were more romantic. We moved on to the S.S. *Vindicatrix* herself, a three-masted hulk slurping up and down alongside the River Severn, where one was taught the practical skills of seamanship. I dashed up the rigging, out along the yard, and shouted 'Land ahoy!' with both lungs.

'Come *down*, Jamieson. We're putting you in charge of the yacht.'

The 'yacht' was an old cabin-cruiser used for navigation lessons. The Captain shouted 'Nor' Nor' East!' and I – straight as a matchstick behind the wheel – had to reply 'Nor' Nor' East, sir!' and turn the 'yacht' in that direction. Every order on the Bridge had to be repeated to ensure there were no errors of communication. At night we fell asleep exhausted, soothed by the creaking of the ship and the sound of water. I loved it all, especially this new experience 'companionship', even when the others bragged about girls and I went peculiar inside. My only reservation was in having to occupy a bunk when most of the class were swinging glamorously in hammocks.

Shore leave came at Christmas but those unable to afford the fare home were allowed to stay on board. It promised to be glum until an extravagant food parcel arrived from John and Edna. Included was a huge fruit cake. I cut myself a slice and passed the rest on. In return, back came a hunk of haggis which I tasted for the first time and found not unpalatable. We shared everything, cracked jokes, and in the evening ambled over to the Mission House where the tea ladies in flimsy paper hats made a sense of occasion out of lemonade and buns. On Boxing Day three of us slipped away to the Bristol pubs and got tiddly: strictly against the rules and therefore essential to do. It was the most delightful Christmas I've ever had. By and large I loathe Christmas, bolt the doors, and watch television until it goes away.

My final report was creditable, apart from knots, which were disastrous. We signed each other's group photograph, pledged eternal friendship, vowed to meet up in Cairo or Rio or Tokyo, and all went home.

A few months later a young man called Colin Shipley, who was a ship's carpenter and yet another of Theresa's fiancés, said, 'There's a place going on my ship for a deck-boy. If you want it.' The next day I picked up my cardboard suitcase, opened the front door of Teynham Crescent, took a deep breath of air, coughed, and set off on the road to Manchester to join the S.S. *Pacific Fortune*.

2 Sea

That was a fast start to life. It slowed up for a moment when on a cold February night in 1952 I found myself with Colin at the entrance to the vast blackness of Manchester docks. In fact my heart almost stopped. It was so dreadfully silent – apart from the squeaking of rats and the ominous ripple of unseen water. Black lines of cranes and sheds fell away into pools of ink. It started to sleet again, softening the smell of resin and old fibre.

A policeman checked our papers from his little sentry-box and let us pass. Colin walked ahead. I screwed up my eyes, stuck my head forward, and stumbled after him into the murk, trying to avoid coils of rope and long cables mooring dead ships to the wharfside. Suddenly the black hull of the *Pacific Fortune* hung over us. Except for half-a-dozen hurricane lamps the ship was in darkness. The sailors were ashore. I followed Colin up the gangplank.

At the top a man stepped out from the shadows. He was about fifty and cube-shaped. Swinging me into the lamplight he looked me up and down, then said over his shoulder in a thick Glaswegian accent, 'Och, Colin, I thought we was gettin' a laddie!' and chuckled. This was Mr Macdonald, my boss, the Bo's'n.

We crossed the deck, went down the gangway, flicked on a light, along passages, down again, along more passages, down, down, to the aft of the ship where the sea crew had their quarters. An iron door was opened and I was shown into a small cabin.

'You'll be all right here. Danny will be back soon – he'll explain everything. Have you eaten? Good. Sign the list tomorrow at 9 a.m. Welcome aboard, laddie.' And the Bo's'n took Colin off for a drink.

There were three bunks in the cabin. The two lower ones had already been taken. I clambered up into mine and sat there nervously swinging my legs.

An hour later the door opened and Danny came in. He was about nineteen or twenty, skinny with an unexpectedly studious air. Danny had a crisp tongue which I later discovered enabled him to hold his own among the bigger, rougher sailors. Robby, a junior like myself but a couple of years older, followed. Robby was amiable enough but overweight and afflicted with boils and indelicate odours. I was the youngest crew member, the only one who had never before been to sea.

Danny showed me where to hang up my toothbrush, all that sort of thing, and said, 'I'm bollocked so it's lights out.' There was no doubt who wore the trousers in our cabin. 'Besides, you should try and get a good night's sleep, you'll need it.' Lying up in the bunk, heartbeat unnaturally loud in my ears, listening to the creaking of the decks, trying to decide whether I should have packed my rosary beads . . . but eventually I faded out.

Suddenly there was a rumpus outside the door. Drunken sailors crashing back from the bars, a sound which was to panic me often in the future. The door sprang open and a light went on. Three young mariners were hooting round the cabin. They weaved across to my bunk and started to tug at the bedclothes. The ringleader, a heavy leathery crewman about twenty-five years old, was bellowing in a Scots slum voice, 'C'mon, let's have a look! Ooh, 'e's wearing pyjamas!' I held on tight and kicked. Danny was shouting, 'Fuck off, Jock! We want our sleep if you want your breakfast!' A group of older crewmen turned up to investigate the noise and they restored order. Robby was giggling uneasily and playing with a boil on his neck.

'Are they always like that?' I wanted to say to Danny, but my mouth had gone so dry that the lips stuck to the teeth.

'They're O.K. really, they're just pissed,' he said, turned over, and fell asleep in seconds.

Clang!!! The alarm shook me rigid. 5.30 a.m. Robby was already pulling on his trousers and saying, 'Get a move on, we've got to get the mess going before the sailors turn up, I'll show you the routine.' I soon realised that one's status on board advanced with the hour one was permitted to rise. We were the first up.

Robby led the way along brilliant red decks and into the sailors' mess, which was spotless and had to be kept that way by us. He showed me how to make the tea, set the table for the crew, trot along – everything was done at a trot – to the Petty Officers' Mess and set it up for the Bo's'n, Colin and the Ship's Electrician (known as 'Sparks'), then along more corridors to meet Chief Ship's Cook Heywood who resembled a barrel of lard. His face opened in a grin and he said, 'Well I'll be blowed, whatever next!'

The stewards were now coming out of their cabins. They lived amidships with their own mess and waited on the officers and passengers. There was a sharp distinction between the sea crew, who actually moved the vessel, and the stewards, who provided service for the elect. The sailors dismissed them as a 'bunch of fairies'. Most of the stewards were English and all the sailors seemed to be Scotsmen called Jock, coarse-grained types yet good at heart. The passengers were even further away, somewhere in heaven – the *Pacific Fortune* was a 9,400 ton freighter carrying general cargo but with room for a dozen or so banana-boat travellers. One never saw them unless 'scruberising' their decks or painting the scuppers where the water ran off. Captain Perry one saw only when he chose to make the ship's round like Matron in a hospital. 'Settling in all right?' he asked with a smile, and passed on without waiting for a reply.

Having been introduced to the hot, steaming galley it was time to trot back to the sailors' mess to clear up the tea and ashtrays. The crew would work until about 8 a.m., when we would serve them breakfast. Afterwards Robby and I had to dash away to serve the Petty Officers. Colin said I had a choice – to call the Bo's'n 'Sir' or 'Bo's'n'. I chose the latter because it sounded so nautical. When all this had been set in motion one was permitted to eat too, for about five minutes, before the clearing up had to be done.

My duties were divided into one week in the mess, one week on deck, plus serving tea and breakfast daily. £10 per week and a monthly allowance of £3. Mess duty was no joy. Waiting on the sailors, cleaning out their quarters, scrubbing floors, polishing brass, waxing teak, lunch, tea – after which many of the sailors would finish for the day – dinner, collapse. Our part of the ship was usually silent by 9 p.m. while the passengers at the other end would be chatting somewhere between the cabinet pudding and the brandy. Scrubbing in the fresh air is more entertaining than scrubbing in the bowels so I preferred deck work, especially when entering or leaving a port. My overseer on deck was a taciturn Scot. I can't remember his name but presume it was Jock. Since he had no regard for words I learnt as I went along.

The first voyage began. The stevedores came on duty and cast us off at dawn. Winding the steel hawsers on to the bollards made my palms bleed. Jock said, 'Put these on', and my hands disappeared up to the elbows in deck gloves. But I lost some of my excruciating shyness and began asking questions which Jock ignored with a friendly smile.

From Manchester along the Ship Canal and out into the River Mersey takes a day of complicated manoeuvres. At Liverpool the ship floated past the green bronze birds on top of the Liver Building. Father said that if one saw them flapping it was a premonition of tragedy at sea.

First week out of port: passed quickly, everything so new, porpoises raced the ship, a white clipper in full sail passed by. In the mornings I ran up to the fo'c's'lehead to retrieve the flying fish which had inadvertently suicided there. First come, first served, delicious for breakfast. And at the end of the day, while the crew were gambling or unwinding in their bunks, I climbed to a secret place on the poop deck and sat on a pile of ropes in my oilskin. Out in the Atlantic after dark the world is eerily bright. I wondered many things – and especially: what on earth am I doing on a poop deck with raw hands?

Ten days out: the weather much warmer. The sailors began to take off their clothes, which was very disconcerting. I clung on to my jumper and black trousers. We worked without shoes or socks unless the steel decks became too hot. We put up a canvas swimming-pool for the passengers.

About two weeks out: I was running along the deck in the early morning when a remarkable smell hit me. The relentlessness of salt had abated, and a heavy scent was in the air. Even the old hands were growing frolicsome on it. Eight hours later – land! On the horizon a low green island wobbled between the blue water and the sky. Haiti. My first palm trees. I had never been anywhere in my entire life and now – whack! Palm trees! Haiti! I kept rushing the sides of the ship and shouting, 'Can't we get off now?' But we cruised on through the Windward Passage, for our port was Kingston, Jamaica.

The ship rode at anchor all day in the Bay of Kingston, waiting for a berth. I asked if we might swim ashore like the sailors do in films with a Polynesian setting. Cook Heywood said, 'Ever seen sharks, laddie?'

I had seen only the fin of one following the ship. An old salt had become very agitated. Apparently the saying goes: aarr, if a shark do follow your ship for three days it do portend a death on board. Ours disappeared on the second night and the old salt lived to sleep again.

Cook Heywood picked up a bucket of bones and offal and tipped it over the side. At once, and I mean *at once*, the water convulsed in paroxysms of pink foam and teeth. It was absolutely mesmerising.

'And be careful when you're ashore,' said Cook. 'It's a popular form of burial hereabouts.'

At about six in the evening we upped anchor and sailed into harbour. The ship was overrun by hawkers in jazzy clothes with whom the crew bartered furiously. Last to arrive was a black woman of enormous size. She wore a peppermint-green blouse which couldn't have been cut lower, a blue skirt daubed with flowers, and a flamingo scarf tied round her head. She flapped on board in sandals. Actually, she sashayed. When she moved *everything* moved because she wore no undergarments. 'Hiya, boys,' she drawled on reaching the top of the gangplank, wheezing and patting beads of moisture from her throat with a hankie.

This was Cynthia, the washerwoman, who had come to take the sailors' laundry ashore. Obviously she was very popular and knew all the men by name. 'Oh!' she boomed, 'I's sure gonna take care ob dis lil baby.' Two black arms heavily laden with flesh cut out the light and I disappeared into a chest which sported the most tremendous pair of breasts I had seen in my life. They were phenomenal, and running down them was an unstoppable exudation of sweat. I emerged damp and red with the promise that 'One night, darlin, I's gonna show you der reeeel Kingston.'

Colin, whose uncle was the Chief of Police, had been invited to a starchy garden party in the grounds of Government House and he took me along. The ladies wore Army & Navy Stores frocks and white gloves, and the gentlemen white dinner-jackets frayed at the cuffs. They looked incongruous, seedy even, in that tropical landscape.

Officially the party was in honour of a Royal Navy battleship anchored in the bay. A group of young matelots moved towards me and I overheard 'Look at that skin!' which is naval slang for 'That's a bit of all right!' They were flirting and asked me what I drank. Only minutes before, I had discovered Coca-Cola, an invention of genius. So Coca-Colas started to arrive. 'This is the life!' I thought, taking in the view with a sweep, then everything went round and I fell over. For the first but not the last time I was horribly sozzled. They had fixed the Cokes with rum.

The next morning I made another discovery. My first hangover. Double agony, because our cabin was at the bottom of the ship, just over the screws, where the heat is at its most aggressive. True, there was a porthole. But this could not be opened in harbour because of rats. In fact it couldn't be opened at sea either because we should have been drowned. But when Cynthia, smoking a cigar, turned up to take me along the Kingston Waterfront, I knew exactly what to order. In and out of the little wooden bars we went, where three-piece tin-can bands make the sound of thirty, and smiles leer at you out of clouds of marijuana smoke – eventually I ordered so many rum and Cokes that I went quite off them.

Next stop: Cristóbal, where South America begins. We went ashore across a solid red carpet of cockroaches the size of sparrows. With every footstep along the wharf there was a ghastly crunch like the cracking of wood, followed by a sickening yellow ooze up around one's pumps.

The Panama Canal: the middle of it is a bayou, a steaming stretch of swampy water strung with liana and full of flying creatures straight from Jules Verne. Here the issue of salt tablets was added to my chores. I hardly needed them myself, being a salt addict. Salt over everything, even over anchovies, even today when I'm supposed to be on a sodium-restricted diet.

Sliding out of the Canal into the boundless blue clarity of the Pacific Ocean, we almost bumped into a whale. 'Slow,' shouted the Officer. The idea was to avoid ramming it. The whale rose out of the sea like a cathedral, waved and gracefully disappeared. This went on for twelve hours because the animal had adopted our ship as a playmate. If you ram them you drive right into a mass of blubber and it sticks, forcing the ship to put into port to have the corpse removed.

The first call on the Pacific Coast was San Pedro/Long Beach, where I stocked up on short-sleeved Californian shirts splashed with cacti, Red Indians and film stars, then three days in San Francisco which the sailors said was *la grande volupté* of the run.

Usually I wouldn't press myself on Danny and Robby when

ashore. In public they were embarrassed by my effeminacy, I think. But the older sailors didn't give a damn. They were amused by the sight of a young thing groping pathetically into the mysteries of alcohol and adult life. But in San Francisco all the sailors had their special banging parlours to visit, so I went into the city alone. From the docks I caught the bus uptown past the gingerbread houses to Union Square where you have to press your face against the bus windows to see the tops of the skyscrapers. I gravitated towards Chinatown. We had one in Liverpool but San Francisco's exploded all over me in a dazzle of Chinese neon. Too young to enter the bars, I walked agog for hours and hours and formed a lifelong friendship with the American hamburger. After the lights, the most noticeable feature of the district was the number of drunks vomiting in doorways.

Then it went very quiet. It must have been the early hours of the morning. I had to return to ship and grew apprehensive between Fisherman's Wharf and dockland. No bright lights here. Out of the gloom, wailing and flashing, a cop car flew at me. Two uniformed immensities jumped out, an entire hardware store hanging from their belts. I hadn't known there could be so many different instruments of persuasion. Hands up, against the wall, frisk; I knew the routine from James Cagney.

'How old are you, kid?'

'Sixteen, sir.'

'Well, at least the kid don't lie.'

It seemed to be an offence in California for anyone under twenty-one to be out so late. They clanked around for a few minutes, checking my papers, expressing surprise at my being at sea 'aweady', and told me to hop in. I was treated to a motor tour of the city before being dropped back at the ship. Their surprise returned when I shook hands and said thank you. Americans, I've since realised, are always impressed by civility. They don't quite know how to cope with it. If ever you find yourself the victim of aggression in the U.S.A., simply say 'I'm awfully sorry' or something like that and they'll blink and fall into the palm of your hand.

As we sailed out under the Golden Gate Bridge I very much hoped Seattle would be as stimulating – one was so inexperienced. But we did see a body float by with a bullet through its head, so even Seattle must have its moments.

Canada. Brrr! And quiet. Our northernmost call was Woodfibre, an isolated lumberjack settlement with one coffee bar, where, surprise, we took on timber. It was in Canada that I gave my first interview. Colin had something to do with it because the radio people were allowed to come on board. They introduced me to the listeners as 'the youngest person to go to sea since child labour was abolished'.

Now the voyage reversed itself.

Haiti was on the horizon for a while.

My seventeeth birthday came and went like a piece of flotsam.

Then only the sea.

Whenever I could I retreated to my secret place on the poop deck. While we were in and out of port, everybody had plenty to occupy his attention but now, back in the small claustrophobic world of a ship in mid-Atlantic, my anxieties proliferated.

At meal times the sailors flaunted their sexual conquests, while I sat in silence and became increasingly choked. With all the toil I should have been developing male muscles but I remained puppyish. Most of the men showered in the evening after work. Always secretive about bathing, I was now so ashamed of my body that I crept out to shower in the middle of the night so that no one would see me unclothed. My behaviour of course only made them more curious. It was always a huge relief when the weather changed to wind and rain, so that everyone was covered in oilskins and there was no pressure for me to take off my top. I was phobic about anyone seeing my chest. Instead of the hard pectoral muscles which all the other sailors loved to display as one of the bonuses of physical labour, there was a pulpiness around my nipples which I took to be rudimentary breasts.

The ragging of that first night was repeated, usually at the instigation of the same young bullying Jock who now frightened me very much. There was always a great commotion. 'Silly fuck' this. 'Sod off' that. Objectively nothing catastrophic happened – a few bruises in the scuffles – and the older men prevented matters getting out of hand. But it made me wretched. Sometimes they blew kisses and said 'Hullo, ducks' or 'girlie'. They would wink, slap my bottom, slip an arm round my waist. What was one supposed to do back? All my wires were tangled up inside because, you see, I was excited by it as well as afraid. Had I been among the stewards, possibly it would have been easier. But I was at the Men's End of the ship, in the throes of a profound identity crisis brought on by puberty but not explained by it (I never completed the proper physical cycle of male adolescence). Why did I have this curvaceous body?

After three months of voyaging, the ship was in a filthy condition. It returned via Antwerp and London to Manchester where one went through the ritual of being paid off (the balance of my wages came to £19. 13*s*. 3*d*). If one wasn't asked to join up again all the fears about not being good enough were confirmed. 'Will you be making another trip with us?' asked the Bo's'n. I had made the grade as far as they were concerned. 'And your monthly pay goes up to £4.'

There were a few weeks' leave so, carrying scent, lace, American groceries, holiday shirts and strings of abalone shells, I went off to put my lightly weatherbeaten face round the door in Teynham Crescent. 'Oh, thanks,' they said when I flung forth my treasures, and then withdrew back into themselves. I couldn't wait to return to the ship.

When I did, it was a comfort to see that the seamen were by and large the same as on the first voyage. At least I knew where I stood with them. And one – tall, too handsome, blond, a friend of the young bully – thrilled me strangely. This could not be openly admitted, especially not to myself, but nor could it be disregarded because I went groggy every time we met.

Half-way along the Ship Canal my overseer knocked me to the deck with one clout. A whirring noise passed overhead, terminated by a violent whipcrack. One of the hawsers securing the ship in the lock had snapped and would have gone through me like a wire through butter. It wasn't a good start. Passing out into the Mersey I scrutinised the Liver Birds. A light flashed from them but did they move? Or was my mind wandering?

Life on board settled down to its jittery routine. One of the stewards I met in the galley presented himself as a suitor but I didn't respond, having adopted the condescension of the sailors with regard to these lesser mortals. Besides, the rejection of all advances had become automatic. Touching people is a very healthy activity. The absence of it made me morbidly sensitive. Nor could I accept my feeling for the Blond Sailor who caused such an upheaval in my prudish breast. I stared at him working on deck. He would look up, wink, and I'd turn away hot and confused. I was convinced a monstrous mistake had been made and only my being a woman would correct it. There were no fantasies about dressing in such and such a way. I merely wanted to be whole.

One night the Blond Sailor opened my cabin door, unbuttoned his shirt and started to kiss me. Two of his friends burst in to see how far he'd got. The Blond Sailor laughed and went off with them. But I was engulfed by shame and driven closer still to paranoia.

In Kingston Cynthia said, 'Why, honey, you sure is gettin' prettier every time I sees yooo.' She calmed me. Cynthia, all Earth Mother and soothing powers. Yet really she could do no more than she already did. Which was my washing, free of charge.

Colin took me up into the Blue Mountains for a drink. We sat on a terrace overlooking a misty valley. The alcohol churned and threw up the conviction that not only should I never be normal but that instead of getting better it was going to get worse (which it did). I experienced an acute attack of panic which suddenly began to break me up from within, the eruption of intolerable pressures, and a compulsion to jump. Reason played no part in it. The compulsion emanated directly from the body.

'Come on, it's time to get back,' said Colin and the brainstorm cleared, leaving me debilitated and depressed.

As we sailed for the Panama Canal on a calm sea I began to vomit from nerves and tried to pass it off as seasickness. The Blond Sailor knew he had broken down my reserve. He appeared to swagger with extra self-assurance. The battle raged on inside me.

In the Pacific the Bo's'n began to realise I was in a pretty bad way. He gave me work which was either alone or with older men but he couldn't isolate me. Knots, always my torture, now I had them in chest, stomach and head and they were getting tighter and tighter.

The sailors must have thought me a very odd kettle of fish. I was over-polite with them through fear of involvement. Physically I had deteriorated, eating little, working feverishly in an attempt to block my thoughts – so much so that the Bo's'n took me aside and told me to take it easy. But I was under excessive emotional strain. The upshot was that, walking down the street in San Pedro, I saw a sign saying 'Doctor' and went in.

After an initial reticence I burst, ending up with 'I want to be a woman!'

'That's insane! . . . I mean, you'll grow out of it.' Which is what they were all to say.

He gave me two sorts of pills, anti-depressant amphetamines and barbiturate sleepers, and told me to visit a psychiatrist as soon as I arrived back in England. He added that he would waive his fee.

Well, I hadn't a clue what a psychiatrist was. It was a new word. The amphetamines shrivelled up what remained of my appetite and shredded what remained of my nerves. The sleeping pills made me dizzier than I already was. By the time we reached Los Angeles I was totally screwed up.

After clearing away the dinner I stayed on board and when my two cabin mates returned I pretended to be asleep. At about 3 a.m. there was a hoo-ha outside the door. It banged open. Panic! They were laughing and stank of drink. I fought like a tiger. As usual the old men broke it up and I was left on the floor with a nosebleed. Later I relaxed sufficiently to weep. But I'd had enough. My mind went cool and I decided to kill myself. On this resolve I fell sound asleep for the first time in weeks.

Next day I worked dispassionately through the schedule and after the last job, which was to clear up when Colin, Sparks and the Bo's'n had dined, I shut myself in the Petty Officers' Mess. No one would return there until the following day. Picture me looking androgynous under a mop of black hair, with a tall glass of water on my right and on a tabletop to my left two piles of pills, one pink, one yellow. It was common knowledge that the way to kill oneself was to swallow an overdose of pills. But which ones? To hedge my bets I decided to swallow both, first a pink, then a yellow, then a pink, then a yellow, until they had all gone. I'd got half-way through when I began to shake, tingle and sweat. My vision flashed on and off. It went into black and white. My final thought was 'This is wrong but so is everything else I do – hope Mum forgives me.' The last thing I remember was falling off a chair.

Strange to say, I didn't blame the sailors. They didn't mean to be unkind and were only being their raunchy selves. Certainly if they'd realised what was really happening they would have done anything to make life easier. But there was no way of getting it across. How could they be expected to understand what I couldn't understand myself? Actually their attempts to make contact with me, however rough and ready, were in fact an example not of their meanness but of their generosity of spirit. Sea people are wonderfully generous. They have simplicity and depth because dealing with the elements is their business. And because of this simplicity they are also touched by romance. I have always admired and loved them. Later on, when I became well-known, I received many letters from sailors and from whole messes.

> 6 Mess, H.M.S. *Crossbow*. Dear Miss Ashley – When you first appeared in the papers we have been collecting your photos and pinning them on our locker doors. Not long ago we decided to form a fan club and all the Mess wholeheartedly agreed. We thought that if you could send us a few autographed pictures . . .

> D4 Mess, H.M.S. *Excellent*, Monday Tot Time. Dear Miss Ashley – It is with hearts full of hope that we write this our first letter to you, an ex-mariner and now a beautiful woman. In our mess deck we have forty-one pin-ups of various young, good-looking women but nowhere among these can be found one such as you. We would willingly tear these down if we could replace them with portraits of yourself . . . We write this letter in the belief that you will treat it as a sincere one, and it is you know. Yours hopefully, Able Seamen Grimwood, Gwent, Sheppard.

> The Lads, H.M.S. *Battleaxe*. Dear Miss Ashley – I wish to thank you on behalf of all the lads for the photographs you very kindly sent. They now occupy a place of honour in the mess, where no matter where we look we can see them, not that we would want it any other way . . . Take good care of yourself and the very best of luck and happiness in all you do. Sincerely yours, A. B. Derek Herron.

Sirens rang in my head. I came to and passed out, over and over again. On the third day I came to and managed to focus on the cheerful face of a middle-aged American nurse in a pale-blue and white uniform. And I was furious!

How stupid to have bungled it – Colin had found me after all and Furness Withy had transplanted me, 8 August 1952, to this David Hockney interior in the Seaside Memorial Hospital, Long Beach, California.

The nurse was saying, 'Oh darling, you've got your whole life in front of you, how can you be so silly, it's a wonderful, *wonderful* world!'

Such rot, but I took to her immediately. She gave me something outlandish to eat called an avocado pear. It was divine. The pear was followed by a priest, blue-eyed American-Irish with a spine-chilling smile. He prefaced all his remarks with 'my child', which drove me up the wall. Eventually I had to say, 'Will you *please* leave me alone!' And when he'd closed the door behind him I tucked into the other half of the avocado.

A faintly embarrassed representative of Furness Withy said that the *Pacific Fortune* had left and I should not be allowed to rejoin it. I must say, Furness Withy's conduct was exemplary through all this. But paradoxically the news saddened me. Despite everything the ship was my only home and contained my only friends. He added that I was being transferred to the Seamen's Mission, San Pedro, to convalesce and should be issued with meal vouchers to the value of three dollars per day. These could be cashed in unofficially so there was pocket money for bus rides out to the beach. The local Samaritans from the Norwegian Seamen's Church introduced me to teenage American voluntary workers who took me to Hollywood, to ball games, to the desert, to the Biggest Big Dipper in the World. With their help my toehold on life returned amazingly quickly. One is so pliable when young. One snaps back.

After months of playing around, I was told without warning to pack my bags for a midnight flight to New York City. I'd never been up before and was treated like God.

The New York mission was grim and in a sinister part of town. Again I managed to cash in my vouchers, lived on hamburgers, hot dogs and french fries, and went into the head of the Statue of Liberty (the arm was closed). The representative told me to pack again. I was on stand-by for the S.S. *America*, which held the Blue Riband for the fastest Atlantic crossing. It was a case of having to take whatever berth was going. This turned out to be a luxury stateroom on U deck with yards and yards of panoramic windows. The menu was an astonishment. Here began my love affair with caviare but I baulked at using the First Class dining-room because my trousers were ragged and my thin freezing Californian shirts frayed to death. However this get-up was perfect for the fancy-dress ball on the last night at sea. I went as Robinson Crusoe. The ship dropped a few passengers at Cóbh on the Irish coast then docked at Southampton.

Another Furness Withy rep met me, with a train ticket to Liverpool plus the balance of my pay, £7. 1*s*. 6*d*. Squaring my shoulders, I opened the front door of Teynham Crescent. They were sitting round the wireless drinking tea.

'What on earth was all that about?' asked Mother.

3 Madness

'Now listen to me, you silly fucking cow. Stop all this shit about wanting to be a woman. You'll grow out of it. Man? Woman? Who cares? You've got it up here, that's what counts. If God had intended the genitals to be as important as the brain He'd have put a skull round them.' Roxy was dispensing advice in a coffee bar, Renshaw Street, one cold November evening.

The first thing I'd done was go for another ship but I'd been given a Dishonourable Discharge. The second thing was to fix up work with John and Edna. And the third was to try and learn to live with the word 'freak', an embarrassment now to my family as well as myself. In this, a positive element had entered my life which was crucial: Roxy.

Slightly built, with a strikingly red face and a pot of green eye-shadow on each eye, he had come to work on one of the stalls in the Market. His forehead was very high with a mass of ginger hair piled precariously above it in oily quiffs. When he was excited they dislodged themselves and wound down over his face, in the centre of which was the foulest mouth I'd ever encountered. From this nervously jerking orifice, night and day, issued a flow of abuse and wisecracks. For Roxy it was a condition of existence, like breathing or the circulation of the blood.

And his hands – when they weren't involved in the reconstitution of his *coiffure*, his hands jumped about in unpredictable staccato, perhaps coming together for a second under the chin like a stunned madonna before shooting off in independent directions, one to the hip, the other to interfere with an earlobe, explore an itchiness in the lumbar region, or simply gouge the air, then they would meet up again behind his neck in a desperate attempt to knot an imaginary turban. I never saw him, one might say, in repose. The animated effect was enhanced by the comparative sobriety of his dress.

Roxy was a new type for me. And in case you imagine him to be of a simpering disposition, I should emphasise that he was as tough as boots. Liverpool can be a mean town for those who stick out like thumbs. But under threat Roxy was at his wildest. 'You touch me, mate, and I'll fucking knock yer face through the back of yer head!' With green eyes blazing in green war-paint, the blood vessels standing out on his scrawny neck, the hands zipping up and down – thugs ran a mile. At first he frightened me too. But the discovery of Roxy's throwaway attitude towards all that was considered reprehensible, well, I simply talked and talked, it was like a bowel movement in my soul.

He invited me to meet his friends in the gay bars. Whenever the doors opened everyone inside would stop talking, turn round to check out who was coming in, and then return to the business of letting off steam among themselves. There were two main haunts: one behind the Market which I was reluctant to use for fear of being spotted, and another at the Stork Hotel. The hubbub! Many of the customers wore cosmetics and semi-drag. The more exaggerated ones had left home and gave parties. I went to one at the flat of two men who lived as women by night. Full of pink satin, white lace, gold tassels, doilies all over the place, it looked as though Mae West had thrown up in there. The atmosphere made me uncomfortable, for my own presentation went much further than Roxy's in formality – a dark box jacket with padded shoulders to make me shapeless, black trousers, hair long on top but cut into a Tony Curtis Boston at the back, and a white untouched face.

There was nothing to do in Liverpool in the early 1950s. The only nightlife was people being beaten up and murdered. After closing time we hung around the Pierhead which was the focus for youthful frustration. Liverpool has tremendous nervous energy. We youngsters brought it to the Pierhead where a dangerous static would build.

Reggie Endicott took me to a boozing party at the house of a friend of his. It was a smart modern one, distinguished by an indoor lavatory. I stood behind a sofa feeling worse and worse and finally went off to this lavatory and locked myself in. For want of anything more constructive to do I took down a bottle of aspirin and swallowed the entire contents. This second suicide attempt was much feebler than the first. In fact it failed to connect at all. I crawled home with Reggie, slept for eighteen hours, and awoke with a monumental headache. It was assumed I had drunk too much, a permissible excess denoting manliness.

. . . We were at the Pierhead. Roxy was bitching with another Liverpudlian queen called Little Gloria (as opposed to Big Gloria who came from Leeds) over a piece of rough trade they both had their teeth into. As usual I was outside it. We had been to the pub behind the Market and had had a few. I loved to drink. My manners had become even more reserved than before. Putting a psychological distance between myself and others was my method of self-protection. Only drink relaxed me, gave me a holiday from myself. But it took quite a lot, half-a-dozen gins before the lights started switching on.

Out there in the keyed-up atmosphere of the Pierhead I overheard two young men discussing marriage plans. I couldn't live that life. On the other side the row between Roxy and Little Gloria grew intolerable. I knew I couldn't live their life either. Despair swept through me like a dry wind. Roxy, Little Gloria, me, everything was so sordid. At eighteen I had no future, no chance for any kind of happiness, so –

I shot like a bullet towards the railings, jumped clear over them and fell thirty feet into the fast current of the Mersey. As I fell through the air I registered the shocked silence of those I'd left behind. My fall was broken by an icy smack. I plunged in and the water carried me off at top speed. Thinks: 'Thank God the tide wasn't out – it's going out now – I'm rushing towards the sea – I'm going like the clappers towards New Brighton – I'll float for a while until my clothes get waterlogged – then I'll be dragged under.' Having analysed the situation, I settled into the current as one would settle into an armchair.

On my way down-river I passed beneath a line of pontoons. As I sped out the other side there was a frightful pull on my hair. For a moment I assumed I had crashed into a post until I found myself rising out of the water. One of the young men contemplating marriage had seen me vanish under the pontoon, calculated the point at which I should emerge, ran about three hundred yards, jumped down to it, and was now hauling me out of one of the most dangerous rivers in the world. I writhed and fought. Chunks of hair came out. But he was so strong, and I ended up at the Ormskirk Mental Hospital. 'Youth Saved by Long Hair', said the *Liverpool Echo*. My first press.

Though sedated I woke up with a start in a soft white gown with no metal fittings on it. In the bed opposite, with jug ears and clawlike hands covered in black hair, a man was tied down and screaming. Some were giggling, or sobbing, or releasing horrible howls from their throats; others shuffled up and down the ward with faces cancelled by drugs. In the bed to my left was a young man with the loveliest pale features. We would chat in the normal way until a fixed stare came into his eyes. He would start to shiver and to mutter. 'Arrgh . . . arrgh . . . I like them black, I like them big, they've got to be big and black, I've got to have them big and black.' Then the fit would pass and he'd continue the conversation as if nothing had happened. His obsession was the breasts of black women, he'd gone over the edge in that respect, and it had disfigured his whole outlook on life. It occurred to me that his best chance of a cure lay not in a madmen's ward but in a ticket on the first boat to Jamaica and Cynthia.

Wanting to go to the lavatory I was distressed to find myself escorted there by two giants in white coats and not allowed to shut the door. The inmates were not permitted to shave themselves either. No knives or forks with the food. One ate with a spoon like a babe in rompers. The screamer opposite had to be fed by one of the giants who wiped the slobbering mouth and chin after every spoonful. This filthy performance effectively put me off food. The ward lacked all adornment and was painted a bleak white. The windows were barred and could open only an inch or two. The doors were bolted shut. I had been imprisoned in a ward for violent maniacs.

When this appalling fact dawned on me I asked to see a doctor, and was told to wait. At last he came and I said, 'Why am I in a place like this?'

'Because if you do stupid things like you do, you *come* to places like this.' Like all the staff he wore a white coat. It was to prevent psychological contamination, to remind themselves they were part of the sane community.

'But I'm not mad. This is a place for raving loonies, this is not for me. I only tried to kill myself because I'm so unhappy.'

He was non-committal, apart from informing me that I'd have to stay where I was, under observation for at least three days.

The two giants took me for a bath, which completed my humiliation. In the ward the lights stayed on all night.

On the fourth day Mother arrived. Bernie was with her in his customary, not-with-it way. She said, 'I wouldn't have come if Bernie hadn't come with me.' I screamed at her. To this day Mother thinks I've let the family down. It was agreed that I could leave, conditional on signing papers committing me to a year's psychiatric treatment as an out-patient at Walton Hospital near by, which had one of the largest psychiatric units in the British Isles. When I got home my brother Freddie said, 'You silly git', and ruffled my hair. It was the nearest the family came to discussing it.

Dr Vaillant was the head of the unit. His dark eyes couldn't rest, least of all on anyone else's, and darted about in terror of everything. Small and twitchy, he reminded me of a rat in distress. After an interview with him I was passed on to a much younger doctor who began the cure by putting a mask over my face and dropping ether on to it. The idea was to release one's hidden depths by getting one high.

'Why do you want to be a woman?' he asked. Claustrophobia began to flow up my nose and oppress my chest. Through the stone walls I could hear someone crying.

'We've got to go and help them! We've got to!' I was babbling like an old wino and tore the sodden mask off my face. There were four or five sessions with the ether mask and I grew to like it. This is fatal for therapeutic probes because it means one has regained one's composure. The doctor asked me about homosexual activity. 'I'm approached nearly every day but I don't like it and I don't do it.'

After a physical examination they put me on a course of male hormones. The dose was massive and might have encouraged a little growth in height but failed to make me shaggy and broad-shouldered. 'No matter what you do, you'll never be able to change my mind,' I said with a knowledge I didn't know I had.

Next on the list was sodium pentothal, the truth drug. It is jabbed into your arm and injected slowly while they ask you questions, questions, always the same ones, always the same answers, over and over again. Eventually they decided to go straight for the Main Nerve. Electro-Convulsive Therapy.

For this I was put in a public ward. Observing those who came out was no encouragement. These blitzed souls returned from the convulsion chamber like zombies, their eyes blinking and heavily bloodshot, with an attendant supporting them on each side. A few hours later they awoke in their beds with murderous headaches in comparison to which an aspirin overdose is like a day at the seaside. When it comes to medical matters I'm usually very brave but on these occasions was not.

You are wheeled into the chamber. Wires are attached to your wrists and ankles. A crown of wires is placed on your head. Heavy canvas straps bind you to a table. Once they press that button it's zonk! out! until you wake up with a head full of cannonballs and broken glass. What theory lies behind E.C.T. I couldn't grasp. It was followed by more talk.

After six months of these mind-bending exercises, the doctor told me there was nothing more they could do without wrecking me physically. The report noted, '. . . he presents a womanish appearance and has little bodily or facial hair.'

Meanwhile I had continued working in the Market. One was really supposed to live on sickness benefit like an invalid, but the work kept me sane. At the same time I had my first clumsy affair with a man. He was called Vic and I'd met him at the Stork Hotel. The barman came across to me and said, 'Someone wants to buy you a drink', which wasn't unusual. Already I was the prettiest and most mysterious of the bunch, but going out of my way to look as straight as possible (although the one thing they always said was, 'You've got a woman's eyes'). Occasionally Vic would crash out on Mother's sofa. She quite liked him. But his insane fits of jealousy killed it before it had a chance to reach anything romantic.

I had also met one of the directors of a local brewery, who offered to put me on a catering course. My first assignment was with Mr and Mrs Leadbetter in Chester at the Commercial pub in St Peter's Graveyard. But when I started to attract an extrovert clientele I got cold feet and asked for a transfer. This was to the Westminster Hotel, Rhyl, to learn dining-rooms and kitchens. It was off-season, dead as dead (roller-skating was the biggest treat in town), so after some months I asked for another transfer. It took me to St Asaph. I didn't get on with the family running the hotel. The last straw came when a horse bolted and dragged me on my back all through the shopping streets one crowded Saturday afternoon. Besides, there's only so much you can learn about a dining-room. I'd run out of ideas; something else had to happen.

Ronnie Cogan, a friend who'd gone to London, would occasionally return north to demonstrate his metropolitan style. Aghast and goggle-eyed, he said, 'You mean you've never *heard* of Cuban heels? Eee, Liverpool's nowhere, kid – if you want to get *somewhere* you've got to come to t'Smoke.'

It seemed the essential move.

Mother refused to lend me a bean, so I boarded the train with fifty shillings in my pocket. At Euston Station Ronnie said, 'We can sleep on the floor of Big Gloria's room in Earl's Court.'

This was it – London. Piccadilly, the Ritz, Her Majesty! The most sensible thing I'd done in my life. It's funny how these changes seem impossibly major while you contemplate them. But when you *do* them, it's so easy – freedom and a floor like Big Gloria's had been waiting there for years. Six-feet-four with a face like Sitting Bull, he didn't seem at all surprised to see us and immediately brewed a cuppa.

Now for a job. Ronnie and I found positions right away as table-wipers at Lyon's Corner House, Coventry Street, the night shift, upstairs. In imitation of Roxy I smeared my lids with green paint, and ate Benzedrine Inhalers to keep me wiping through the night (you took out the wad of inhaler, cut it up with scissors and swallowed the pieces with water). It caught on. In 1953 if you wanted a cup of tea in Central London at 4 a.m. you went upstairs at the Lyon's Corner House to be greeted by a squad of painted macaws screeching about on speed. My section was soon filled with fans, little old men and women to whom I gave free cups of tea from a gigantic metal teapot. They sat there all night drinking tea and going to the lavatory, and at dawn they melted away.

With Ronnie I took a small flat in Westgate Terrace. In the morning after work we'd fly back in a fever to scrub it, hoping to exhaust ourselves for sleep. My God, those Benzedrine Inhalers. Three days later you'd be all of a pother and still going! One drank excessively to smooth it off round the edges. Sometimes I ploughed through a whole bottle of vodka before work.

No, London was not disappointing. I learned all that was free if you were prepared to walk and can still surprise Londoners with odd corners they didn't know existed. The pubs we frequented were the

Fitzroy and the Marquis of Granby north of Soho, in a district hung over from Bloomsbury days and known to us as Fitzravia. The Fitzroy was the most outrageous pub in London and often raided. The police entered, the place fell silent, they bolted the doors, and anyone without identification was taken off in a Black Maria. 'Are you old enough to be drinking here?' they would ask – I always carried my passport in case of these interrogations. It was in the Fitzroy that I met Rock Hudson and Ava Gardner. After hours a mixed bag, including Danny La Rue and Tommy Osborne, congregated in the Snake Pit, a Soho bomb-site with railings round it and a tea caravan in the middle behind St Anne's Church. London was of course littered with bomb-sites. Soho I never really took to, despite spending considerable time there. But I did meet a famous scientist in a restaurant in Dean Street.

'Is it Mr Einstein?'

He turned and said, 'Are you a boy or a girl?'

'I think I'm a girl.'

'Whatever you are, you should be Madame Butterfly with those long eyelashes.'

'Can I have your autograph?'

'But I don't like to do that, it embarrasses me so much.'

'Oh, go on . . .'

'Oh, all right . . .' He gave me five, one each for our table, some kind of record for him.

Little Gloria came south too and brought the news that Vic had committed suicide on a camping holiday. At lunchtime he'd walked into a Welsh reservoir. 'Don't be too long, food's almost ready,' his friends cried. He called out, 'That's O.K. I'll not be back.' The body was found a few days afterwards.

The first Christmas, I went home, laden with gifts (for Mother a £5 box of chocolates the size of a cartwheel), showing off in a royal-blue box jacket and slip-on shoes. Slip-ons had recently come into the London shops. Before it had always been lace-ups.

I arrived on Christmas Eve. Ivor turned up blind drunk, ready for Midnight Mass.

'No, Ivor, I'm not coming with you, I'm an atheist now.'

'I'll thump you if you don't come, you great cissy!'

'Not very spiritual talk for a Christmas Eve.'

'No fancy London stuff here, thank you very much,' said Mother. 'You *are* going with Ivor.'

'Well, what's happened to you all of a sudden? You're not even a Catholic. You're famous for encouraging people to defect! So leave me alone. I just want a quiet Christmas.'

Feeble as it was, such confidence astounded Mother. 'Get out of this house!' she bawled. 'And never *ever* come back!'

Luckily I hadn't unpacked. Ivor sloshed along the hall walls behind me, attempting to get to the church across the way. He zig-zagged all over the road. Mother was pushing him, abusing him, trying to stop him collapsing before he reached a pew. The two of them fell up the steps, he crashed into the door, and she shoved him inside.

I turned and called out, 'Are you sure you never want to see me again? Because if you say yes, you never will.'

Mother was out of breath at the head of the church steps, framed in the light of the doorway. 'I *never* want to see you again, d'you hear? I've hated you from the second you were born!'

This moment had been a long time coming. But there was no mistaking that it had arrived. I walked a mile or so to Broadway where Ronnie was spending Christmas with his lot. When he opened the door he was horrified to see me with my suitcase but Mrs Cogan was marvellous. 'You come in, love, we'll give you your Christmas,' she said.

Back in London, while elbowing tea stains off the formica at five in the morning, a very pretty girl called Sylvia drifted in for a cup of tea and said, 'Wouldn't you prefer office work to this?'

'This is O.K. I wouldn't mind a change.'

'I'm sure my boss would *love* you.'

Which is how I came to operate the switchboard at J. Rowland Sales Ltd, a theatrical agency in Charing Cross Road. I gave up the Benzedrine and the eye-shadow and went legit. There had been inducements – I gave an Inhaler to a fellow worker and he ran into a bus and was killed. Finally, when Ronnie metamorphosed into Humphrey Bogart under my very eyes, I knew I'd overdone the drink, drugs and sleeplessness. It was at this agency that I met Duncan Melvin, a musical and ballet impresario whose wife owned Le Petit Club Français in St James's, a fashionable dining-club for politicians and civil servants. Duncan looked like a little leprechaun, which is what I called him. Pink and chubby, always chuckling, he wanted to be my sugar-daddy but I said no. I was too romantic to make it as a tart.

The agency was perfectly situated when the coffee-bar boom happened. Our favourites were nearby in Old Compton Street, the Two Eyes where Tommy Steele used to sing before he became famous, and the Kaleidoscope round the corner. Here I first met my great friend Rita Wallace (*née* Farrell). Like Big Gloria she came from Leeds. Like Duncan she looked like a leprechaun. Like me she was a teenager, but half my height with wild red hair, ravishingly pretty and usually hysterical with manic laughter. Rita was doing the same as I'd done, waitressing all hours, Benzedrine Inhalers, have another coffee on the house, have another Danish, have you met Betty the Berk? One was always being introduced to people with names like that. Betty grunted and carried on spooning piles of sugar into his coffee.

When Ronnie moved on I couldn't afford to keep the flat. A transvestite hooker friend, Tristram, who had a record of petty-mongering as long as your leg, said I could take a room in his basement in Victoria. After a while I had to put it to him.

'Tristram, I think somebody's been sleeping in my bed.'

'Oh yes, Eyelashes [my latest sobriquet],' 'this couple I know, she's a doll, he's a dish, so in love, so romantic, they had nowhere to go, sorry, I meant to tell you.'

'And Tristram, you've given up going to work – how are you living?'

'Didn't you know, sweet? I have this private income.' He was a crashing snob, gave himself such airs.

A few weeks later, coming down the street after work a little earlier than usual, I spotted a young woman coming up the area steps. Nothing romantic about *her* and she was with a man a hundred years old at least. And something else bothered me. I went up to Bill, one of the boys who lived upstairs, and said, 'Do you know, I got the most shocking bill from our grocer. It's £43 and I hardly eat.'

'Haven't you any idea what's going on?'

'What do you mean?'

'You're in a very dangerous position. Tristram's letting your room to whores during the day. By the hour. By the half-hour when he can.'

'You haven't missed much, have you.'

'They must be using your account at the grocer's too. And the house, you realise it's being watched.'

I went cold. Who would have believed I was innocent? Who *ever* believes it?

'I'm getting the night boat to Jersey tomorrow,' said Bill. 'Why don't you come?'

Bill regularly went there to work the summer season. The night boat appealed to my sense of drama. A few days afterwards Tristram was arrested. He was described in one newspaper as appearing in court 'with heavy black beard poking through heavy white make-up'.

We floated into St Hélier at eight in the morning feeling gorgeous. The following day I was washing dishes. The day after that the bush telegraph informed me of a more amusing job out at La Corbière.

The hotel there was unfinished, plonked by itself on the edge of a cliff, with the lighthouse rising theatrically opposite. It was owned by Mr and Mrs Wormold who lived in St Hélier. He was a charming softie from the North of England. She had more zap, the double of Ginger Rogers, and was having a duet with his business partner.

'We want someone who can do everything,' he said.

'That's me.'

'So far only one bedroom's finished. You can have it as general manager and caretaker. Breakfasts, morning coffee, lunches, teas and the bar.'

'When do you want me to start?'

'How about now?'

Under me were a part-time barman, a woman in the kitchen and a cleaner. Among my customers were the lighthouse-keepers, a tourist called Clare Cork who was passing through and an Italian waiter who was her lover. But at night I was alone, with only a black cat and a tortoise for company. I'd start the day with an early-morning swim, then open up, take in the milk, tidy the bar, put the chairs and tables out on the terrace, put on tea and coffee, cut bread for toasting, heat the fat in case anyone ordered a cooked breakfast, and sit there eating pieces of orange in summery bliss. Apart from the vagrant staff, the first in would often not be until 11 a.m., the new shift for the lighthouse wanting a drink. A few for lunch, mostly salads. Tea-time was busiest, cream teas on the terrace, but the nights alone could get very gothic.

On my Sundays off I'd sit in the Red Cabin Bar of the Royal Yacht

Hotel and be sociable. Imagine my joy when Rita and the gang pranced in at the tops of their voices. 'Dwahling, it was such a good idea, we're going to slave here too.' After work they'd come out to La Corbière to keep me company, turning up with the Sarah Vaughan records around midnight and ready for a party. Mr Wormold normally left at 11 p.m. He knew about these *dansants* but didn't mind because I was such a godsend during the day.

'All I ask is you don't forget to lock up last thing.'

'I wouldn't, Mr Wormold. And after midnight I'll turn the lights out too, in case the police get nosey. I shouldn't want to distract them from their duties.' Besides, the lighthouse cast such a poetic light through the large window it would have been criminal not to exploit it.

One night I'd gone up early to ease my head – the lighthouse men had been in and out and I was whoozy from drinking with them. Hearing a noise below, I went to the top of the staircase wound in a sheet. The party people were arriving. Raising my hand I said 'Welcome, darlings!', tripped, and fell all the way to the bottom where I rolled under the piano. Dazed momentarily, I grabbed one of the piano legs to raise myself up. It moved. I noticed it was covered in black cloth. My eyes travelled up it to where a powerful thigh stretched tight the fabric in an outward curve, up to where it joined another leg and bulged menacingly as a beam from the lighthouse moved slowly across the jutting pelvis, and from there to a narrow leather belt, a stark white shirt suggesting the shadows of a heavily muscled trunk, up towards an open collar and a dark throat kissed by the sun, two ropes of muscle between which an Adam's apple was gently swallowing, and on to a strong jawline, wide mobile mouth with brilliant sudden teeth, a nose slightly fleshy but only so much as to render all the rest more huggable, and proceeded to the magnificent eyes in whose endless green depths birds sang and lions roared and dreams slid to and fro. The head was square, covered in tight glittering curls, and set rocklike on straight shoulders. For me the rest of the room had vanished into silence. All I could hear was, 'Let go of my leg, you bloody idiot.' He was young and sturdy. Rita had brought him.

A week later, while I was working late in the bar, he walked in. Rolling golden body, deep deep tan. Taken unawares, I stuck my head in a glass of gin and scrutinised him out of the side of one eye.

'Remember me?' he said.

Knives switched under my ribs. I'd forgotten the tonic.

'Can I get you a drink?' I said.

He jumped up on a bar-stool and sat there grinning. 'Just a beer.'

I grabbed a bottle, snapped off the cap and sent it frothing across the bar. 'Oh here, you do it.' I was pumping shots of gin into my glass with the other hand and failing to be blasé. I was tongue-tied. Whenever his own patter ground to a halt, which was quite often, he would look down and brush non-existent specks of dust from his thighs.

Once the gin began to soak in, I relaxed a little. His name was Joey, a Cockney boy from the Isle of Dogs in the East End of London. Italian and Irish blood splashed together with the English inside him. He was so tremendously bright and alive that he seemed to trigger a phosphorescence in the air. He was working in St Hélier in the office of a boatyard. And I was, I was –

'They call me Eyelashes!' I blurted out, reeling inside.

'That's a funny sort of name. Can I have another beer?'

Yes!!

. . . That is, 'Sure you can.'

After closing I walked with him to the bus-stop. Before he climbed aboard he kissed me. In front of all the passengers. I was completely floored. When I fell into bed I thought, 'What *is* going on?' He had walked into my mind and now squatted there. I didn't sleep.

When I met Rita in a coffee bar in St Hélier, Joey was with her.

'Hi, Joey,' I said in my most nonchalant breeze.

'I don't want to know *you*,' he said. 'Eye-bloody-lashes!'

Horribly crushed I returned to La Corbière. But in a few days, much to my surprise, he called in again. After spinning a silver coin in the bar for half an hour he said, 'I wanted to say sorry.'

'What for?'

'For being a prick in that coffee bar.'

'Oh that. Don't worry. I'd forgotten about it.'

'No, you hadn't. I thought you were a girl, then Rita told me . . . Oh it doesn't matter.'

At the time I was dressing in a very non-committal way: slacks and a sweater. The Tony Curtis hair-do had grown into an Audrey Hepburn. I let people decide for themselves what sex I was, behaving accordingly. On the beach I hid under an all-over singlet.

Joey didn't catch the bus back that night. He stayed quite a few times from then on, despite plenty of girlfriends back in St Hélier. Yes, he was sensationally handsome. With an unavoidable body. But in no sense was it easy. Because of my loathing for my own flesh, for my genitals especially, I was a terribly uncertain lover, no lover at all really. Joey didn't know what he was supposed to do, what I would allow him to do, or what he wanted to do either. What we did most that summer was talk about it. Hours and hours of talk going round in huge circles on the sand.

At the end of the season, we found ourselves on the beach. Joey came out of the water. I stared at him as he stood dripping in sky-blue briefs, covered in gooseflesh.

'One day,' I said, 'I'm going to be a woman. I promise you because I love you.'

'Ha, you're ridiculous,' he said, rubbing his golden pectorals with a towel.

'Oh, I know that only too well.'

In London I obtained work at Waitrose grocer's in Gloucester Road, slicing bacon – would I never escape that bacon? Ronnie brought his mother to my bedsitter and in honour of this Liverpudlian reunion I cooked on the single ring a pan of Scouse (like Irish stew, you throw in the lot and braise). Just before they left, Rita showed up.

'Have you heard?' she said. 'Joey was dancing and his back went.'

He was in St Bartholomew's Hospital. At last, unable to restrain myself, I went over one evening. His parents were coming out of the room so I hung back until they'd left. Joey looked grey and thin and had broken out in spots. He was covered with sweat. All his vigour had gone.

'What the hell are you doing here? My parents might have seen you. I don't want any visits, understand? Now get out!'

His embarrassment over me was understandable. More distressing was his loss of confidence in himself. He was going through an emotional crisis because he believed his back would never fully mend. I sent him notes and left it at that.

A Windmill girl asked me if I'd like to occupy her flat while she spent Christmas with her family in Dorking and then went on tour. We lived like gypsies then, throwing things into a suitcase at the drop of a hat. So much so that for a long time I deliberately didn't acquire more than one suitcaseful of possessions.

What a gloomy basement it turned out to be, livened up only by a coal fire which I kept on the roar. Not long after moving in, I had a late-night visitor. It was Clare Cork.

'I'm sorry, I'm terribly ill,' she said. She was panting, fainting, the sweat pouring off her.

'My God, come in.'

The problem was pregnancy, thanks to the Italian waiter. In fact she was on the verge of labour.

'Quickly, lie down, get into my bed, I'll call an ambulance.'

'No! I can handle this. No ambulances.'

'But, Clare, I've got no idea what to do!'

'Look, it's O.K., false alarm, please, I'd like some tea . . .'

While I was in the kitchen there was a scream and I dashed back. Clare was looking ghastly. 'It's hurting,' she said. 'They wouldn't understand in Ireland, for months I've been trying to abort it. I think I've done something to myself. Can you look to see if I'm all right?'

As I examined her, she burst. The bed filled up with blood and water and the baby's head began to emerge.

'I don't care what you say, I'm going to get an ambulance.'

'No, darlin', it's too late, I need your help here. Now go and boil as much water as you can.'

Hot water. The number one priority in every film you ever saw. My first birth! And at Christmas too. It was turning out to be an occasion after all. The kitchen rang with pans. The water took an eternity to boil. I unearthed some fresh towels and steamed back in to assist. Clare was lying exhausted on the bed.

'You've done it! Is it a boy or a girl?'

She looked at me from under her lids and said, 'It's neither.'

'What do you mean it's neither? Let's have a look.'

But that wasn't possible. Clare had wrapped it up in lots and lots of newspaper and thrown it on the fire. Just like that. She said it died a few minutes after birth, but I wasn't so sure. Clare wouldn't let me touch the fire. She sat beside it for two days, obsessively poking the ashes, then she left for Ireland, relieved that her ordeal was over, and that she could now face her mother as a good Catholic.

Without explaining why, I said to Little Gloria, 'I've got to get out of Olympia, it's driving me nuts.' Actually I was having nightmares and daytime horrors about the burnt baby. He said there was a room going where he lived.

7 Nevern Square. The basement and the ground floor were

inhabited by a Polish family who acted as caretakers. They would have ignored an atomic bomb so long as it paid the rent. Which was a blessing because from the first floor upwards it was bedlam. Prostitutes, transvestites, drug addicts, petty crooks, and their guests, a non-stop party, doors banging, music blasting, lights on, twenty-four hours a day.

Little Gloria, with pin eyes either side of an enormous rotting nose and no mouth at all, had come a long way since the Pierhead. At night he donned a shift, a stole and a wig and went out on the bash. He was tiny and I'm sure this helped – short people get away with drag more easily than tall people. He was also a kleptomaniac and his room was an Aladdin's cave of glittering trash hoisted from Woolworth's. Little Gloria invited you in for coffee and then gave it to you out of one of your own cups. The form was: don't bother to say anything, just pick up your own bits and pieces on the way out. Hoisting (shop-lifting) and kiting (a spending spree with a stolen cheque-book) were his two stand-bys when trade was thin on the pavement.

My room was towards the top of the house and underneath it, 'making ends meet, darlink', was Sheherazade, a towering Titian redhead from the North, a lesbian and a harlot. Most of the women prostitutes were blatant men-haters. Yet, no, she was not so much a lesbian as prodigiously kinky. You name it, Sheherazade loved it. However, her predilection was for sado-masochism. With boots, leather and whips, she ran a prosperous business out of her severely furnished bedsitter. Apart from height, Sheherazade's most conspicuous asset was the bulk of her breasts, strapped up in a brassière like a black-leather hammock to render them more victimising. They were magnificent, even better than Lana Turner's in *They Won't Forget*. On duty she added a pair of black-leather briefs with apertures let into them front and back and decorated with curlicues of metal studs, Prince Charming boots (seven-inch stiletto heels) reaching to her strong upper thighs, and round her wrists and neck coils of chain cut to the correct length by a man in the hardware department of Harrods, himself a suppliant. A true exhibitionist, Sherry often patrolled the streets attired thus, with a trenchcoat over the top to prevent arrest.

Once she called me in as I was walking downstairs. A client was with her.

'Look at that!' she said. 'I mean, Toni [I'd lately rechristened myself], just look at it! What garbage we've got in today. Doesn't it make you want to spew all over it? Disgusting little worm! It's fit for nothing but the shit pit!'

The man's eyes were paralysed with fear. He was lying naked on his back on the bed. A leather thong had been tied fast round his flame-red testicles. This thong was looped over the old-fashioned light bracket in the centre of the ceiling and pulled tight by the weight of a heavy flat-iron hanging in mid-air from the other end. Every so often, mouthing cruelties and curses, slapping her thigh with a riding crop, Sherry strode up to the flat-iron and gave it a yank.

'There! Serves it right for being such a pile of bile! Go on, love, you give it a yank.'

'I don't like to, Sherry.'

'No? Do you want to whip him then? Is that what you want to do? Go on, give him one. Give him several. Give him the bloody lot, the stinking heap of fishheads!'

Sherry was marching up and down with a blood-curdling sneer on her face. I didn't know whether to laugh or run away.

'No? Well, watch.' She struck him smartly across the testicles with her crop and a charge of ecstasy rippled through his body.

'I was only on my way out to buy some Jaffa Cakes,' I mumbled.

'Don't fret, darlink,' she said by way of an aside. 'He has to lie like that for an hour or more before he gets the inspiration. Then I give him one good tug, he comes, and pays me fifty quid. Sometimes it takes hours and hours. I tell you, it's no cinch this work, but it makes ends meet.'

To me Sheherazade had passed on to the Higher Wisdom. She was so at home in strange waters. We always knew when she'd had a good day because that splendid red head appeared in the doorway, announcing in the vaguely Central European accent she affected, 'I've got an itsy bitsy bottle of bevvy.' From behind her back she would produce a magnum of champagne. Nothing about Sherry was small.

On my floor lived Pussy and Ernestine, both waiters and apart from myself the only inhabitants in bona fide employment. Pussy was so named because he had the face of a Persian cat, the features all squashed into the centre by two large round cheeks. Ernestine was an alcoholic who eventually drank himself to death. Next to them was Jicky, who named himself after the scent by Guerlain. He had a

Garbo fixation and his room was improvised from packing-cases in the Scandinavian style. He would sit in it and say, 'Yes, sweetheart, today I'm suicidal, I think I must kill myself.' In the end he did of course. Jicky was very beautiful, in the cold hard way that a plate can be beautiful, and affected dead-white *maquillage*. To everyone's disgust he insisted on storing it in the communal fridge. With Jicky everything had to be cold, even his pots of paint.

Our resident junkie was Dawn Roberts, much older than the rest of us, about forty. Dawn was a bony little blonde, actressy, with a slash of red lipstick for a mouth and blue skin. No one knew where her money came from but she was a close friend of the famous Society drug addict Brenda Dean Paul. Brenda was always being arrested on charges of possession. She was the daughter of Sir Aubrey Dean Paul and his Polish wife, the pianist Lady Irène. Looking like Veronica Lake in dark glasses, Brenda made one feel that her life was all tragedy. In 1959 she was found dead in her flat just before her fiftieth birthday.

Dawn was very far gone in the needle game, jabbing herself in the bottom several times a day; not bothering to lift up her skirt and slip down her panties, she simply jabbed it in through the worsted. On one occasion, a boy called Hilary stood to inherit quite a few thousand pounds if he married. For a fee, Sheherazade came to the rescue and we all filed off to the Kensington Register Office. Dawn was a witness. Half-way through the ceremony she took a syringe out of her black suede handbag and stuck it into her bottom. It was the middle of winter, she was in thick tweeds, so it took a bit of muscle. The registrar looked up, blinked, and carried on. He can't have missed it. Presumably he couldn't believe the evidence of his senses.

As a safeguard against incapacity, Dawn taught everyone in the house how to do it for her. Heat up the drug in a spoon over a burner, pull it up into the syringe, and so on. When drunk, in bits and pieces, or first thing most mornings, she was unable to supply enough will-power and co-ordination to her limbs to fix herself.

The most glamorous of the drag queens by far was Tallulah, so called because he modelled his voice on Miss Bankhead's. His big blue eyes, high cheekbones and mouthful of white teeth set in a jaw of granite gave him immediate distinction. While the rest of us were talking it was Tallulah's pleasure to flick his tongue in and out over scarlet lips so gummed with gloss you could see your face in them, and then slowly draw the lips back like stage curtains to expose the brilliant teeth. These would be held on view from ear to ear for as long as it was necessary to fill the room with white light, a glorious phenomenon on a dull winter's day. In addition to the smile, there was the walk, an effortless glide which conveyed the impression that he was moving forward on ball-bearings.

Tallulah's dilemma was that in drag he looked like a man and out of it, like a woman. He was especially fond of black men – 'goolies' as they were called. Oh, they *all* loved the goolies whose constant presence in the house was indicated by the aroma of hashish on the staircase. Black women also came on occasions. One went by the name of Verne[illegible] She had short curly hair dyed pink and always laughed instead [illegible]peaking. I took this for confidence at the time but now realise that it must have been tremendous insecurity.

I never knew what I'd find on returning from Waitrose. We didn't lock our doors, were constantly rushing in and out of each other's rooms. Someone would say, 'We're all going to Jicky's for coffee, are you coming?' Jicky was only across the landing but we'd make an outing of it. Anyone might be in there – Rita Hayworth, Marilyn Monroe, Judy Garland. They were extraordinarily gifted mimics.

Usually after work I went to Tallulah's room, which was the most comfortable as well as the most bilious. He'd draped tangerine and shocking-pink chiffon over the lights, covered the bed with leopardette scatter cushions, congeries of lace frothed at the windows picked out with velvet bows, hundreds of bottles of scent and cosmetics, a plastic Jesus that lit up from inside, coloured stills from the film musicals on the wall, frilly frocks which gave you migraine, and wigs on the window-sill: a style known as 'Hollywoochie'. Tallulah would be at his dressing-table practising The Smile, whose only drawback was laugh lines which he attempted to defeat with endless face-packs.

'Perhaps I should forget the smile and go po like Jicky.'

'You mustn't, Tallulah.'

'You're right, honey – it's my glory – but in the wrong light I look as though I've been garotted – this new Leichner's bona on the eke – what do you think? – and you haven't mentioned the ria – navy blue is really me, isn't it.' But after a few hours he would decide that really navy blue wasn't him after all and the following day his hair would have changed to grass green or lemon.

The slang was known as 'parliare' and seems to have been linked with Italian, from the days when travelling players came over from Italy. For example:

bona	good
cod	bad
eke	face
homey	man
lallies	legs
nanti	not
ogles	eyes
pelucca	wig
polone	woman
the ria	hair
varda	look

Tallulah, Little Gloria and Roxy used it constantly and were terribly, terribly funny. With them it amounted to a minor art form. But disinclined to go too far into the homosexual subculture, I didn't adopt it myself. As well as being the youngest I was also the most sober (apart from drink!). Occasionally I went moral on them and said they should take proper jobs.

'Hark at her! Proper jobs! What d'you think I'm doing every night bashing my feet to pulp? Window-shopping?'

It was the same with drag. Pussy in particular was always trying to get me into it but I preferred to look androgynous. Sometimes I put the slap on with them. 'Cor blimey, Gloria, go and get Sherry in for a varda. Oh, Tone, you should go all the way, you really should, you look like Lena Horne.' Which was true. The foundation was much too dark. But my thought was, 'The day I dress as a woman is the day I discover I can become one.'

Visitors to Nevern Square included Ina and Audrey. Big Gloria brought them along. They were both in the R.A.F. Audrey had the largest feet you ever saw. He was from Leeds too and sometimes appeared in uniform. Ina, who was from Newcastle, would never do that. When going on leave he always popped into the lavatory to change into something more *louche*. Audrey enjoyed his National Service because he had the pick of the men. Ina however was a true transsexual and very unhappy, as I had been in the Merchant Navy. He didn't want to be discharged for being a homosexual because he didn't consider himself one.

Incidentally, all these female names – it was an important part of sloughing off one's old identity. If you really wished to be cruel to someone you called him 'Brian' or 'Henry' or whatever. I loathed being called 'George'. People still do it now and again for a cheap insult. We referred to each other as 'she' and 'her', a convention it would be too confusing to adopt here. My own choice of name, Toni, was the counterpart of my style of dress. Non-committal, unisexual.

When rock 'n' roll burst we burst with it. Little Gloria gave a party with 'Rock Around The Clock', his only record, played over and over again on Tallulah's gramophone. Plus gin and 'poppers'. These are fine glass phials of amyl nitrite (intended by the medical profession for those whose hearts are wont to flag) which you crack and sniff. The heart leaps out of your chest and the body is swamped by a rush of intense glow. For a few moments you gibber inanely, then you go sky high. After a while you have another one. We were all popped out of our heads. One o'clock – two o'clock – three o'clock – CRACK! . . . slobber . . . How that house shook! Sherry was terrific at the jive. She loved to take the lead. Only Dawn couldn't make it to her feet – she clapped and chortled in the corner like something from the funny farm.

'Little Gloria,' I said, 'there's an awful smell of burning.'

'Have another popper, Daddy-O, and shut yer eke. Poppers, everybody! Where's my drink, oops, oh ah oh, that's, mmm, ah, ooo,' and he charged through Ernestine's legs.

But the room went up in flames. There was a terrible scramble to escape. Chiffon and tulle flew in all directions. By the time the firemen arrived most of the party-goers had gone to ground in the back streets of Earl's Court. The room was gutted.

Nevern Square saw me nicely through a winter without Joey. It was a happy house, there were fewer fights than you would imagine and most of them were over peluccas. But in the spring of 1956 Tallulah began to get into deep water. His boyfriends deserted him and he owed three months' rent.

'Well, there's always the night boat to Jersey,' I said. We looked at each other and took a taxi to Victoria Station.

When the island police saw Tallulah they almost fainted. Chrome-yellow hair, plucked eyebrows, see-through plastic mac (these were known as French Letters), the smile and the walk, a touch of rouge –

he couldn't bear to look pale. We washed dishes. The manager of the hotel, Mr Pomfret, took a violent dislike to Tallulah, who was inclined to be over-careful with his hands.

'Can't you wash dishes like a man, you fucking freak!'

'Listen to this, Tone. Pumfry's gone all Hercules, he's been at the pills again.'

'Freak freak freak!'

'Don't you call my friend a freak,' I said. 'He's a very nice person.' I hit Pumfry round the face with a wet tea-cloth. There was a scuffle and he locked us both in a cupboard.

'I'm calling the police,' he shouted through the wood.

'Fine. And hurry up about it because we want to get out of this cupboard.'

He didn't call the police, he sacked us instead. As a result I transferred to washing dishes at a small hotel at Grève-de-Lecq run by Mr and Mrs Craven. I'd not been washing-up long when their chef went sick.

'Who on earth is going to cook the two hundred lobsters every day?' said Mrs Craven. Lobster teas were the house speciality.

'I'll do it,' I piped. I knew roughly from my brothers that it takes twelve minutes to boil a lobster, that they have to be boiled alive. And I was the only person who didn't mind the screaming noise as the air forces itself out of the shells, although Rita tells me I used to weep over the pans. Later Mrs Craven took me aside and said, 'Would you like to run the dining-room? And with the season coming up, do you know anyone who could help you?'

By this time Pussy and Ernestine had arrived on the island, also because of rent trouble. I met them with Tallulah at the Red Cabin Bar and said, 'Would you all like a job with me?'

A small staff cottage was set aside for us. Every morning I turned on the record player and woke them with 'The Farmer And The Cowhand Must Be Friends' at full blast. It wasn't popular because they drank like fish and always awoke with ghastly hangovers (but by 10.30 a.m. they were blotto and happy again). One of the things which fascinated me was that although I received higher wages they all seemed to be better off.

'Now listen, what's going on? How come you've all got this dough to throw around?'

Tallulah looked me straight in the eye, opened those pearly gates, and said, 'We thieve £5 a day from the till. £5 each.'

How could I have been so dim? 'O.K.' I said, 'that's what you do, well, carry on I suppose, but you're not to take so much or I'll sack you, and you're not to let me see how you do it or I'll sack you again. Now back to work!'

As a troupe we were a great hit in the dining-room. The more flagrant we became the more the tills rang. But poor Tallulah, he went up and down like a yo-yo. Either he was camping it up like crazy or in the deepest of blues. With the sea so adjacent he found trying to drown himself an irresistible proposition. Twice I retrieved him from the waves and whispered thanks to my bronze medal. One Saturday night we built a bonfire on the beach for a barbecue. It was a great success – baked potatoes, sausages, chops – until Tallulah came out of the shadows, drunk, wearing a white sheet.

'This is the end,' he announced and delicately lifting the hem of the sheet walked straight into the bonfire. It must have roused him from his sorrows because he came out the other side like an express train, but he couldn't walk on his feet for weeks and served the customers standing in enormous blocks of bandage.

Joey turned up and presented me to his fiancée. I swallowed hard. He looked ill and was cold. We walked along the beach, drawing in deep breaths of air and letting them out again without speaking. For a long time he didn't realise how completely I had fallen for him.

By the end of the season I was very tired. Money was still disappearing from the till in large amounts. Short of shopping my friends, there was nothing I could do. That bubble would soon burst, I was convinced. And I'd started brooding again about Joey. He didn't want me. Since I'd saved well I decided to go to Cannes for a holiday.

Being a freak has its compensations on the Côte d'Azur. In singlet and Audrey Hepburn hair I walked out of the *pension*, down to the Eden Plage, and into a crowd of faces from London. Eric Lindsay and Ray Jackson, who ran the Heaven and Hell Coffee Bar next to the Two Eyes, were among them.

'Why don't you go to Le Carrousel?'

'Le Carrousel?'

'The most famous nightclub in the world for female and male impersonators. They'd love you. We're driving to Paris, we'll give you a lift.'

I cashed in my air ticket (which one could do in those days) and jumped in the car. Paris! The Eiffel Tower looked unutterably smart.

We went to the club's 11 p.m. floor show. Through the foyer, through the Long Bar, to the tables and chairs for about a hundred. The interior was Parisian red plush and gilt, with a small stage and band at one end. The curtains opened and I was transfixed. It was more than I'd ever imagined. Not the bewigged and painted dames of Nevern Square but beautiful girls. Two of them, 'Coccinelle' and 'Bambi' according to the programme, held my attention throughout.

'They can't be men,' I said to Eric.

'Of course they are. That's the whole point. Except that one there. Micky Mercer. He's a woman. Let's come back tomorrow and see if we can get you backstage.'

'But I can't dance, I can't sing, I can't do that stuff.' The whole idea petrified me.

Yet I did return. The Artistic Director, Monsieur Lasquin, agreed to see me. He called in a Canadian, Les Lee, to act as translator and to check the credentials on my passport. 'Brother,' said Les, turning towards me a frightening visage, half-in, half-out of drag, 'you'll knock 'em dead.'

Bambi came in, pursed his/her mouth at me, and started speaking huffily to Monsieur Lasquin.

'Il faut attendre le patron – Monsieur Marcel,' said Lasquin.

The boss took hours to show. I was a dither of nerves. A tough French Algerian, he barged in scowling. He looked me over as if I were a piece of furniture, went out, came back, and said in broken English, 'So what you do?'

'Nothing, monsieur.'

'Nothing. I see. Nothing . . .'

Monsieur Marcel frowned, walked behind his desk and scratched his square blue chin, muttering, ' . . . nothing . . . nothing . . . '

Then he looked up and burst out laughing: 'O.K., we teach you.'

4 Paris

In the 1960s it was in London; in the 1970s it moved to New York; but in the 1950s 'it' was in Paris – you smelt it in the streets, you saw it in the faces in the cafés, you trod in it the moment you went out of the door: a feeling that to be elsewhere was to be in Siberia.

I'd read about the beatniks and existentialism in the newspapers (I read newspapers cover-to-cover, plus Georgette Heyer novels) and knew that 'Left Bank' meant dressing in a black sweater and black slacks and regarding the world as your oyster. Already I had the wardrobe. Now I wanted to try out the behaviour. So I took a room in the heart of it, in the Hôtel Jacob, rue Jacob, off the Place St Germain. It was winter and the cafés were glassed-in but this didn't discourage the human traffic up and down the wide purpose-built pavements of the Boulevard St Germain, existentialism's main trawl.

The first place I went into was the Café Flore and gosh! There was Françoise Sagan sucking an *apéritif* with Simone de Beauvoir, and an American in white basketball boots looking on through a hang-over – Rod McKuen, yet to be acclaimed. Too intense. So on to the Café Turnot and ordered a Kir, chatted to a black American. An ordinary black American? Not here, not in 1956. His name was Richard Wright and in 1940 he'd published the first big black American novel, *Native Son*. But he looked sad, a long way from home.

'Then why don't you go back to Mississippi?' I asked.

'And wipe spit off my face all day?'

Expatriate Americans and English tended to accumulate at the Café Odéon. Many had deserted the Korean War. Hemingway materialised there occasionally, still the great literatus but increasingly lushed to bits and surrounded by nobodies and even, sometimes, Parisians. The form was very *débonnaire*. You didn't make a song and dance, you sat down, and hey presto, became part of it. A tab accompanied each drink and in due course they would all find their way across to Hemingway's area of table. By the end of a stint he'd often have fifty or sixty under his chin. Before his eyes finally glazed over he would pay them all and stumble out. Someone might shout 'La musique!' as a way of clearing the slightly perplexed air Hemingway always left behind him. We'd be off to the Club Tabou or to L'Ange Bleu, or the Club St Germain where Stephane Grappelli swung his violin, or uptown to Le Boeuf sur le Toit where Juliette Greco sang her *chansons réalistes* as if she were hacking her way through a jungle.

After Hemingway the other great figure was of course Jean-Paul Sartre. On the tourist map he was taken in between the Louvre and the Hôtel des Invalides, by way of the Brasserie Lipp where he lunched in his dingy overcoat. If only he'd left a hat on the floor he could have made a fortune from the perpetual file-past of Americans.

'Is that Sartre the Great Thinker?'

'Well, Martha, it doesn't say anything here about it, but I suppose it must be because he looks so *unattractive*.'

I never saw Sartre wear anything other than this overcoat, whatever the weather, whatever the time of year. And there was no question of small talk. Basically you collected a cup of coffee and sat down at his feet. At this time I believe he was being watched because of his opposition to French policy in Algeria so his eminence was tinged with insurrection, which further excited his disciples.

These famous men and women, with whom one rubbed elbows but was not on terms of intimacy, regarded me as a surreal object. They did make the moment ring with a certain éclat. But my own business was on the other side of the river in the Huitième district.

As a beginner, I was paid about £12 per week by Le Carrousel. My room was a couple of miles from the club and in order to save the Métro fare I'd walk to rehearsals each morning along the Boulevard St Germain, across the Seine to the Place de la Concorde (where the most famous guillotine of the Reign of Terror chopped 1,343 heads), up the Avenue des Champs-Élysées to the club at 40 rue du Colisée. Even by Parisian standards I was an odd-looking creature, yet I always felt safe walking. Only once was there trouble. Walking to work at night, taking a short cut down a side street, a man put a gun in my back. It was the time of the White Slave Trade scandal. I saw myself caged in an Oriental harem with a potentate who would beat his gong and demand my favours. It was a tiresome prospect and I screamed 'Damn! Damn! Damn!' very fast, very loud. The gunman was so startled he ran off and I dived into the nearest *boîte* for a cognac.

The dressing-room was divided in half by a row of back-to-back dressing-tables. On one side were the stars like Coccinelle and Bambi and on the other the polloi: two rows of narcissists transported in mirrors. Fortunately for my *savoir-faire* as well as my *amour-propre* I was seated with the stars, who were to instruct me in the techniques of make-up and presentation.

Bambi took me along to Dr Four once a week for expensive shots of the female hormone oestrogen. These assist feminisation, but not fundamentally. The most important effect is the promotion of breast development. As the breasts enlarge they redden and become sore. The nipples become particularly touchy. Oestrogen must affect people differently because my breasts never amounted to much whereas Ruby, another of the female impersonators, had overwhelming dugs, pendulous in character. She'd take off her brassière and wail, 'My God, the floor's cold!'

Coccinelle's were quite a bagful too, the consistency of india-rubber because she'd had them pumped up with silicone. You could knock them and they wouldn't budge. Eventually of course they would begin to sag and Coxy had to return for boosters. Oh, dear, this dilemma again: is it 'he' or is it 'she'? Really, I should try to stick to 'he' until they've had their operations, but sometimes that simply doesn't sound right. So if I should lapse into 'she' again do regard it as the triumph of verisimilitude over pedantry.

Monsieur Marcel was pleased to see me become friendly with Bambi who, unlike most of them, was half-way respectable, didn't go in for harlotry after hours, didn't have a team of sugar-daddies in train. Bambi lived quietly with his mother, both of them refugees from Algeria. He was the most beautiful of the troupe.

The most striking was Everest, six feet five inches without heels. He was from Switzerland and, despite being brought up in a mountainous air, suffered from asthma. Everest was sheer pantomime – he performed a brilliant strip with clouds of talcum powder puffing out from all the naughty places in his body-stocking. I asked to do it on those days when Everest was absent but the management said it would undermine the image of my routine, which was to be, God help us, 'M'Lady'. Les Lee had a lot of raucous comedy in him too, although his expression was often that disquieting mixture of toughness and melancholy which one saw often on the faces of the transvestites.

Indisputably the star was Coccinelle, known to us as Monique or Coxy, and baptismally Jacques. He was Parisian by birth and had been raised among strumpets so that the ethics of their system came naturally to him. While constantly in pursuit of the rich, he kept a whole string of *amours* for his own pleasure. They frequently came to the club full of grievance because it was Coxy's fancy to coerce them into women's clothes from time to time. Being so full of machismo they fretted terribly in frillies. But of course they needed their keep. Coxy was nuts about drag. He thought the whole world should be in it.

He had a sensational collection of minks, all dyed different colours, which could have been why he owed Monsieur Marcel so much money. Marcel didn't mind because it guaranteed Coxy's permanence in the show. He was a great performer in the vaudeville tradition, ostentatiously vulgar. He liked to blow raspberries in the middle of his lilting rendition of 'Love's A Many Splendoured Thing'. At premières it was the same – a rubbery breast would topple out in front of the cameras, which he would thereby hog. All his frocks were cut low enough to reveal nipple when he exhaled. Lips were Coxy's obsession because he had virtually none of his own and therefore spent hours with a scarlet lipstick, smearing it on, layer upon layer, spreading it up to his nose and down to his chin like strawberry jam on toast, glossing it over, then applying yet more layers of lipstick, until in the end he'd achieved his objective, a mouth like a baboon's bottom.

Later Coxy had a sex-change and married her favourite boy, François. Being a faithful child of the Church, she booked Notre-Dame Cathedral for the ceremony (which she attended in another off-the-nipple gown). When the newlyweds appeared on the Cathedral steps for photographs, the crowd gave them a terrific send-off, apart from those who pelted them with tomatoes.

Since it was the most expensive club in a wildly expensive city, the *régime* at Le Carrousel was very strict. If you missed a rehearsal or a performance without notification you would be suspended without pay. For fighting, the suspension was ten days. Since most of us were living hand-to-mouth in hotels, suspension could be a disaster. No drink backstage and no visitors except by permission of M. Marcel, and absolutely no fraternising in the *salle* (where the public sat), again except with his permission. He was quite the autocrat. I was trying to think of whom he reminded me and then watching *Key Largo* on television it hit me: Edward G. Robinson at his most tongue-in-cheekily pugnacious. Marcel's aspect was even more forbidding when he wore 'shades' because his true nature, deeply ironical, which otherwise showed in his eyes, was concealed. His wife owned Madame Arthur's, Le Carrousel's poor relation in Pigalle specialising in grotesques. They could be a fierce couple.

Only Bambi and Coccinelle addressed him without the title Monsieur, until one night he popped into the dressing-room and I said, 'I'd really like a new frock, Marcel, I'm fully bored with this one.'

Coxy's lipstick stopped dead in mid-air for the first time in history; he didn't take his face out of the mirror but I knew what he was thinking: 'That cow's got a bloody nerve!'

'Yes, you crazy English,' said Marcel, 'I think you look tacky too. Get off to the fitters tomorrow. Will you stop grumbling now? Can I have some damn peace?' I went off to the dressmaker's in Montmartre and called him Marcel from then on.

I made a quick visit to London to collect the rest of my things.

'For Christ's sake, why the hell are you going to work in a drag club?' grimaced Joey. Such a sulky boy at times. At least the fiancée had vanished, with a little help from me.

'Do stop being so *farouche*, Joey.' One learned new words every day in Paris.

'What's that mean?'

'Miseryguts! . . . The club's not perfect but it's one step nearer my goal.'

'Big deal. I'm hungry.' He winked at me and tucked his shirt in. Here I was, about to enter upon a crucial new chapter in my life, and all he could think of was bacon and eggs with plenty of fried bread. If I'd waited for Joey's approval I'd have been stacked with the dishes in Jersey to this day.

But Rita bounced up and down like a beach-ball, rushed at me, hugged me, stared up at something in her mind's eye which none the less seemed to be positioned about a foot above my head, and declared: 'It's the most romantic thing in the world. Paris. Paree . . . I'll never see you again, ever . . . yes, I will! It isn't far, is it?'

A new show was unveiled every January and this is what I began to rehearse, starting at ten in the morning. Everyone had solo parts and we all bundled together for a finale. My spot, Monsieur Lasquin decided, would consist of dancing a mambo in printed leopardskin trews and a tied-shirt top, followed by singing 'Venus, if you will, please send a little boy for me to love', in a long white Grecian dress.

'It's a nice contrast, don't you think?' said M. Lasquin, tearing the leg off a *croissant* and dipping it in his coffee, 'the animal and the cerebral, the concupiscent and the virginal, the . . .'

'The dirty and the clean?'

'That's so English of you. Now run through it again with Monsieur Tarquin.'

Monsieur Tarquin was the choreographer who felt he was the new Massine and that it was only a matter of time before . . . Meanwhile he fluttered with zeal.

Opening night – was I on hot bricks. I danced that mambo like a leaping thyroid, so fast that the band were still playing it long after I'd fled the stage.

'How d'I do, how d'I do?' But they were speechless with laughter, all except Tarquin who'd stuffed a silk *fichu* into his mouth and was hissing at me through it, *'Merde, merde!'*

Then, having changed into the white cerebral, I slapped my thigh, did a mental giddy-up, and reared back on to the stage to slaughter the song. Again I dispatched it so quickly that the band were in the middle of the last verse when I was back in the wings. Tarquin was jabbering from a corner with tufts of hair in his hands. 'Bow-wow, bow-wow, you forgot to take a bow-wow, you, you . . .' I thought he'd flipped and I'd be given the sack.

In fact 'Toni April' never overcame stage-fright ('April' after the month of my birth). Not being an exhibitionist was decidedly a drawback but I didn't dare take a drink until the show was over. Only once did I turn up drunk, so late that I had to dash straight on stage, stumbled and fell into the orchestra pit – never again. As always, the band were saints, four little old men doing their Palm Court best, slightly forlorn, with oppressive bills to pay and wives and families to whom they returned in the early hours of the morning.

If ever anyone got by on looks alone it was I. It would pass through my mind while I was up there on the shiny wooden stage, rasping and twirling in silks: 'I'm getting paid for this rubbish – it can't be true!' Speaking came easier than singing and dancing. Later on, in the south of France, when I introduced the acts in English while Gérard did so in French and we soaped up a little repartee, then I felt I'd done a successful job. But otherwise I wouldn't call myself an artiste.

Monsieur Tarquin wasn't overflowing with the gifts either. He was happy for the show to be a string of solos plus finale. I said to Marcel, 'I'm frightful at this mambo and Venus thing.'

'Of course you are.'

'Can't I do something more interesting? A sketch with some of the others?'

'Have you tried working with them? They're monsters. Underneath they're all trying to slit each other's throats. They all want to be big solo stars, they refuse to share the spotlight with anyone.'

'But I don't mind working with someone else. I'd love it.'

'You find someone and maybe we try it out. Talk to M. Lasquin about it, I haven't time for this, where's my taxi?'

Audrey came over to Paris. He'd been training at the Royal Ballet in London and I grabbed him. Monsieur Lasquin worked out a routine based on *My Fair Lady* . Eliza Doolittle is a bit corny now but she was a hot property in the 1950s. It involved fast, dramatic costume changes for me and was a great success with the audience because it provided a change of pace from all the drag queens trying to be Marlene Dietrich taking her clothes off. After this, if ever the cast thought I was getting above myself, they'd address me as 'M'Lady' in scornful tones. 'Look at M'Lady, she's just off to Heaven to have lunch with God.'

But under their healthy chastening there was perhaps a genuine resentment because I was now dressing full-time as a woman and looked authentic, whereas most of the others were buffoons in the glare of the day. They murdered their features with paint, wore dresses of staggering grossness, forced their boobs up and out – I was never a great one for cleavage. Among them only Bambi could also get away with it off-duty, although he cultivated a fringe because he had a receding hairline. I didn't and wore my hair scraped back in a bun or chignon to prove it.

Coccinelle had real talent, and eventually published his memoirs, but the others had only their talent for disguise, for turning their dreams into illusions. But the public was fascinated by it. The stars who came thought they were being very existentialist and avant-garde. We always knew when they were out there because the buzz from the *salle* would flow backstage. They timed their entrances considerately, coming in about 10.45 p.m. for the 11 o'clock show, so as not to steal the limelight from us. Ginger Rogers, Claudette Colbert, Marlene Dietrich, all alarmingly tiny. Marlene thought there should be a 'lesbian cabaret' club too (she had put up money for such an enterprise but I don't know if it came to anything). Les Lee introduced me to Rex Harrison who thought it 'all too intriguing', while Kay Kendall sat there looking haggard (she was very ill). When Schiaparelli came she was wearing a rose in her hair. But being 'Skap', it had to be sticking straight up on a stalk so that it looked as if it were growing out of the top of her head. Coccinelle noticed it, grabbed a bunch of roses from the bar, and distributed them backstage. We went on in the finale, a row of roses nodding on the tops of our heads. Schiaparelli ripped the rose from her hair and noisily stamped out – she adored being given the opportunity to do this sort of thing.

One afternoon I was sitting outside the Café Flore, having coffee with Steve, an American writer for Maurice Girodias and the Olympia Press. He was saying, 'I've written so much porn I can't get it up any more.'

'What a pity. You should try falling in love – it's not comfortable but it's wonderfully bracing. Have you ever been in love?'

'It gave me insomnia, I ran up debts and took to the bottle – I expect that was love. Her name was Linden Travers. Did you know her? But love is out of date now . . . Have you?'

'I'm in love at the moment. But he's in London.'

'Does he love you?'

'I don't think so. Well, maybe, in a funny sort of way – I think I'll have a *Parfait d'Amour*' (a rather sweet drink, purple in colour; it suited my mood).

I recall this desultory conversation because what happened next was straight out of a movie. Rita and Joey walked by carrying luggage.

'It was pouring with rain in London so we've come to live with you. Do you mind?'

My room at the Hôtel Jacob was strictly single, so we moved next door to the Hôtel d'Isly where they had rooms-for-three.

'Do you think I'll ever fall in love?' said Rita. She and Joey were just good friends and she had yet to be deflowered.

Rita – or Gigi as we began to call her – was determined to make Paris a success. We went to the Café Odéon. While Rita was rolling her green eyes and being enchanted by a big Jewish American with a gap in his front teeth, I said to Joey like Scarlett O'Hara: 'You'll never be free of me as long as you live. I'll always be there. I'm the only person you'll ever really love.'

'I can't think like that, I want to go and look at the Venus de Milo.'

'Steal some bread from the table. We can feed the carp in the Tuileries fountains. Gigi, we're going to the Louvre.'

'Can I see you again?' asked her American.

Rita's lovely round pink face turned white. Then red. 'Well, Lover of the Nile,' she replied, 'I'm going to the museums now. Art, you know. I need it. But I plan to be around . . .'

By the time we got outside she was giggling hysterically. 'Did you see that?' she said. 'He's called Marcel. I virtually had to drag myself out of his teeth, the dreamboat!'

Joey was disappointed by the Venus. He screwed up his face and said, 'I shouldn't like to fight her for a piece of meat.'

'But look at the skin, it's extraordinary.'

'Where's the Mona Lisa?'

'Where's Gigi?'

We tracked her down in the Salles des Cariatides, transfixed by the Discobolus. 'That's my kind of man,' she said.

'Oh Gigi, it'll happen to you one day. But I've got to get ready for work now.' And I did, so that we could eat. It was always such a wrench, just as the evening was taking off. I don't know how we survived. But we were young of course, and over the moon, which makes things much easier. They always met me at the club afterwards and we'd walk home together, stealing milk from the crates to go with our bread and cheese. Rita became adept at sneaking tomatoes and apples from the stalls, but there was never enough to eat.

By now I'd attracted my first stage-door Johnny. We called him the King of the Penguins because he waddled, hopped and flapped his arms and was never seen out of white tie and tails. On his black oiled hair perched a top hat, in his hand were gloves and a cane, around his shoulders was an opera cloak, in his buttonhole a red carnation, and across his breast a blue sash bearing a bogus decoration. He was very fat and wore white make-up rouged on the cheeks and on the end of the nose like a clown. Not only did he himself flap but he was the cause of flapping in others. Around him was always a commotion of waiters, taxi-drivers, slamming doors, popping corks. In a high squeaky voice he told me how much he loved me.

'Oh I don't mind if you're in love with me,' I said, 'so long as Rita and Joey can come along too.' We capered all over the cafés of St Germain, but always ordering the cheapest item on the menu, which was usually soup, filling ourselves up with bread, or as a treat bowls of chilli washed down with red wine in the student/Moroccan quarter of St Michel. When the three of us went out alone it was one cup of coffee shared between three and loaded up with sugar for energy – my sugar habit today, at least four heaped teaspoonsful per cup, must be a legacy from this period.

Joey cattily suggested Rita went out on the bash. 'If Toni can earn money to keep us, so can you.'

'How dare you, you lazy sod! I'm not like that, I'm saving myself. At least I've tried to get a job. Have you?' The problem was that neither of them could obtain work permits. But Joey wasn't ashamed of wanting merely to chase the Parisian girls. He wasn't conceited, he just knew how toothsome he was. I would have walked off a cliff for him.

One morning after a long night Les Lee decided to take us all for *le petit déjeuner* at the Flea Market. When we came out the sun was up. Joey said, 'You look as though you've got a suntan. I think I'm rubbing off on you at last!'

'Take off your glasses,' said Les. I always wore dark glasses in the early mornings when I still had full stage make-up on. 'Oh shit, your eyeballs are bright yellow – you're ill!'

I'd been feeling lethargic and losing weight. Hepatitis was confirmed when the results of the blood tests came through. I was told to go on a special diet – no fats, no chocolate, no alcohol. But imagining hepatitis was akin to sea-sickness, that is, something which went away by itself, I ignored the doctor's orders.

Rita had more or less left us for her young Jewish American, Marcel Wallace, who between classes in French Literature at the Sorbonne was courting her heavily and taking her everywhere.

'Do you know what he told me in the bar of the Ritz?' said Rita.

'That a woman should be able to make a man come just by trembling. He's teaching me so much. He introduced me to Sartre the other day.'

'Dingy overcoat in the Brasserie Lipp?'

'That's right. How did you know?'

Joey and I moved to a cheaper hotel where we were robbed of everything. They even stole Joey's soiled underpants. It was all getting rather desperate.

Les Lee pulled me up sharply: 'Unless you're prepared to be very ill indeed, that boy must fend for himself. You've got to eat properly.' Les was always enormously kind to me. He had all the old-fashioned vices but all the old-fashioned virtues too. He sent money home to his parents every month. He saved, had a budget for everything, made all his own dresses, sewed every sequin on himself. The first Christmas in Paris, Les took Joey and myself under his wing and fed us up. Joey, whose stomach had shrunk, ate so much that he vomited all over the taxi on the way home. I remember crashing out in Les's bed one night. He'd just had his eyes lifted by a plastic surgeon. When I awoke I thought he was dead on his back. His eyes were open and rolled back into his head showing only the whites. After such an operation you cannot close the eyes for a few days because the lids won't stretch, so you must sleep with them open.

Joey returned to London, and Les found me a room in the Hôtel de la Paix in the rue Roquepine, next door to his hotel so that he could keep an eye on me. Very run down, I was put on a course of vitamins and plain-boiled foods. If I went for a glass of wine Les would snatch it away saying, 'You look ugly with yellow eyes – remember that!' I soon got the idea.

The hotel was run by Mme Petit, a bright Frenchwoman in basic black and pearls. My room was in the attic with a view across the rooftops to the neo-classical Église de la Madeleine, a vision of glory when my latest acquisition, a record of *La Bohème*, turned on the second-hand gramophone which went with the room. I played it every night while up there composing myself for work and knew that for me opera was the ultimate theatrical and musical experience. But I missed the madness of St Germain, its irreverence.

It took me nearly six months to recover but at the end of that time I was rewarded by being chosen to play Le Carrousel's summer season at Juan-les-Pins on the Côte d'Azur.

Before we boarded *le train bleu* I visited Rita in the American Hospital. She had married Marcel in Jersey and was now sitting up in bed holding her first son, David. She looked so like the all-American mother with piles of paper hankies on either side of the bed. Even her voice was changing, Leeds having been nudged out by a definite twang.

'That was fast work. Are you happy, Gigi?'

'I think so, Toni. I want *lots* of babies.'

'I *do* hope you're happy, more than anything!'

'I am, I am, I told you! But my youth is over now. Marcel's going to teach at the University of Arizona and I'm going to be a good campus wife. Doesn't that make you smile?'

'No more stolen milk . . .'

'No more stolen tomatoes either. Marcel's father invented sonic radar, they're multi-millionaires. Isn't that a bonus? It's rather frightening but I'm sure I'll take to it. We're off in a couple of weeks.'

'Good luck, Gigi.'

'Good luck, Toni.'

I felt that my youth was over too.

The season down south meant promotion and more money. While Coxy remained with the show in Paris, Bambi and I stopped the traffic (literally) along the Côte d'Azur. Part of our job was to be seen in the best places so that folk would say, 'It can't be true – surely they're girls', and come along to the show. Often we'd drive half an hour along the coast in Bambi's Simca and sit drinking cocktails on the terrace of the Carlton Hotel in Cannes like a couple of neon lights. Everywhere we were importuned. Our strategy was to say, 'O.K. – for £1,000.' Even then we had takers and so resorted to our second line of defence: *'Mais, monsieur, nous avons une petite inconvenance.'*

'Oh, I see, you're two lesbians?'

'No!' and we would crook our little fingers, hoping the penny would drop. If it didn't I would yell in frustration, '*Nous sommes garçons*!' which of course didn't bother them at all and in the end we'd invariably have to tell them outright to get lost. You can imagine how good-looking they were, those men in the south of France – I'd give my eyeballs for one or two of them now.

Juan was the nicest of the resorts because it was relatively undeveloped. Le Carrousel's premises there were not as opulent as in Paris but attracted a similar mix of the straight, the bent, the curious, the young and old, plus a quota of celebrities. Bob Hope and his wife came and took me out for breakfast. He didn't crack one joke. Les Lee explained that his wit was thin without cue cards. Margaret Lockwood brought her daughter Julia or 'Toots' as she was known. As I squeezed past her Margaret said, 'I've been dying to ask you, I hope you don't mind, but what' – she put her nose in the air and swooned like one of the Bisto kids – 'is that divine scent you're wearing?'

'*Ma Griffe* by Carven,' I answered bashfully (because Margaret Lockwood had been a big star ever since *The Wicked Lady* in 1945).

While Margaret sat in a deckchair doing endless crossword puzzles, Bambi and I joined Toots and her boyfriend Simon Gough on the beach near the Lockwoods' summer villa at Cap d'Antibes. It was very private, unlike the beaches in Juan where we were mobbed by trippers and photographers, especially when we wore bikinis. They would point at our knickers, say 'Where is it?', and we'd have to bombard them with the contents of our picnic lunch.

When work was over at two or three in the morning, we'd drive off again to Cannes, to Le Whisky A-Go-Go on Palm Beach. If the others in the show came with us they usually changed into men's clothes. At the Whisky it was all fizz and cha-cha-cha. And men. The whole atmosphere along that coast was so importunate – I could have been a great courtesan if only I'd known how to cope in bed. Les Lee was quite different. I shared a big apartment with him and had hardly any sleep. There were troops of men through the flat all night long while I snuggled up to Frou-Frou, Les Lee's dog, christened after the underskirt of a cancan dancer.

When there was time, my greatest diversion was Amateur Strip Night at La Vieille Colombieuse nightclub – secretaries *en vacances* would mysteriously get the call, jump on to the stage and start to disrobe. Half-way through they invariably froze, looked down at themselves in horror and fled the stage in tears.

In the club next to ours Edith Piaf was singing. After her show she always left with a group of muscular Ganymedes, the sensible woman. Apart from opiates, her favourite tipple was vigorous young men from underprivileged backgrounds. She flaunted them on the beach. When she'd had a few drinks you could hear her ranting at them: 'Yes, go and brag to your friends how you've had the Great Edith Piaf! I don't care. You can't break me. I'm broken already. But try! Try!'

Joey arrived for the summer, bringing yet another girl with him.

'I've got V.D.,' he said.

'You're full of encouraging news.'

'Don't be like that. I was hoping you'd lend me some cash to get it cured. It's not very nice, you know.'

'I don't *know*. I've never had it. What about this girl?'

'She's nothing really.'

'O.K. – you get rid of the girl and I'll pay for the treatment.' I had to help him out – he was wearing a white tennis top, with three mother-of-pearl buttons up to a darling little collar. His looks, as always, hypnotised me.

A German woman called Ariane came to the club. She had a brandy-coloured suntan which showed off her platinum hair. We took to one another immediately and met for lunches and drinks. After a while she said to me, 'You're English and I'm German – the war was a terrible thing.'

'But it's over now.'

'Yes. And I've an awful secret to tell you. I'm Goebbels's sister-in-law. My sister was married to him.'

'But how come you're alive? I thought the entire family committed suicide in the Berlin Bunker.'

'I was in the Bunker at the end. Goebbels and my sister, they murdered their six children and then poisoned themselves. But I was only twelve. They said: "You are not immediate family, you leave." They sent me away in a car. My sister was one of the most beautiful women in Germany . . .'

Ariane had splendid jewels which I suspect were the remains of the family fortune. She also had a marvellous sense of humour, refused to brood on the past, and visited me later in Paris: 'I live in Düsseldorf but I always do my shopping in Paris.'

Meanwhile Bambi and I continued our search for the miraculous surgeon who would, we imagined, enable us to lead a normal life. The details of the Christine Jorgensen story had now become familiar and strengthened our resolve. We were told of such a doctor in Nice and visited him. He gave us hormone implants. A small cut is made along the pubic bone and pellets are inserted which operate on a slow-release principle. They last much longer than the shots.

'Not only can I perform surgery on your genitals,' he added, 'but also I want to transplant wombs.'

'How wonderful,' said Bambi.

'Wonderful? You're crazy! Bambi, if you want to give birth to monsters and maybe die on the slab, you go ahead. But count me out.'

My pay should have dropped when we returned to Paris but it didn't, which was tantamount to a rise. Off the breadline at last! It's a glorious moment in anyone's life when this happens. And I could begin to save.

Mme Petit knew this and gave me a better room on a lower floor. There was an informal procedure in these small Parisian *pensions*. Because there were no lifts and only one bathroom, as one's money went up the position of one's room came down. The hotel was tall and narrow and as I prospered I found myself descending it until I was sandwiched on the second floor.

One noontide, sitting up in bed with a cup of coffee, poking my hair, meditating on the start of a new day and springtime in Paris, with the sun flooding across my counterpane, I was astounded to see somebody drop past the window. This was followed by an ear-splitting crash. Grabbing my *robe de chambre* I ran to the window. A man was spreadeagled face-downwards on the roof of Mme Petit's dining-room, which was made of netted glass. The courtyard had filled with gesticulating French. The man was semi-conscious, he made no noise, not even a moaning. But when he stirred I could see that the front of him, especially face and hands, was pouring with blood from a thousand cuts.

Mme Petit told me he was a Pole. His wife and son were still in Poland but he had sought political asylum in France. That morning he'd heard he couldn't have it.

The incident galvanised me into doing what I'd long wanted to do: move back up to the top. Being so utterly French, Mme Petit was shocked that I should want my unchic rooftops back but I was determined and began to unpin the *Bohème* and *Traviata* posters. The French and their chic! It was relentless. As a gesture of defiant individuality I found myself including in my dress one item that didn't go – a necklace that was too bulky, an evening bag in the daytime, a clashing scarf, the wrong gloves – anything to antagonise perfect taste. 'Vulgarity is the garlic in the salad of charm' (St Bumpus).

After work Audrey and I began to frequent Le Bantu, a late-late nightclub behind the Lido where artistes unwound when their shows were over. I first went with Hary Laubscher, a London friend in the throes of depression. As we left, the manager called me over and gave me a wadge of francs.

'What's this for?'

'You work at Le Carrousel, don't you?'

'Yes, but . . .'

'Well, that's for bringing in a customer.'

'But he's my friend.'

'Is he? He gets charged the same anyway. So you might as well take your cut. That's what happens here.'

If you were in the business yourself and introduced business to another club, you received your cut. Presumably it's this kind of practice which makes Parisian nightclubs such an exorbitant night out. The cut was a lot of money. A third of the bill. Hence Le Bantu became my regular move-on after work and although it seemed to come close to prostitution I was soon earning as much money there as at Le Carrousel. If Audrey came too we'd treat them to a few wild rumbas – the management used to ply us with champagne to get us going.

They did the same with the strippers who came on from the Crazy Horse Saloon: Dodo Hamburg whose angle was to strip off widow's weeds out of a coffin, Rita Renoir wearing dark body make-up and whooping around as if she had live fish in her knickers, and Rita Cadillac, a tall, pouting blonde. I became quite friendly with Miss Cadillac. We went to Joffo's Salon together where Robert did our hair and we once spent a weekend at Joffo's château near Tours. She turned out to be a superb shot, bagging six rabbits to my one.

The Alaria Ballet, an exotic South American macambo troupe, came to Le Bantu when they were performing at the Lido. Jean Marais kissed my feet there. Geneviève Fath gave me her earrings to dance in, two pearls the size of ping-pong balls, one white, the other black. Geneviève was said to have the largest single-piece marble dining-table in Paris.

Who else? The Bluebell Girls, of course, who worked at the Lido, and the Showgirls Sandra Lebroque and Candy Seymour-Smith (deb-turned-coryphée), accompanied by an American male dancer called Skippy. He was slim and fair with feet like razorblades. The Bluebell Girls should have been nicely tucked up in bed by this time. Their boss, Margaret Kelly, a Liverpudlian, was very tough with them, desperate that none should go astray. But Elvis Presley had quite a few. He was stationed in Germany at the time and flew to Paris with an entourage for dirty weekends. His military crew-cut made him strikingly boyish and it stunned you to realise what a looker he was. The most remarkable thing about his looks was their colouring: blue-black hair, golden skin, lips so cherry-red they looked artificial, and brilliant green eyes. One of his aides took me aside and asked if I were prepared to 'go with Elvis'. 'Going with Elvis' wasn't something you had to think about for very long but I thought it only cricket to explain who, or rather what, I was. There was consternation in the Elvis camp. Presley, puritan as hell but a polite Southern boy none the less, came across and said, 'I hope my friend didn't embarrass you. Do have a drink.' There were no more approaches, but his party always sent a drink across when we coincided. He was always sober, looked slightly uncomfortable, but loaded with charisma even in that dark glittering den.

Le Carrousel kept one tied down during the civilised hours, seven nights a week, but every few months I'd take a night off and there were treats. A performance of *La Traviata* at l'Opéra – at last. Judy Garland at the Palais de Chaillot. Meeting Anton Dolin at Bill Taylor's flat – 'You look like my father,' I said to him. He thought I was trying to be the smart alec until I showed him Father's photograph which I always carried. Since then he's always been 'Daddy Pat' Dolin.

A Russian Prince took me to Shéhérazade for dinner, Old Russia recreated, gypsy violins drooling schmaltz, and the tables bathed in blue fire from sizzling *flambés*. The Prince kissed my knuckles and said, 'I know I'm dull, I know I'm not handsome, *mais vous êtes ma honeybunch* and I'll do anything if only you'd go to bed with me.'

While we tangoed on the dance-floor I thought about it and said, 'O.K., Dmitri – if you eat a glass for me.' At once he tucked into a brandy balloon. After three or four bites there was blood everywhere. They brought the restaurant's first-aid kit to mend his mouth. It was a gallant effort, I couldn't deny him.

But these incidents were exceptional. And there were few major dramas inside the club itself. Capucine (not the film star but one of us) did once try to kill himself – I hope you aren't becoming too fatigued by these suicide attempts. They were always happening around me. Life seethed with private tragedies. But I'll try to thin them out from here on. Anyway, Capucine's heart was pierced by a conflict: the ancient sugar-daddy and luxury, or the young blades and penury? Of course the luxury always won in the end because Capucine's keeper was a very famous millionaire, enabling Capsy to compete with and overtake Coxy's mink collection. But unlike Coxy, Capsy wanted to be 'a lady' as well. This put him into agonising quandaries when he fell for a bricklayer or a road-digger (which was frequently, because Capsy couldn't resist the *boue*).

So it was no surprise when M. Lasquin announced, 'Capucine won't be in tonight. She's taken an overdose of pills and is being pumped out in the clinic.'

However, Capucine wasn't going to leave the ground clear for sympathy or bitchery and came striding in wearing a whole mink farm and all the crown jewels. His mouth was swollen and bruised where the stomach pump had been forced in (sometimes in an emergency, if the jaw is clenched, they have to break the teeth to do this).

'The show must go on!' he said in English, throwing off his pelts. And he passed out cold on the floor.

Marcel entered, looked down scornfully, looked at us, looked at the dressers and said, 'Take her knickers off.'

Capucine was on his feet in a twinkling – he wasn't going to let anyone see his *zee-zee*. He flew out to a cab and made a complete recovery at home. But Capsy had his moment a few months later when Callas gave a charity concert at l'Opéra. Tickets were several hundred pounds each. Coxy poo-pooed Callas but Capucine was in fact the only one who could afford to go. Once there he dropped a shoulder strap, out they fell, and he was all over the newspapers the next day. This kind of frantic oneupmanship was the least attractive side of Carrousel life. I suppose fame and attention gave them a feeling of reality they didn't otherwise possess.

Of all the people Les Lee introduced me to, Josephine Baker was the one I liked most. Before the war she *was* Paris, the most celebrated of the black dancers who bewitched Europe in the 1920s. She had been nicknamed the Black Pearl and compared to a figurine from Tanagra. In my time she contrived a comeback show, *Paris, Mes Amours*, and took it to the Folies Bergères, the scene of her original triumphs, but they said, 'Sorry, Josephine, you're past it.' She booked the Olympia off her own bat, put it on and broke all records there. Then she took it on tour and came back for a second season. I asked her why she'd gone back into show business and she said,

'Because I was broke.' The reason she was broke was that she'd taken on masses of orphans and refugee children.

Towards the end of my stretch at Le Carrousel I became chums with a new member of the troupe, Peki d'Oslo, otherwise Alain Tapp, later Amanda Lear.

Audrey said to me, 'You must meet this young painter I know. He wants to become a woman.' Peki's Franco-Oriental family lived in southern France and he was pursuing art in Paris, surviving by painting delightful postcards of Paris scenes. I said, 'But, my dear, these are lovely – you must stay as you are, you must develop your talent, you mustn't waste yourself in cabaret.' In addition to being a painter he was a talented polyglot. But Peki was adamant and so joined the show. *Sayonara*, starring Marlon Brando, had just hit the screens – wasn't he gorgeous in that military uniform? – and because of Peki's features M. Lasquin gave him an Oriental spot.

Salvador Dali visited the club. He said, 'Gold is the most beautiful thing in the world, and the next most beautiful thing in the world is to wake up in the morning and find lots and lots of cheques in the post.' Mr Dali hoped to paint me unclad as *Hermaphroditos* but the possibility of being immortalised in my half-way house on the walls of the Tate Gallery was too horrible to contemplate. Dali's cousin was much weirder than the painter. He invited me for dinner at his flat and served spaghetti. Instead of Parmesan cheese, he took out a box and sprinkled tin-tacks all over his and walloped the lot down while giving a monologue on horse-racing.

It was Peki whom Dali came to know really well. I don't think they were ever what the Americans refer to as 'an item' but they were close. Peki told me hair-raising stories of Dali's artistic orgies staged outside Paris and attended by Pompidou and other *éminences*. One was an exercise in symmetry. The maestro arranged two beds in the centre of the room, co-opted two pairs of twins, one male, the other female, and urged them to make love with their opposites.

Le Carrousel organised tours to Germany, Scandinavia, Italy and South America. In the autumn of 1959, after the regular season at Juan, the promoters of the Italian tour specified in the contract that both Coxy and I had to be part of the package. The tour opened and closed with long runs in Milan at La Porta del Ora, a lavish club with plaster scrollwork on the walls, mock Louis Seize furniture, and a barman who seduced me with a stream of Dry Martinis.

In Milan I digged with Audrey. He had a maddening habit of jumping out of his bed at 4 a.m. shouting, 'I've got to have a man, I've got to!' and charging out of the door.

So when Peki said to me, 'I want to be a lady just like you,' I replied, 'In that case, *chéri*, when we move on, you become my room-mate because I tell you, Audrey's driving me round the twist with these gigantic Italians rolling in at all hours.' And so, for the rest of the tour Peki became my *protégé*.

Between the two runs in Milan came Bologna, Viareggio, Naples and Florence. Not Rome. It was the Papal City and the Church didn't want types like us in it.

The manager of La Porta del Ora indicated that it was part of our job to sit with the customers, encourage them to order champagne (on which the mark-up was always immense), sleep with them if possible, and drag them back in again the following day.

'I'm not sitting with those smelly old tramps after a hard day's work!'

'Butta you musta. Eet's expected.'

'Ees eet? It was never done at Le Carrousel and I'm not doing it here.'

'At leest, won't you eet dinner out there?'

'I'll eat dinner out there but it's going to be alone, just with Peki.'

Out there, a gentleman of mature years sitting with Coxy and Kiki Moustique (another of the turns; and who, incidentally, was married to a sweet young girl) came across and introduced himself: 'Are you English? I was educated in England.'

That seemed tolerable so we permitted him to join us. His name was Enrico Paradi, a frightfully rich industrialist. Later the manager came up and said that Coccinelle wanted to see me in the dressing-room.

'You two-faced English bitch!' she yelped. 'You're on the first fucking train back to Paris!'

'Coxy, what are you talking about?'

'My name's not Coxy!'

'O.K. – Monique . . .'

'To you it's Coccinelle – *the* Coccinelle!'

'Look, Jacques, is there something I can do for you?'

Everyone was frightened of Coccinelle, who was powerful enough to pick up the phone and say 'Marcel, I want So-and-so exchanged.' But I wasn't frightened because I knew my name was on that contract alongside hers.

Finally, after plenty of ugly grimaces, French slang and general dementia, she came out with it: 'What the hell are you doing stealing my *micheton*?'

'It's a sad thing, Jacques, when people as famous as *the* Coccinelle can no longer hold on to their men!' Sometimes one has to flourish one's claws in this life or else be swallowed alive.

'You wait, I'll get you, back in Paris. In fact I'm phoning Marcel right now!'

'Do your worst – I wouldn't mind leaving this grotty little tour.'

I was called to the phone and Marcel said, '*Ma petite foule Anglaise*, what is going on now?'

'Monique's accusing me of stealing her moneypot.'

He spoke again to Coccinelle, who then stalked off the premises crashing every door she could lay her hands on. From sheer cussedness, I now determined to make a better acquaintance with Enrico, who turned out to be a dear old thing. There were a few days' break before Bologna and he invited Kiki and myself down to Rome for a slap-up weekend at the Excelsior Hotel on the Via Veneto. At Milan station we found two first-class sleeper berths booked for us. Inside were bottles of champagne, red and white roses and two purple-velvet boxes of Suchard chocolates with our names spelt out on them in semi-precious stones.

When we reached the Excelsior we handed over our passports, changed, and took Kiki's Pomeranian walkies along the Via Sistina. At the top of the Spanish Steps I saw, wouldn't you guess, Anna Magnani, one of my favourite actresses in over-emotional parts, seemingly dressed in mourning (the women so often are in Italy). We chatted while she was waiting for her son; she was mad about everything English including the people. However, when Kiki turned up in full slap and falsies Anna changed completely and that was the end of that.

As we continued our promenade, the *paparazzi*, always to be my bane, got wind of who we were in that telepathic way for which they're renowned, so we decided to retreat to the hotel – where we were arrested (as undesirables, the nerve!) and put back on the train for Milan. My experience of the Eternal City had been very brief indeed; it was too galling and Coxy of course was thrilled – until the *paparazzi* sold their pictures and Kiki and I found ourselves featured in all the popular magazines.

Bologna was freezing. The club was snowed in so practically no one saw us. In Naples the club was run by a countess who always had a dead rose in her hair and a dead cigar in her mouth. After Milan, Naples had the best audience in Italy. Florence was chaos. There were no dressing-rooms. We had to hang our G-strings and wigs in the Ladies. The Florentine women continued using it and we had to stand over our make-up to prevent pilfering. But the audience was perked up by several tables of crooks who had trailed us from Naples. Then back to Milan, where Shirley Bassey followed our act. Shirley didn't understand the Italian audience and, thinking the incessant talk was disrespect for her voice, hit one of them round the head with a stick.

One day in Milan I announced I was leaving the show to have a sex-change operation. They gasped, though their reason for doing so was: 'If you leave the show, they'll cancel the contract and we'll all be out of work.'

'I made a pact with myself a long time ago – to have this operation by my twenty-fifth birthday or kill myself. I've saved enough money and I'm twenty-five at the end of this month.'

'A few more weeks won't kill you!'

'Well, all right, but then I promise I'm off.'

Let me tell you how this came about.

5 To the *Wizard of Casablanca*

> And why beholdest thou the mote that is in thy brother's eye, but considerest not the beam that is in thine own eye?
>
> Matthew vii 3

Though sex-change operations in 1960 were associated in the public imagination with Dr Frankenstein (and still are very often), they were not brand new. The first report of one was made by a German, F. Z. Abraham, in 1931, but he gives no details. The first popular account was in 1933 in Niels Hoyer's book *Man Into Woman*. It is the story of a Danish painter, male, who became Lili Elbe after a series of operations only vaguely described.

The term 'transsexualism' was invented in 1949 by Dr D. O. Cauldwell who wished to describe a girl who obsessively wanted to become a boy (the incidence of transsexualism in males however is much higher than in females, about four or five to one). A few years later the word was taken up by Dr Harry Benjamin whose researches led eventually to the first systematic study in 1966, *The Transsexual Phenomenon*.

In 1952 a team of Danish surgeons under Christian Hamburger performed the operations on George (later Christine) Jorgensen which established the general blueprint for transsexual surgery and post-operational treatment. Publicity of the case the following year brought the matter before the whole world for the first time.

The subject of sexual ambiguity was publicised in Britain by two unusual cases. In 1952 Elizabeth Forbes-Sempill, daughter of the 18th Baron Sempill, issued a statement to the effect that she had been re-registered on her birth certificate as a male (taking the Christian name 'Ewan'), thereby becoming heir-presumptive to the baronetcy of Forbes of Craigievar, a junior title held by Ewan's brother, the 19th Baron Sempill. Whereas the barony was one of those rare British titles which can pass through the female line, the baronetcy could not. So when the 19th Baron died in 1965 having sired only daughters, his daughter Ann became Lady Sempill and his reassigned brother became, after some litigation, the Hon. Sir Ewan Forbes, 11th Baronet. Ewan married and now lives as a farmer in the Highlands, shooting and fishing, skiing and skating.

The second case is that of Roberta Cowell. Born Robert, the son of Major-General Sir Ernest Cowell, she had been raised as a boy, and in an effort to establish masculinity became a wartime fighter pilot and a motor-racing driver. However the façade was impossible to sustain and when advised by doctors that she was more properly a woman she tried to kill herself. Roberta Cowell eventually adjusted to her new role after a series of operations and the story was published in *Picture Post* in 1954.

Both these cases were the result of ambiguous genital formation at birth, resulting in incorrect sex identification. They are not to be confused with cases like my own, those of transsexualism, which so far as doctors have determined are primarily of psychological origin (abetted to a greater or lesser extent by physiological factors according to each individual case) and therefore, as the law stands, do not entitle one to a change of birth certificate. I mention them in order to clarify such confusion, since many readers will have been introduced to the subject by these two cases.

Church and State demand that we be either male or female. But Dr Armstrong's 'Sexual Rainbow' or 'Spectrum of Sex' notices seventeen physical states ranging from the normal female to the normal male. Most people fall comfortably at one end or the other but a small number fall into the intervening states known as 'intersex'. It was Dr Armstrong's belief that I was among this small number (although very few transsexuals are) and therefore entitled to surgery to eliminate my physical limbo and underline my psychological orientation, which was female. Unfortunately, at the time I was being handled by the Walton Hospital, medicine lacked the finesse necessary for addressing itself to this question – if it hadn't, I might have been spared much upset. It would be interesting to know in what way I could have been classified as a physical intersex, before taking the matter into my own hands and thus making it impossible to verify.

Interesting but not crucial. A male or a female? I feel that, despite my great social confusion in the early years, the question was settled in the subconscious long before doctors entered my life, perhaps even before birth. The subject is still very contentious because it raises fundamental questions such as the relationship between mind and matter. The medical theories were exhaustively debated in my divorce case, and the various arguments will be tartly summarised in that chapter. For the time being it seems best to describe what was happening to me.

I started out life as a boy. As I grew up I turned into a feminine-looking boy. Perhaps I should have accepted my androgynous nature – most feminine-looking boys do, both heterosexual and homosexual ones. But I couldn't accept it because I felt myself to be essentially female. Why, I don't know. But I did. And the feeling went as deep as feelings can go. Doctors could argue among themselves for ever. Meanwhile I came to realise what I had to do to sort myself out.

The taking of oestrogen satisfied the transvestites but not the transsexuals. I've seen men who've been taking hormones for twenty-five years and they still look like men with breasts stuck on to them. But my mind had made an internal choice of sex to which the external did not conform. My male genitals were quite alien to me. I would never let anyone touch them, not even when we slept together, not even Joey. And I never once went to bed with a man without being blind drunk. As I grew older this physical secretiveness grew worse. The elimination of these organs became essential to my finding life tolerable. It wasn't a matter of: wouldn't it be fun to have a vagina? Possibly for people like Coccinelle, but not for me, and I doubt it even for her because transsexual surgery is no joke. My early life had been such agony that it seems the psyche had said to itself, 'This life is shaping up into no shape at all. Something has got to take charge, so I'm going to', which resulted in great strength of purpose. Little wonder that among less single-minded transsexuals, self-mutilation and suicide are so common.

The horror of a life of ambiguity and disguise, the constant fear of being exposed – one could not live with it and remain sane. You see, I would attract men to whom I was attracted, but when the moment came to go beyond kissing, the illusion would fall apart and I would be utterly lost. Even when they said it didn't matter that I was a boy, it did to me. I regarded myself as neither transvestite nor homosexual, although aspects of my life perforce overlapped with these.

You may feel, 'Oh, terms like intersex and transsexual, they're only words, they don't really mean anything.' And you would be wrong. Of course they are words, but that is a tremendous encouragement because it means that instead of my being a freak, modern knowledge has identified syndromes and named them, has evolved concepts to deal with conditions such as mine. You cannot imagine the comfort in knowing that one is *something*, and not merely monstrous. My distress at sea was so much the worse for having nothing, not even catchphrases, to hold on to and steady the mind. One is a rarity, which makes learning to cope a very hard lesson, but one is not outside the discernible laws of nature.

Sexual trauma was paralleled by social trauma on those occasions when I had to identify myself formally. 'George Jamieson' was on my passport, though I had long ceased to resemble the picture inside it. In Milan I visited the British Consul to see if it were possible to be issued with a new passport in the name of 'Toni April'.

'Heavens above!' he said. 'What on earth are you going about like this for? Don't you realise it's illegal? You can't go round dressed as a woman!'

'Yes I can. I've got permission from the Italian Government. For everywhere except Rome.'

But a new passport was not possible.

For fear of the questioning it might involve and possible refusal, I did not apply for a French work-permit. Instead I would get Robert, the hairdresser, to drive me to Brussels every three months. The words of Lady Georgia Blueharnis came back to me: 'I can hardly imagine anyone setting out *deliberately* for Brussels.' But so long as one was out of France for at least twenty-four hours they would renew the visa and the question of a work-permit could be avoided. For the journey to serve its purpose the passport had to be stamped. I cowered in the back of the car, looking like a young lesbian in harsh black male clothes. I had no confidence in myself dressed this way, I'd walk hunched-up, furtively, jumping at the slightest noise. My self-possession returned only when I slipped back into my proper clothes. Robert would tell the passport officer that I wanted the stamp as a souvenir.

'But this passport is full of souvenirs!'

'Yes, well, she, er, he collects them.'

Fortunately there was never any major aggravation. I relied on the prestige of the British passport to get me through, which it did. By now I'd be aching for a pee – the nerves – but held on until the hotel. I never used public lavatories; anyway they were disgusting in France and easy to eliminate from one's routine. In bars and foyers I'd use the Ladies if I had to, but circumstances had developed in me a bladder of iron.

As the presentation of myself as a woman became more convincing the fear of exposure became more acute. I'd given myself a deadline. I had saved the money. But where was the surgeon?

A few months before the Italian tour, Coccinelle had vanished. When she reappeared she was smirking her head off. What had changed? Coccinelle was in no mood to keep it a secret. She threw off her clothes, fell backwards on to a sofa with her legs in the air and wide apart, and pointed between them with a long carmine fingernail. 'Now, M'Lady, what do you think of THAT!'

'Jesus, Monique . . .' I'd never before seen her without her *cache-sexe*. She had a very pretty body (with remarkably beautiful feet) and now there was no doubting the brilliance of the work between her legs. She had, as far as one could see without getting too close, a five-star vagina.

'Where did you get it?'

'Aha, that would be telling. I've been sworn to secrecy!' She could be such a tiresome beast. Coxy donned a blue chiffon *robe* trimmed with ostrich feathers. It was ultra-see-through and she posed about in it so that everyone could see that there was nothing a-dangle.

I knew then that I had found my doctor.

Coccinelle had paved the way as a result of the extraordinary degree to which she regarded her body as an adjustable object. She'd had masses of silicone injections in her breasts. She'd had five nose jobs – transvestites and transsexuals are obsessed with remodelling the nose. When her nose collapsed to nothing, she tried to have a sixth to build it up again but it wasn't possible with mere nostrils to work with. As a young boy Coxy had been ugly, with a nose that went on for miles, hence, her passion for having it sawn down until nothing was left, just two holes that glared at you in the front of her face. She later had a face lift which honestly she didn't need. She'd had an ear job (the ears are trimmed and pulled back flatter to the skull). She'd had an eye job. She'd had electrolysis on her facial and bodily hair. Somehow the eyebrows had become involved in this. They'd disappeared and she would paint them on wherever the fashion of the moment dictated. There is so much they can do these days – operations on the jaws, operations to remove the Adam's apple, operations which shorten the vocal cords and raise the voice one or two tones. They can even reduce height by chopping bits of bone out of the legs (but they can't do the same to the arms so the result is ape-like). I'm sure Coxy has kept up with all the developments. The only thing they can't do is sew on lips, which is the one she's really waiting for (although they can inject silicone into them). There are dangers, of course. One Paris doctor, known as 'the Tit Man', killed someone with a silicone needle. It pierced the heart.

In our priggish way, Bambi and I disapproved of Coccinelle. We'd sit in the Calvados Bar opposite the George V Hotel, listening to Salena Jones at the microphone, and pose there, me as Audrey Hepburn, Bambi as Grace Kelly, and talk about it all. We did what we did in Paris, Milan and Juan because we had to earn a living. But at heart we felt we were true ladies. After the show I'd go off to Le Bantu and dance away my surplus energy with Audrey or Skippy. And Bambi would go home to Mother and her steady penniless boyfriend. In our conversation we came to the conclusion that not only was Coxy an exhibitionist of the *demi-monde* but, underneath it all, she was also a man, a homosexual transvestite whose passion for the knife was driven by vanity, the desperate need to be admired.

How prissy we were! How sure and how simple-minded. Coxy was far more complex than that. It would have taken twenty-five psychiatrists to sort her out. Compared to us little puritans, she was awesomely liberated, always floating around in big cars, swathed in minks, oozing sex. The last I heard of her she was still pulling out her tit at first nights. Only since have I come to recognise how magnificent Coccinelle was.

Coxy was also perplexed by me. She could not understand why I had no *michetons*, why I was so in love with Joey who was poor and visited me so rarely, why I'd never had my nose bobbed. 'Darling,' she would say, blinking her bloodshot eyes and placing her finger on the tip of my nose, 'you must, really you must, I have the marvellous doctor for this.' One look at Coxy's and I knew my nose was fine. But I envied her glorious lack of inhibition.

I was driven out of my wits by her refusal to name the surgeon who had operated on her *zee-zee*. All she'd tell me was: 'It cost £1,500, so that rather cuts you out, doesn't it?'

'No, it doesn't, Monique.'

She raised her painted eyebrows. 'So you have the *micheton* after all?'

'No, I don't.' But I wasn't going to tell her I'd saved over £2,000.

'Well, he wants to remain anonymous. But he is the best in the world and despises his fellow medics. They despise him too because they know he's a genius!'

I pestered and pestered because it was time to make my move from Shangri-La to Nirvana, but the row with Coxy over Enrico closed her up altogether. It was Kiki Moustique who obtained the information.

'Toni, I think this is what you want,' she said.

My eyes dilated in wonder. Dr Burou, Clinique du Parc, 13 rue Lapébie, Casablanca, Morocco.

That evening I wrote: *Dear Dr Burou, I got your address from Coccinelle. I am twenty-four years old. I want a sex-change operation. Would you accept me for an interview? It's very important.*

A secretary replied. It was brief and to the point. I was to present myself at the Clinic on 11 April. Having had it out with my colleagues, I told the Clinic I'd be there on 11 May.

Back in Paris I explained my intention to Marcel. 'And so, Marcel, would you be prepared to advance me some extra money if I run out while I'm there?'

'No, I wouldn't be prepared, you crazy English! I'll lend you money for clothes, for a car, even for an apartment if you like, but not for that. I've seen a lot of strange people pass through this place. And no good ever comes of this operation. Stay as you are or you'll ruin your young life.'

'You don't understand. There is no life for me without this. I've only got one life and it's my only chance for happiness. I can't be a freak for ever.'

'The operation – *that* will make you a freak for all time.'

'Perhaps you're right. But I can live with that. Have I got to jump off a bridge before people understand that I can't go on living as I am? Only I'm not going to jump off a bridge – I'm going to Casablanca!'

The whole club tried to dissuade me. Les Lee said, 'Honey, when you see that knife, you'll be back.' It was different for Les. He had adjusted to being what he was. But for me the idea of flouncing round Le Carrousel in drag for the rest of my life was totally unacceptable. There was a big daylight world outside and I had to face it, I wanted to explore it, it *fascinated* me.

I said, 'Well, Bambi, aren't you coming too?'

She looked at me with the big blue eyes. I thought she was going to burst into tears but she said, 'No, it's becoming too fashionable.'

I couldn't believe what I was hearing. 'Fashion? What's fashion got to do with it? This is our future, our destiny, you've got to see it through. This is what we've talked about for years.'

But Bambi didn't want to talk about it any more. Then the Bluebell Girls heard. Sandra Lebroque and Gloria Paul came at me like a delegation: 'You're not going, and that's that!'

All this opposition had a consolidating effect. I'd never before felt so calm, so centred. Toots Lockwood was sweet and girlish on the phone: 'If it's what your heart tells you, Toni, then follow your heart.'

And Coccinelle was downright positive. 'Yes! Go!' was what she said before flying off to do a show in Berlin.

I bought a Casablanca street-map and studied it at night, trying to imagine myself there. A French-Moroccan boy working at the club supplied the address of a clean, cheap hotel. At the Hôtel de la Paix I packed my worldly goods into a trunk and took it down to the basement while Madame Petit followed me whimpering.

On the morning of 10 May 1960 I went to Orly Airport. I thought it appropriate to go alone but Les, Peki and Skippy insisted on coming and really I was grateful. Because of my passport I again had to adopt the lesbian gear – there were to be no last-minute hitches.

Les kept up a patter. 'But Africa, dear! And all by yourself! It's a disgusting thought. You'll be murdered at least twice. I know it's not *darkest* Africa but there are no smart bits, you know, to hide in. Have you thought about dirt? There will be heaps of it everywhere. And you'll catch something incurable from a camel – people always do in Morocco. Oh – what a husky porter – grab him. My God, you fool, Africa! They'll put you in a cage and sell you in the market like a parrot. How can you bear the idea of it? All those Arabs with V.D. . . . wanting to touch you. They say it's just reached the stage Europe reached in the Middle Ages – the plague waiting for you round every corner. Bambi must have told you about Camus – '

'Stop it, Les! I'm petrified as it is.'

Then they all broke down in tears.

'And stop crying – just help me get on to this bloody Caravelle jet! I'm petrified in case passport control asks me to take my hat off.'

'But honey, you don't know what Africa's like!' sobbed Les, kohl smudged across his face.

'Neither do you, *mon ange*. Now where do I go in?'

We all kissed and hugged and as I was about to go through the departure lounge, Skippy held me by the arm. 'Just one more thing,' he said; 'when you get back, can I be the first?'

'Oh, Skippy . . .' and my rib-cage collapsed and I wept like a baby.

The flight was ghastly. Six hours of the worst stage-fright. My stomach was a fist and would admit no food. A glass of gin and tonic fizzed and went flat on the pull-down in front of me – I couldn't even drink. But such fear and adrenalin – it brings you alive to your fingertips!

It was tea-time when I descended to the tarmac of Casablanca and the heat slapped me in the face. At the hotel the young Arab desk-boy took my passport and asked if I wanted a jug of water. Les Lee loomed before my eyes saying, 'Don't! It will be full of filthy organisms!' So I asked for a bottle of Perrier and went up to my room.

All I wanted was rest, to lock myself in this room in a strange city where I knew no one and doze until the following morning. I'd been dozing pretty effectively for about an hour when my eyelids slid open and I thought, 'You lazy, miserable sod! This is Casablanca, this is Ingrid and Humphrey, the Atlantic coast of Africa! It's time to stop flopping on the bed, time to stop hiding. This is Dream-Come-True Eve. So go out and celebrate for Chrissakes!'

I set about myself with alacrity. In another hour I appeared at the top of the staircase groomed to kill. A black cocktail dress with a cute bosom, six rows of artificial pearls cooling the lower throat, a chignon so sleek it might have been painted on with a brush, my most regal *maquillage*, and a tiny evening bag filled with crisp banknotes. Perfection.

Descending slowly the stairs, I saw the jaw of the desk-boy drop lower with every step I took. He was thinking: 'Where on earth did this bit of stuff come from? Two hours ago the dregs of something disappeared into that room – and now! The Paris clothes, the hair-do, the eyes, the eyes . . .'

Glowing with self-assurance in the warm evening, I tell you, I took my time with those stairs. But staircases can't last for ever and at the bottom I realised with sudden pleasure that I was starving. I asked him for directions to the very best Moroccan restaurant (not tourist) where a lady might be seen dining on couscous alone (it had been lavished on me in St Germain days). I daresay such a place doesn't exist in the whole of Africa, women dining alone being so modern a development, but I soon found myself bumping through the streets in a cab and was dropped at a gilded doorway. It was the best couscous I've ever had. And being alone didn't ruffle me at all. There are not many moments in life when one can dine thus in public, talking to no one, fidgeting not in the slightest, with heaven moving sweetly through the veins. Perhaps this is how enlightened Zen monks spend their entire life. If so, they're having a whale of a time.

The cab returned via the Clinic – I got out and gazed at it under an African moon against a navy-blue sky riddled with stars, expecting it to have been transformed into an Egyptian temple, but it just looked like a clinic. That night I had no sleep at all, listening to the low whirr of the city, car headlights moving every so often across the bedroom ceiling. I heard a man's footsteps climbing the stairs, the rattle of a key in his door, door closed, and wondered what his secret might be. Everyone should have a secret. It gives a person depth, possibilities, something to tell a lover.

Up early, I arrived at the Clinic with fifteen minutes to spare. A rather too voluptuous blonde receptionist asked me to wait in the waiting-room but I couldn't sit down. The Clinique du Parc is basically a maternity clinic for Moroccans on whom fortune has smiled and the place was filled with the bawling of the rich new-born. Eventually a nurse beckoned.

Dr Burou's consulting room was reassuring. Calf-bound reference books and old French furniture whispered 'quality'. Two things struck me when the nurse had closed the door behind her. Firstly, the silence. The room must have been sound-proofed. Secondly, Dr Burou. He was facing the window, then turned round dramatically. I'd been told that he was handsome but I wasn't expecting . . . an Alain Delon. Classic French features, dark-brown hair and a smooth-smooth tan were the idyllic landscape from which shone two aquamarine eyes and two white rows of teeth more devastating than Tallulah's. He beamed *health*. He made you think of American bathrooms and candlelit dinners at the Château de Madrid all at once. In fresh linen beach-clothes, with a blue shirt whose top button was undone to intimate a furry chest smelling of Chanel, he could have been a playboy who'd just sauntered over from Monte Carlo in his yachting sneakers. I discovered later that he had a love of water sports and water-skied every day at the local yacht club.

He was, I suppose, about forty-five years old and I had only two reservations. One, he dressed slightly younger than his years; two, he was on the short side: there was something in the way he held his athletic body which suggested that subtly he was trying to stretch it, that his lack of height was the only thing in the world which bothered him. None the less, I was awed.

Dr Burou greeted me with a simple handshake, and with his hands slung in his pockets started to walk round me as if I were an exhibit in an art gallery – or a zoo. His hands were muscular, expensively manicured, and every so often he'd pull one of them out and make a slight gesture with it as if to emphasise a point to himself.

'*Vous êtes le spécimen parfait*. Please take your clothes off and lie down over there,' he said, indicating a couch covered with a starched linen cloth. Everything he said was in a sardonic, slightly flirtatious tone. It was immensely attractive, not in the least off-putting, and he soon had me giggling. He examined me from top to toe to make sure I was all real and expressed pleasure in the fact that I'd had no cosmetic surgery.

'How old are you?'

'Twenty-five.'

'Oh yes, this letter. Family?'

I lied and said I hadn't seen my family since I was fifteen.

'Are you prepared to sign a paper absolving myself and the Clinic from all responsibility should anything go wrong?'

'Yes.'

'Are you absolutely sure you want this operation?'

'Yes.'

'How?'

'Because I'll kill myself if I don't.'

'Don't talk nonsense. What illnesses have you had?'

'Hepatitis.' I didn't mention calcium deficiency or the Walton Hospital.

'When was that?'

'Three years ago.'

'Any serious maladies, allergies, heart trouble?'

'No.'

'Are you afraid?'

'Yes, I am.'

'Do you realise you might die?'

Apparently there is a huge loss of blood.

'I accept the risks.'

'Do you realise that I haven't done many of these operations, that you are a guinea pig?'

I believe I was Dr Burou's ninth sex-conversion.

'Are you prepared for a shock?' he said. 'Right now?'

'Yes – what?'

He went to a desk and took out a file of photographs, handing them to me one by one. They were pictures of the operation, cut by cut, in vehement technicolour. The gore, the blood, the knives, if one had the tiniest reservation these pictures would have flushed it out.

All I could think of saying was, 'Are these pictures of Coccinelle?' Because if they were she'd had the most enormous *zee-zee*. He laughed and ignored my question.

'There's only one thing I want from you, Dr Burou.'

'What's that?'

'A promise.'

'What promise?'

'That you do not photograph me.'

'But I photograph all my patients – '

'I want you to give me your word that you will not photograph me.'

'But the records, they should be complete. One day, you never know . . .'

'I *do* know. This is too important to me, too private, too mysterious – for snaps.'

'O.K. I give you that promise. You know, I think you're quite special. When would you like this operation?'

'As soon as possible.'

'Move into the Clinic this evening. We operate tomorrow morning at seven.'

Stunned, I floated out into the sunshine and walked and walked. I'd expected weeks of psychiatric tests and clinical run-up. There were a thousand questions suddenly. Money, for example. He hadn't mentioned it. I thought of my family, one of the occasions when I was glad to be utterly free of them, not to have to try and explain.

The desk-boy said, 'But, Madame, why aren't you staying longer, where are you going so soon?'

'You wouldn't believe me if I told you.'

At the Clinic Dr Burou introduced me to his wife. She was a compact middle-aged Frenchwoman with short, mousey hair beautifully set, a Dior suit, and small pieces of high-grade jewellery. She pottered around being 'Madame Burou', helping with the administration of the Clinic, helping me to fill in forms. She came across as one of the unhappiest women I'd ever met and one of the reasons, I discovered, was that Dr Burou, for whom she was abject with love, had eyes elsewhere. Later I would take tea with her in the Burous' flashy penthouse, which ran across the top floor of the building, and listen to her tales of woe.

Then Dr Burou introduced me to Marie, the Matron, six feet tall with heavy shoulders which pumped when she laughed. A young nurse, Jeanne, who was to look after me at night-time, took me up to my room past the Arab cleaners shuffling about with buckets and mops.

The rooms were not numbered on my floor but identified by a panel of flowers on the door – otherwise the place was plain and functional. Mine was 'African Violets', very appropriate, and decorated in mauve, with french windows on to a balcony with a view straight into an apartment block opposite. The room had a radio and a private bathroom, the last word in hospital luxury after my previous experiences, but no air-conditioning, so in that climate it inclined to stuffiness.

Accompanied by two nurses as witnesses, Marie came with papers for me to sign. Dr Burou returned, all flirtatiousness gone, and again went through the reasons why I should not have the operation. At the end of his lecture I asked for a bite to eat.

'Not before an operation – the anaesthetic would make you vomit into your lungs and you'd suffocate to death.'

I went out on to the balcony and absorbed the city – it was a balmy evening, pregnant with omens. A young boy stared at me from across the street, a monkey on his shoulder, a fixed smile on his face like a pagan doll.

At about 10 p.m. a nurse appeared with a syringe in a metal dish. 'I expect you didn't get much sleep last night – this will help.'

12 May 1960, 6 a.m. Two nurses woke me. 'We must shave you. Down there.'

'Could I shave myself? Do you mind?'

Next the pre-med injection. Bliss.

When they came for me I said, 'Can I walk to the theatre?' I must have been having a limelight fantasy.

'You must go by trolley.' Two girls in blue coats wheeled me along the corridors on my back. I counted off the lights as they flicked overhead. Into a lift – but whether it went up or down was impossible to gauge. Then more corridors. It was rather like being swept pleasantly out to sea and by the time I rolled into the theatre I was grinning from ear to ear. The anaesthetist, another dreamy male, a Mediterranean Dr Kildare, and in fact the only other man I ever saw in the Clinic, said '*Bonjour, monsieur.*' It struck me as hilarious, a game of charades.

With a mask across his face Dr Burou said, 'I must ask you again, any doubts . . .'

'Do your finest work, Doctor.'

Then they gave me the final jab.

As I murmured, 'One . . . two . . . three . . .' Dr Burou bent over and breathed, '*Au revoir, monsieur.*' He smelt of gardens.

The operation lasted seven hours and involved removal of the testes, surgery on the outer genitalia and the construction of a vagina. No ovaries, no womb of course. The brilliance of Dr Burou's technique was that he did this retaining the maximum nerve tissue and inverting it into a vaginal lining so that erogenous sensitivity was not destroyed. The adrenal glands continue to produce sufficient androgen for orgasm to be possible by stimulation of these nerve endings. And afterwards the taking of oestrogen is no longer necessary.

Some sex-changes claim that the operation makes them more sensitive than ordinary women, although I find comparisons of this sort pretentious because sexual responsiveness is such a personal quality, being the product of psychological as well as physiological factors. I did ask Dr Burou if it would be possible for me to make love and achieve orgasm and he said, 'Theoretically there's nothing to stop you. Whether you do, and how often, is entirely up to you.'

Do you want diagrams of the procedure? I can't supply them. Dr Burou kept the precise details secret, apart from the aerial photographs. He is generally regarded as the most brilliant man in his field. I don't think his technique departs radically from that used elsewhere: I don't think there are any major 'secret ingredients'. He has simply refined it and is more adept at it than the others.

As I came round I was not aware of my body, which was immobilised by bandages. The first words were Dr Burou's: *'Bonjour, mademoiselle.'*

I heard myself, far off, saying, 'Was it successful?'

'Indeed it was. I'm very proud of you.'

Then I passed out with relief. I kept coming to and passing out, realising what had happened, unable to believe it. Whenever I attained consciousness I experienced what can only be described as overwhelming rushes of deep peace and these would phase me out again.

The following day my brain was clear enough to dispatch the telegrams I'd promised. To Les Lee, Sandra and Gloria, Julia Lockwood. I wanted to send one to Joey because I knew that I could now make him happy. But for him I felt too much emotion for a telegram. In a few days I wrote to him in London. I can't remember what I actually said. 'Darling, it's going to be all right now' was what I felt.

As the anaesthetic wore off I became aware of a most hideous pain. It was unlike anything in my previous experience or, I suspect, in yours. It was as if branding irons were being vigorously applied to the middle part of my body. I screamed and a nurse came quickly with a pain-killing injection.

'You are going to have to be *very* brave,' said Dr Burou, 'because we can give you these pain-killing shots for three days only. Otherwise you'll develop an addiction to them.'

The injections stilled the pain but put everything else at a distance too, as if the world were taking place in slow motion on a screen. They did however allow sufficient respite for me to give myself a superficial examination. My middle was grotesquely swollen and bound inches deep with bandages into which blood continuously spilt and congealed. A rubber tube for peeing came out of it. Pints of sweat poured off me and this was exacerbated by the oppressive heat of the day. The noise of carts, donkeys and motor cars came through the balcony windows and the crying of babies through the walls.

Feverishly I was running my fingers through my hair. It came out in handfuls. My lovely thick black hair, it covered the pillow. 'Nurse! Nurse! I must have a hand mirror!' My hair was in patches from the shock of the surgery. She assured me it would grow back again. It did but was never afterwards thick and healthy and soon went grey.

My face was puffy with drugs and sleeplessness. The skin looked bruised and drained, as if I'd been in a car crash.

Les Lee and Julia phoned. I couldn't make much sense of what I was saying or hearing but it was a comfort to know they were out there. When I replaced the telephone I thought, 'Those new-born babies bursting into life – yes, I've just been born too – I am a woman in Casablanca and I'm in agony but my spirit is soaring and when I get out of here, World, I'm going to knock you for six!'

The World had to wait however because I had an appointment with Torture. On the fourth day, as the branding irons descended and sizzled across my body, I screamed as usual for the nurse. Instead of a jab she gave me tablets. The pain mounted and closed in on me. She held my hand and said, 'Scream, yes, scream, it helps.' It rang throughout the building, a terrible roar of pain, and the poor women waiting for the onset of labour must have shuddered with anxiety. The nurse tried to mop my brow as I threw my head from side to side, clenched in spasms, and gave issue to long gurgling groans. The pain, which came in waves like everything else in life, was aggravated by movement of the hips. The slightest shift would set it off. Night-times were the worst and I must thank Jeanne for helping me through them. She kept going above my dreadful moans, chatting about her son who loved mathematics, who wanted to be a racing driver, who wanted to go to college in England, and how wonderful it would be if he could, and would I teach her some English? I looked at her as if she were mad and then the pain hit me again. Occasionally my eyes lost focus, ceased to convey coherent information to my brain, and I would go into a semi-blind hysterical state which was usually followed by unconsciousness. I was soggy the whole time. It was delightful when they came to wash me, even though the refreshment was brief. Lightweight European meals appeared and were taken away barely touched.

Then came the first of what I shall call 'the horrors'. At the end of the operation a speculum had been inserted into the vagina. This is a beak-like instrument which can be screwed open and closed. I called

With Duncan Fallowell on the set of *Coronation Street*, 1980

Left: V. E. Day, May 1945, George Jamieson at St Theresa's Primary School, Liverpool

Below left: George Jamieson, aged thirteen, with brother Ivor (nine) and sister Marjorie (seven) at home, Norris Green

Right: George Jamieson, aged fourteen, playing Bassanio in *The Merchant of Venice* at St Theresa's

Far right: George Jamieson, aged fifteen, at school

Below: Cadet class of the S.S. *Vindicatrix* 1950–51, George Jamieson standing seventh from the right

Right: The first year at Juan-les-Pins, 1956, 'Toni April' aged twenty-one

Opposite: Second summer at Juan, with Les Lee (*left, en femme*) and Margaret Lockwood (*centre*), 1957

Below: The second year at Juan-les-Pins, with Julia Lockwood, 1957

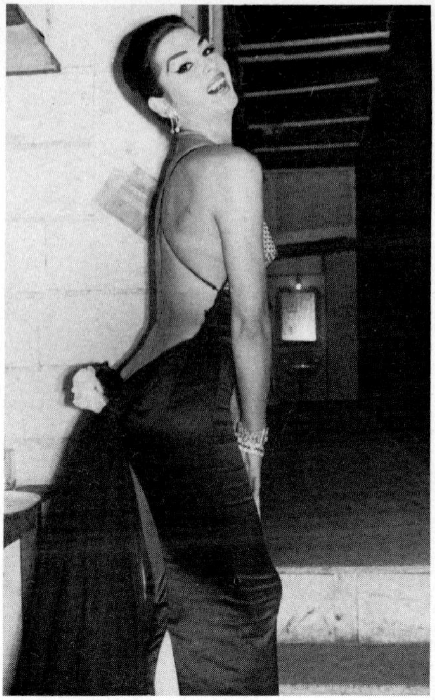

Above left: At Le Carrousel, Paris, 1958, aged twenty-two

Above right: On stage at Le Carrousel, aged twenty-three

Backstage at Le Carrousel, Paris, 1958

Opposite: At La Porta del Ora, Milan, with Kiki Moustique, 1959

Above left: Waiting for Geronimo, Milan, 1959

Above right: After the show in Bologna, 1959.
Left to right: Peki (kneeling), April, Novak, Coccinelle, Kiki

Pasta with Peki (now Amanda Lear), Milan, 1959

it my Oscar, after the film award. Later I christened it Donald Duck. It is needed to prevent the vagina from closing up and to guarantee the smooth healing of the vaginal walls which are heavily clotted with blood while the blood-vessels realign themselves.

From now on it had to be removed every morning to allow for examination, ventilation and mopping up. This was Marie's job. She stuffed a hankie into my mouth and told me to grip the bedrails behind my head. Marie was built like a bull and her movements had great physical assurance which was a comfort. You don't want ditherers on this sort of work. She unbandaged me, removed the speculum, and then the nurses swabbed me. Tablets cannot touch pain at this level. Worse followed in the evening when she came to replace it.

'There are two ways of doing it. Slow – which takes a long time and is very painful. Or fast – which is much more painful but soon done. Whichever way you choose, you must get accustomed to it.'

'Fast,' I gurgled through the hankie. She didn't wait a second. Bang! My head hit the rails behind the bed so hard that I almost concussed myself. We took more care in future over the arrangement of the pillows. Then I was rebound tightly and she wished me a good night's sleep.

Those awful nights . . . you lie there hot and soaking, you scream, you moan, you smell foul with clogged blood, you're bruised and swollen. And yet you are pitifully grateful too. Elated, completed at last, a relief so all-embracing that you imagine nothing will ever hurt you again. But these *petites opérations* as Marie called them – I started to quake an hour before she arrived.

In two weeks I was allowed up to bathe and with a nurse in each armpit take a few disorientated steps across the floor. Another shock waited for me in the bathroom. A looking-glass. Always slender, I was now a configuration of bones. It was suggested that I might like to take the air. Since there was no garden (apart from the Burous' planted roof-terrace) this meant hobbling into the street. Making myself as presentable as possible, but slandering a Balmain suit all the same, we began this epic voyage through the Clinic to the outside world. My legs were ropes of jelly and pains shot upward from thighs to chest. Laughing and screwing up my face with discomfort, we made it out into the sunshine, an explosion of dazzling images, and I woke up in the gutter.

'What happened?'

'You fainted. We better get you back to bed.'

I was just sitting there, chuckling in the road like a drunkard. But it wasn't good P.R. to have loonies falling about outside the Clinic.

Each day they encouraged me to walk further. Dr Burou visited me with pep talks and as life seeped back slowly into my system he christened me 'Mademoiselle Glamour Girl'. His wife also began to visit me. On the first occasion a nurse showed her in. She asked how I was, was I comfortable, did I need anything, going through all the motions of seeming to be involved, but no sooner had the nurse left us together than Madame Burou began to change her tack and within minutes was raving about '*Cette blonde! Cette femme! Sur la plage, toujours cette blonde*!'

It took me some time to work out what was going on. 'The receptionist?'

'*La réceptioniste? Aussi? Non, non, non! Je veux mourir, mourir!*' And she burst into tears.

'*Cette blonde*' was the Great Doctor's mistress, with whom he kept trysts on the beach several times a week. Madame Burou was frightfully overwrought about it and whenever I had tea with her up in the penthouse she would always get round to this subject and end up weeping. She belonged neither to her husband nor to the Clinic. I never saw her with any friends of her own. She was utterly lost and the loneliness vaporised off her like ether, depressing the atmosphere wherever she walked, the sort of woman who silenced birds.

Julia telephoned. She was between jobs and coming over. This was a real bonus. I asked Dr Burou if she could stay in the Clinic. He went one better and said they would put her up in my room at no extra charge.

When Julia arrived she was full of schoolgirl gush. Nothing in her manner betrayed shock or disgust at what she found. Though still a teenager, she capably took over from Jeanne as comforter and friend. I'll never forget it. Even the *petites opérations* didn't throw her out of gear. It was quite remarkable for one so young. And Dr Burou took a definite shine to her – we saw rather more of him in my room after she arrived. He suggested she take me out for dinner and he made all the arrangements. I felt emotionally strong and Julia didn't stop talking.

'You must meet my great friend Sarah Churchill, the daughter of Him, as she puts it, Winston that is. He's always just "Him". She's my A.M. [adopted mother] and I'm her A.D. [adopted daughter].

You could be Sarah's A.D. if you liked. And you are my A.B.S. [adopted big sister].' She could go on for hours with these games. Julia was an only child and had been brought up by a nanny. It must have been a lonely childhood. Margaret was a tough career woman (look at that aggressive beauty spot!) and though she was never unkind to Julia I never thought of her as an especially warm mother. Toots was not starved of love but she'd been short of affectionate companionship. 'And,' she went on, 'I think you should leave Le Carrousel, I mean, I adore Les Lee and all that, and I *adore* Everest, but I think, now, really, I don't think it's the life for you any more.'

'Toots, you don't have to tell me that. I want to marry Joey, adopt children, be the housewife.'

'No, I didn't mean that either.'

'To be suburban – such a luxury . . .'

Dr Burou followed up dinner-therapy by suggesting that sunshine would be salubrious. Julia and I scrambled into a cab and drove to one of the many swimming-pools along Casablanca's ugly polluted coast. I looked like a ghoul in a bikini but was not ashamed, except perhaps of my knee-caps which looked abnormally large.

Julia dived in. Like her mother, she was a fish. How I craved the crisp water in that glutinous heat.

'Come on, Toni, give it a try.'

'No, Dr Burou didn't say go *in*.'

'I'll hold you, come along.'

'Julia, I'm scared to.'

After ten minutes of watching her sport about I said, 'Hey, I'll sit on the edge and let my poor little ankles sort of dawdle.'

A waiter turned up with two Singapore Slings on a silver tray. I drank eagerly. 'Yes, you're right, Toots, I've got to take the plunge sometime. Get ready in case I sink straight to the bottom.'

'Oh, well, no, perhaps it would be better to wait until you've asked the doctor.'

The 'no' was all I needed. Carefully I lowered myself in and managed a few paddles. 'Well, at least it's watertight!' My sense of humour had returned.

At the end of the week Julia had to go back to London but offered to travel via Paris if I'd like to be escorted there. Dr Burou said I should stay an extra two weeks but I was running out of money and told him so. He waved the subject aside but I didn't want to enter my new life shackled to debts. When the bill came it was a surprise to read that the operation itself cost only £70. But Coccinelle was right, the subsequent treatment boosted the total to over £1,500.

On leaving they presented me with the Oscar. Dr Burou, as godlike as ever, kissed me on both cheeks and said, 'I hope you find your happiness now – and remember, it's all up to you.'

. . . Again the flight was terrible. Air France were having a strike of ground staff and we circled Orly for an eternity while they improvised below. The delay meant that Julia had to board her connection directly and so I re-entered Paris alone.

At the Hôtel de la Paix, Madame Petit and her daughter, Sophie, greeted me with four extended arms. 'You look so well!' I didn't. 'And there's a letter waiting for you.'

It was from Joey. I recognised his writing at once, like a lot of baby matchsticks falling over. Our letters must have crossed in the post. A thrill ran through me. The past month had been so extraordinary, I needed to feel him close and I couldn't wait, I opened the letter on the spot:

Darling Toni – I hope you are well, I'm sure you are. I am, thank God. I wanted to write before but plans got in the way. Well, I've got to tell you, last week I got married to . . .

I collapsed in the hallway.

For four days, I stayed in bed, refusing visitors. The letter – I read it again and again and cried and cried. It was so awful, the timing of it, everything. On the fifth day Les Lee forced his way in.

'What's happened?' he said.

I told him.

'No, no – I mean Casablanca, the operation.'

'Les, I'm so mixed up now, Joey's gone, and – yes, Casablanca, it's done, it's wonderful, but . . .' And I started crying again.

'What are we going to do with you, eh? You've just gone through the most amazing experience in the world and all you can think about is some bum who's married some slag!'

This was the treatment I needed. Les brought the gang to see me for reports. Besides, reality wouldn't let me wail for long – I was almost out of money. Joey's marriage was the greatest shock of all but I returned to working at Le Carrousel in order to earn the money that would enable me to leave it.

After a few days I collapsed again. Marcel said, 'You need a holiday, I'll lend you some cash.' Robert Bodin agreed to take time off from coiffing the rich and famous and drove me south and along the coast to St Tropez, but the Brigitte Bardot set were screeching into the early hours and I couldn't get any English tea in the place.

'Let's go to Juan, Robert. Joffo's there. And Le Carrousel are coming down.' We did all the tourist spots as well: Villefranche when the French fleet was in, St Raphael, Cagnes, Antibes. At Vence we joined the queue of trippers to see Picasso making ceramics in his studio – he looked like a Gila monster in shorts. At Menton the harbour was dominated by the *Creole*, Stavros Niarchos's three-masted black yacht, the world's most beautiful ship. In Juan I had a platonic liaison with Tom who came from north Paris. He tried to seduce me but I wasn't ready and explained my history. Tom was sweet and told me that he was separated from his wife who lived on the other side of Juan. A few days after I left, I read in the papers that he'd stabbed his wife's lover to death outside La Vieille Colombieuse.

On Bastille Night, 14 July, the club was booked solid. This is the night when all French citizens run completely wild – every country should have one night like this per year, preferably several. Audrey and I caught the atmosphere and went straight to Le Bantu at 3 a.m., my first night out in Paris since Casablanca. The Bluebell Girls, the Alaria Ballet, everyone was there, wound in streamers, high on champagne. But I still tired easily. As I was leaving, Skippy tapped me on the shoulder. He was as skinny and speedy as ever, with a little golden moustache, and said, 'You're coming with me.'

'Skippy, I know what I promised but please, not yet.'

'Don't be chicken, honey, it doesn't suit you. You've got to find out sooner or later.'

'Well, bring a bottle . . .'

'There's plenty at my flat.'

I was a basket of nerves. Very gently he undressed me. Despite the wine I was over-tense.

'Come on, relax. I'm not going to hurt you. If I do, I won't insist.'

He made love to me so tenderly. Afterwards he said, 'Was it O.K.?'

I was sobbing and laughing. I couldn't stop. 'It's the happiest moment of my life!' I howled. As we lay side by side, stroking each other, he said, 'Listen, honey.' The window was open. Cars hooting, fire crackers, shouting and singing in the streets. He led me to the window. The bars were a-hop and everywhere flags flew, rockets shot into the sky. 'Well I'll be damned, they're celebrating the loss of your virginity.' He was so American. Wherever you are, Skippy, many dear kisses for being so kind on that miraculous night in Paris and helping me along the road to womanhood.

Julia appeared again and announced that Sarah Churchill was coming to meet me. As children we had been brought up with two gods: God and Winston Churchill. Now I was to meet his daughter. The three of us met at the Hôtel Bristol where the Churchill family usually stayed.

In 1936 at the age of twenty-one she'd dashed to America on board the *Bremen* to marry a Jewish comedian called Vic Oliver, hotly pursued on the *Queen Mary* by her brother Randolph who said she was too young to know her own mind. Vic Oliver only had $60 to his name when they were married – it was the kind of thing which impressed me.

Now, aged about forty-five, she was a natural aristocrat with Titian hair and brilliant green eyes emphasised by a green silk dress.

'How wonderful to meet you,' she said. 'Julia's told me so much I had to fly over and see for myself.'

I went all silly and said, 'I never thought a Churchill would ever travel ten feet to meet me.' But Sarah cured my shyness with that uniquely English charm, a combination of elegance and sauciness, innocence and worldliness. She had a light fruity voice, lyrical and gay, and used it to great effect without overdoing the theatricality. Her gait was that of a young girl, bouncy and enthusiastic. Yet there was in her a streak of melancholy, I felt, which all the Churchills had except Mary. Sarah's sister, Diana, committed suicide, and as everyone knows poor Randolph's life was no advert. Of Marigold, the one who died young, there was little mention. It must have been oppressive to the point of despair, having so illustrious a parent. Perhaps that was why Winston detached himself from them, gave them total rope.

Julia was A.M.-ing it like crazy. They discussed the theatre, rather breathlessly (underneath Sarah's veneer of breeding was a highly-strung woman), who was in what, who was getting good or bad notices. Sarah told me that in Hollywood she'd danced in a film with Fred Astaire, and was terribly proud of being a quarter American (through her grandmother Jenny Jerome, Lady Randolph Churchill).

Lunch was in a modest bistro in St Germain where Sarah was known and treated like a significant deity. 'Whatever you're eating,' she said, 'we must have red wine – it's so full of *goodness*.' She was the first woman I'd met who openly declared that she never wanted to have children: 'I quite like them actually but whenever I try to make friends they run off shrieking in the opposite direction.' Her plane was at 5 p.m. and she was gone.

'Flying to Paris just for lunch – that's so stylish,' I said to Julia, for Sarah had made an enormous impression on me. In due course she was to teach me much about how to conduct myself in Society. And how not to.

The new sensations to which Skippy had introduced me I explored with a young Roman-about-Paris called Giancarlo. He was very vain in a simple-minded way, always smartly dressed, would come and go as he pleased, zipping from place to place, a frightful tease who could be outrageously rude to strangers for no reason whatsoever. He was hopeless at conversation but tireless in love. I never discovered what he did for a living. He said he was kept by a woman. Once I went to his rooms a couple of blocks from the Hôtel de la Paix. When the concierge rang up to announce me, Giancarlo gave strict instructions that I was not to be allowed upstairs, thus compounding the mystery. He must have been up to something fairly acrobatic because he was always appearing with sprained wrists, bruises on his legs, nail-parings embedded in his back.

By the autumn I'd saved several hundred pounds. It was time to face England. Paris had been marvellous to me – I could never have earned the money that I did in any other city. And I had acquired a lot of know-how through Le Carrousel. But I was determined to strike out, even though I hadn't the foggiest idea how I was to go about it. Marcel offered to double my wages but money was no longer the important thing. Besides, change was afoot in the club too. It was situated on the ground floor of a block of offices. These were now being turned into flats and the new inmates didn't take to the club at all, they thought it lowered the tone of their property. Angered by the noise, they began to throw old tin cans and dead cats down into the courtyard. Coccinelle kept a trumpet by her in the dressing-room. Whenever the flat-owners started to rebel she'd throw up the window, stick out her trumpet and blow. It was clear that the club's lease would not be renewed, that it would have to move. The discipline slackened, there was misbehaviour. None the less Marcel said to me in his swaggering but affectionate way, 'You'll be back, *ma chérie*, I don't doubt it.'

What finally persuaded me to cut loose was Julia's offer to put me up temporarily at her flat in Dolphin Square. She came over to accompany me on the journey. I said my goodbyes without ceremony. They were all sure I'd be back.

We took sleeper berths on the Flèche d'Argent. At Dover, I struck them as questionable, all in black, wearing dark glasses. 'I'm sorry,' said the officer, 'but I can't accept this as your picture.' I started to panic. 'Take your glasses off,' he said. Julia was behind me, blocking the view of the others in the queue who were beginning to crane. 'This is *not* you – please take your hat off!' He was getting aggressive. My long dark hair cascaded to my shoulders. 'I knew it,' he said in triumph. The picture was six years old. I felt my legs going and held on to his desk, saying almost under my breath, 'A great deal has changed since that picture was taken . . .'

He looked at me long and hard, then suddenly his whole expression altered. 'Oh,' he said, 'oh, oh, I apologise, I'm so sorry, forgive me if I embarrassed you.' He took me by the arm and rushed us both through. I was in England, shaking from head to toe, but deliriously happy.

6 Scandal

Dolphin Square is one of the leading eyesores on that brutish stretch of the Embankment known as Grosvenor Road which runs from Vauxhall Bridge to Ranelagh Gardens in a part of London that fails to be either Chelsea or even – which is staggering – Pimlico. I always think of it as properly belonging to East Berlin (it is characteristic that living in the Square at the time, in addition to the gin soaks with their polka-dot gloves and cork-tip cigarettes, was the spy William Vassall, making solitary love to his pin-ups of soccer and rugby-football stars, though no one knew it until 1962).

Julia had a small flat full of dolls. She was rehearsing *Peter Pan* at the Scala Theatre. Twice she'd played Wendy, once to her mother's Peter, once to Sarah Churchill's. Now she was Peter himself and looked it, with her thin boyish body, and honey hair sliced in to the neck.

Sarah had a flat on the river side of the Square. When the porter discovered that she and I were friends he started to ring me up. 'Miss Churchill's gone out again – could you help?' I'd go in search because she could get up to tricks after a drink or two. Once I found her directing traffic on the Embankment in her nightie.

I decided to change my name by deed poll. 'April' I retained, but as a Christian name. Followed by 'Ashley' in deference to noble good-egg Leslie Howard, 'Ashley Wilkes' in *Gone With The Wind*. It cost £13. I still think it a good name. Distinctive, yet not *de trop*. The two 'A's place me at the top of invitation lists alphabetically arranged And foreigners find it very easy to remember and pronounce too . . .

Next – find Joey. I wrote care of his parents on the Isle of Dogs.

He was living in Wapping and invited me to a party there to meet his wife. Eunice was small, sweet, Anglo-Saxon, unmemorable – no, I don't want to be sour, I became fond of her in a roundabout way, but Joey wouldn't let her wear make-up and she should have ignored him.

He was looking prosperous in a 'Prince de Galles' check suit. I'd bought him his first in Paris and he'd adopted the fabric – it did suit him, noticeable but not noisy, warm and tactile without the murk of tweed.

'Have you heard from Rita?' he said.

'No – have you?'

'No one's heard then.'

'She must be up to her neck in it.' But it wasn't Rita's neck which preoccupied me, it was Joey's, thrusting out of his white collar like a lion's on an Assyrian bas-relief, made in heaven for lips and teeth, and the eyes brimming with larks. The dark beast! All his male beauty and self-possession were back. He well knew his powers because after showing me round the chums I was cornered; he slid out of his jacket, sort of slung himself against the wall, flexing his shoulders, absently fingering something in his pocket.

'You're looking well,' I said.

'So are you. My back's O.K. But I find I'm walking a bit twisted to one side. I didn't have it in Paris. You probably haven't noticed.'

Of course I'd noticed. I shouldn't have changed it for the world. It was unutterably sexy. It made him appear to be always on the verge of stripping off his shirt and swinging at a tree with an axe.

We began seeing each other again and made love to Renata Tebaldi records, arias from *La Bohème* and *Manon Lescaut* . . .

Which was all very divine – and yes, it was, Mother Nature had equipped Joey magnificently for love, and I felt it fully for the first time – but I needed to eat. Work. What was I fit for? I gathered I was interesting. How could I be profitable?

At night Julia often returned with members of the cast who said, 'What are you? An actress or a model?'

'Ac-tu-ally . . .'

'She's a model!' interjected Julia.

I grinned my gratitude and thought – why not? Modelling was quicker than actressing – and I've always liked things to happen fast.

A photographer printed up a box of test shots, I asked which was the best agency in London, was told Cherry Marshall's, and went along. Miss Marshall asked me to twirl. 'You're a natural,' she said and took me on the spot. This was a surprise because modelling was then far more formal than it is now, training was considered essential, but again I had been dropping heavily the magic name . . . 'Paris, yes, I've been working in Paris for the past four years, Miss Marshall, that's why you don't know me – Paris and Milan – appearing for Schiaparelli, that sort of thing . . .'

Two days later the agency rang and asked me to go in the following morning. My first booking. I was up at dawn, painting a masterpiece. When I walked into Miss Marshall's office she was sitting upright and immobile. 'Is it true, April, that you worked at Le Carrousel?' It was as if a statue had spoken! I felt sick. Yes, it was true. 'Then I must tell you, I can't have you on my books.' She wouldn't reveal the source of her intelligence.

There was no time to dally with hurt feelings – I'd taken on a small flat of my own at 14 Harrington Gardens, a house filled with Persian students. Again my *gîte* was right at the top. I do hate people walking over my head.

The next agency down the list was Fashion Models, run by Signon, a Eurasian who had been the Queen Mother's favourite mannequin. Her mouth was done up like Coccinelle's and generated almost as many curses. Despite the effing and blinding, Signon was Graciousness Itself to behold, jet hair sleeked into a chignon and always pinned with an orchid, fine pearls at the neck.

Signon called in her Scandinavian partner and said, 'We could use this, Ingrid, couldn't we?'

'Ve bloody vell could, Signon,' said Ingrid, because she copied her boss right down to the mouth.

Fashion in 1960 was only just coming out of the rigorous Barbara Golan look, dresses with twenty yards of material in the skirt, stiff underskirts, dozens of matching accessories. They warned me of the risks of the modelling business, amphetamine slimming pills followed by too much to drink in order to relax, the perils of the casting couch, but what I liked least were the auditions. A mass of girls would clog a hallway until a hard-bitten bat came along and shouted, 'Throw up the bars, let them through one by one.' The big models – Sandra Paul, Bronwen Pugh, Grace Coddington, Sue Lloyd – were only the crest of a neurotic, hard-working groundswell, every one of whom had to be up early and perfectly groomed in case a call came through. Our heroine was Fiona Campbell-Walter who in 1956 had married Baron Heinrich von Thyssen, a magnate whose family fortune had survived the war more or less intact. Marriage was the way up and out into the world of reality. Sandra Paul became Mrs Robin Douglas-Home, Bronwen Pugh Viscountess Astor, and Maggie Simmonds Countess of Kimberley.

And I had Joey and Eunice to sort out. The more I loved being with Joey the more heart-breaking it was when he left. A back-street romance had not been my intention. I wanted to do things with him. He was quite unlike anybody else I knew.

'April, I feel sorry for you,' said Eunice, 'Joey's going places.'

'Sorry for me?' I towered over that little face. 'You know nothing. Feel sorry for yourself. He belongs to me and always will.'

In fact Joey belonged to no one but himself – it was one of the most attractive things about him, that wilfulness. But Eunice's remark stuck and it depressed me. Joey could do anything with me, so I knew I had to be extra strong, make a decision and act on it, or else we should drift in no-man's-land for ever. I was listening to Elvis Presley's 'Mess of Blues' on the radio when I decided to finish it, to see him no more . . .

To help me make the break – and this is something I advise for anyone who feels that their emotions need to be disciplined by reason – I deliberately took another lover. He could not compete with Joey deep down of course, which is exactly what I wanted: Enrique Fernandez, a Spanish waiter, no fuss. I was introduced to him by an Australian model and knew at once that he was the one to refresh and simplify the air. Apart from being very good-looking – he had to be that – he was uncomplicated company. We went window-shopping in the drizzle, then on to the flicks.

'You're too fine a man to be a waiter, Enrique.'

I took him along to Signon who said, 'What a corker!' He didn't have a work-permit but she still found him plenty to do. He became so successful that he gave up modelling, married an English girl and bought an hotel in Austria.

My very first job was a three-day fashion show in the Stratford Court Hotel in Oxford Street for a manufacturer from the North of England. Brown twin-sets, grey trews, plaid skirts and pleated shirt-waisters: country-bumpkin couture in the first flush of man-made fibres.

Signon trained me in how to show off a hat, how to throw off a coat or jacket – it was essential to look down at the lapel and feel it compulsively with your fingers, as if apprising the audience of its fetishistic sumptuousness before slipping it off your shoulders, catching it by the tab, standing immobile for a moment with one foot pointing out, turning, and walking off.

Photo sessions I had least flair for, because I was used to an audience and didn't know how to play to a machine. I tended to freeze. Terence Donovan once photographed me in a poncho for a cigar advertisement and in order to make me react without premeditation he had two cowboys fire blanks across my face with six-shooters. Though young, Terry was already very successful, roly-poly belly, a Rolls-Royce and a studio in Yeoman's Row, the first of a new breed of self-made photographers.

Occasionally one froze literally, since I became one of *Vogue*'s favourite girls for underwear, photographed by Duffy or Honeywell. I saw Bronwen Pugh coming out of a Ladies Room and she said, 'Darling, don't *do* underwear. You'll never get back into clothes.' It didn't bother me. I mentioned this to Signon who said, 'I'm inclined to agree with you, April. Who gives a fuck when you're being paid eight guineas an hour? And they've booked you for the whole day.'

That led to a soap advertisement with nothing on at all, except a towel strategically draped. They stood me in a bath which was so slippery I kept falling over. Instead of running to help, they all gasped and turned away every time I went flying. They were only trying to preserve my modesty but I was black and blue by the end of the session.

Television commercials were more prestigious because you moved. This form of advertising was still new to England and they were hopelessly amateurish. Arrid Underarm Spray Deodorant: the rulebook did not allow one to be filmed in the fully frontal act of spraying one's pits. They shot the underarm, then cut to one's hand going 'psh! psh!' with the cannister against a blank background. Armpit and hand could not figure in the same shot because it was considered obscene; whereas I feel that the way they did it was far more salacious because of the prurience it implied. It was a civilisation ago and will give you an idea of the traumas they all underwent when my past hit the headlines.

This commercial was to be screened during a sweaty summer. Typically, they shot it all in winter clothes. When Mr Arrid turned up he had puppies and it had to be completely re-shot. I've never earned more for a day's work. £160, with a free carton of cannisters thrown in. No good to me because I always use roll-on. It's healthier and more effective.

Heated hair-rollers: they wanted a glamorous type but when the client saw me he said, 'No, no, we don't want Cleopatra, we want a middle-class housewife, Mrs Upper-Average. Comb out the hair, blot the lips, pat out the eyes.' It took them hours to make me nondescript. My line was to open a door and say, 'Hullo, come in.' Then open a door again and say, 'Goodbye. Wasn't it a lovely evening.' The gist of it was that I'd had a perfect cardboard head throughout the evening thanks to their heated rollers.

It was through television commercials that one dreamed of rocketing into films. When the word went out that United Artists were looking for six beauties for *The Road to Hong Kong*, filming at Shepperton, every girl in London with a portfolio put on her best sling-backs and marched towards Mayfair.

I was early by twenty minutes and went for a cup of coffee. The steam went up my nose, I sneezed violently, and one of my eyelashes flew off and landed in the breakfast of a man opposite. Fortunately I always carried spares.

Over two hundred of London's finest were compressed into the hall and up the staircase, frantically retouching themselves with compacts and lipsticks. The noise was enough to give one mumps because, naturally, they were all insulting each other. I almost turned back but didn't because I couldn't afford to waste the taxi fare.

The six beauties were supposedly Chinese but fidelity was not the prime consideration. A scout was scrutinising from the gallery and I was one of those summoned upstairs, past a line of put-out noses, to the drawing-room which was first base. A short dark-haired girl stood beside me, taking pert puffs on cigarette after cigarette like Bette Davis in *All About Eve*.

'Are you an actress then?' she said in a madly affected voice that drawled ten feet behind her meaning.

'No, I'm a model.'

'Well, why don't you sod off! I'm an actress and actresses need work. I've been *trained* to be an actress.'

'We're all here for the same reason.'

'This is actress territory. You've got a bloody nerve, you models.' On and on she went at me – her name was Sarah Miles, by the way – until I was called. Telling her to drop dead, which is a request often made of Sarah, I went in.

'She's very tall,' I heard someone say.

'Lovely face, nice figure,' said another.

'And divine legs,' I added.

'Say that again!'

'Say what?'

'Is that voice real?'

'What do you mean?'

'We've got to give her a speaking part. Let's see those legs then.'

Damn the legs. A speaking part. Undreamt-of-grandeur. What I had to do was ask an imaginary Bob Hope to 'Follow me, sir, please.' I said it half-a-dozen times.

'We'd love you to have a speaking part but we must see your walk first. Pretend that clock's Bob Hope and approach it.'

'Follow . . . me, sir, please.'

'She hasn't got a very sexy walk.'

'Would you do it again – and make it sexier.'

'. . . Follow me . . . sir – please.'

'I think she's got a sexy walk. Kinda snooty sexy.'

'No, I don't think she has.'

'What do you think, Lorna?'

'Follow me, sir . . . *please*.'

But the hooker's roll didn't come naturally to me, and even in make-up I didn't look remotely Chinese, so this helluva speaking part went to an Oriental girl.

I was, however, cast as one of the six beauties. We had to geisha around Bing Crosby and Bob Hope in a futuristic hideaway and my special task was to feed Bing marshmallows with a pair of tongs.

We were collected at five in the morning for make-up. There was a fabulous hairpiece sitting in the dressing-room. It was huge and matched my hair perfectly.

'That's a super hairpiece,' I said. 'Can I wear it? It would be fantastic down my back.'

'I'm sorry, Miss Ashley,' said the hairdresser, 'but that's Miss Collins's fringe.'

Joan Collins was in effect the star because Dorothy Lamour was making only a guest appearance.

My greatest fear was that Bob Hope would remember me from Paris. If he did there was no mention of it, although I began to wonder when Bing crooned 'April in Paris' at me. In fact the nearest I ever came to being a movie star was playing one, on a flying visit to London in 1959, in a mock newsreel that was incorporated into the stage performance of John Osborne's *The World of Paul Slickey*. Despite claiming to abhor America and the Americans, John Osborne then owned a king-size American sedan. I was filmed getting out of it, acknowledging the adoration of the masses, and walking into the première at the Odeon, Leicester Square. Duncan Melvin also performed in a newsreel, playing a cleric who'd been arrested for jumping on choirboys. *Slickey* was said to be the West End's most disastrous first night since the war. The boos were deafening. At the end of it, confronting an audience in which reclined Noël Coward, Lord and Lady Montagu of Beaulieu, the Marquess of Milford Haven and the Duke of Bedford, Adrienne Corri went out front, threw up two pairs of fingers and bellowed until the veins started out of her neck, 'Darlings, fuck you all!'

Live fashion shows were my bread-and-butter and the best of these were for Roter Models, owned by Mr and Mrs Schroter, a Jewish couple from Vienna. Their top designer was very highly-strung, so it all came pouring out in those crazy frocks. He had every design book in Europe and he'd take features from Chanel, Givenchy, Cardin, Courrèges, push them together and then EXPLODE them. Like most clothes designed by men they were wonderful for wearing on marble staircases, impossible to shop in.

The atmosphere at Roter Models was unusually good-natured. Pauline Moore and Sue Pratt became my cronies, along with Ina Barton who was in the throes of a marathon sex transformation, the speciality of London's Charing Cross Hospital. They insist on lengthy intervals between each stage and use skin grafts from the legs which leave tell-tale scars on the thighs. So much messier than Dr Burou's technique. But her doctor, John Randell, was very solicitous for her well-being and wrote her letters which began, 'My dearest Galatea . . .'

The four of us went on pub-crawls after work, teasing the men by crossing our legs and ignoring them. Conversation was very open in the dressing-rooms. Women when they forgather can be quite as filthy as men. A German model, Hildegard, complained: 'My husband, he fuck me every morning before work, every night after work, I'm so sore, so fed up with it, he have such big dick.'

'How big?' I asked, filing a nail, one eyebrow raised.

'I don't know. Eeenormous!'

'Get a tape-measure out tonight,' said another.

The other girls must have overheard because the next morning all of them had measured their husbands and lovers. Hildegard got more sympathy after this. Her Englishman won with 9¾ inches. (However I always feel that girth is every bit as important as length. The long stiletto can be just as untrustworthy as the little stabber.)

Mr and Mrs Schroter were very hard workers. But so were those Spanish and Greek women who were paid peanuts in the backroom. I'd go behind the scenes and say 'Angels, how's the sewing coming along?' Or if I were wearing one of the frocks, I'd throw up my arms: 'You made it – how does it look?'

My most important show was a charity at the Dorchester Hotel in front of Alice, Duchess of Gloucester. I was arrayed in Deanfield furs and Kuchinksy jewels and was accompanied by two detectives to and from the Ballroom. I said to one of them, 'Listen, how much stuff have I got on?'

'At the moment you're wearing over £150,000 worth of swag.' Have you noticed how policemen and criminals so often talk in the same way?

'What happens if I walk straight across the Ballroom, out the front door, and shout taxi?'

'Try it and find out.'

As I was the only dark model they gave me the only white mink. 'How stupid,' I said, 'I haven't got a black skirt to show it off.' I borrowed a pencil one which was far too tight.

When you do a royal show, you ignore everyone else, walk right up to the royals, do a deep curtsey, and trail round the riff-raff afterwards. With my legs in bondage it was bad enough trying to walk, but when I curtseyed there was a long ripping noise muffled by mink. My first thought was: 'Oh my God, I bet the Duchess thinks I've broken wind.' My second thought was: 'I can't get up.' I seemed to be stuck there long enough for a civilisation to rise and fall and rise again. While I made rapid calculations, the Duchess must have thought I was seeking some kind of acknowledgment because she finally muttered, 'Yes, it's very nice, dear.'

It broke the ice. I pushed hard, shot upwards, drew my legs smartly together, and made a controlled exit.

Charity balls were very common. Signon would be given a bunch of passes and there we'd be looking ravishing among the columns.

At the Bubbly Ball for Cancer Research, Lance Callingham, Lady Docker's son, trod on my foot. It didn't matter because the organisers had laid on 'foot revivers', electric plates which warmed one's feet back to life so that the dancing need never end. But the reason I recall this occasion was because it was when the scales dropped from my eyes with regard to the press. One had tended to assume, halfwit that one was, that whatever appeared in the newspapers was more or less true. At the Ball a gossip columnist asked me for my name. 'Agatha Christie,' I said. My picture appeared in the *Tatler* and under it: Miss A. Christie.

It is so easy to gull the press. This anecdote suggests two other characteristics which I have found to be true of gossip columnists particularly. They are appallingly ill-read. And while being overloaded with cynicism they have no sense of humour whatsoever.

You can see I was growing in confidence. With each job, I made further advances in my campaign against shyness, learned more, and found myself entering . . . Society?

Peter Finch wasn't 'Society' exactly. He'd get drunk at Churchill's rather than the 400 and he drank like a bat out of hell. 'Doing anything tonight?' he'd say over the phone. 'Come on then, let's go to Winston's and push the boat out – Danny La Rue's appearing there.' Before the wild people and discothèques somehow restricted closing-time in London to three in the morning, nightclubs always wound up at four or five, so it would be fairly late when Finchie dropped me back again at Harrington Gardens. One night he decided he was coming in and paid off the cab.

My landlady was a foreigner who specialised in Muslim gentlewomen studying English and there was a house rule: no men after 11 p.m. But Finchie was making such a hullabaloo on the steps I thought I'd better smuggle him in before there was a scene. Once in my room he threw off his clothes and said, 'Right, take yours off now and get down on the bed so I can screw you.' He'd only recently made *The Trials of Oscar Wilde* but none of the phraseology had rubbed off. Finchie was of course an Australian. 'You don't beat about the bush in the Bush,' he used to say. Oozed charm none the less.

'No, you won't, Finchie.'

He nodded.

'Stop nodding!'

He bulged his eyes instead and his tongue fell out like a furry animal.

I did my usual trick and pointed between his legs: 'You couldn't, even if you wanted to. Get out before you get me evicted.'

We started laughing and he crawled round the floor, pulling on his jacket, trousers and shoes. Everything else was stuffed into pockets and he bade me a good night, blowing kisses and bowing from the waist like an eighteenth-century admiral. His departure was followed by a sequence of wincing crashes. I rushed on to the landing. Finchie was sprawling at the bottom of the stairs with a nosebleed. 'Sh, sh, sh,' he whispered at the top of his voice and I heard the door close.

The next morning while preparing myself for work there was a knock on the door. It was 9 a.m. precisely. At the age of twenty-five one managed on so little sleep. The landlady, a spinster and a religious maniac, stood in the doorway with an expression of utmost disquiet on her – for want of a better word – face. It was more like a battlefield across which nausea and rage fought for supremacy.

'Do you know anything about these?' she said, holding up between finger and thumb a pair of sky-blue knickers as perhaps she had once held a dead rat by the tail in Old Istanbul. Finchie's Y-fronts.

Thus was I persuaded to search for accommodation less *en croûte* and in due course moved to an airy flat in Emperor's Gate, sharing it with fellow-model Della Young. But before I did, I was walking along Walton Street in Chelsea on a spring day, one of those vigorous London spring days when the shoots peep up to a sky of turbulent greys and the wind comes howling across from the Urals, when I fell over Duncan Melvin. Duncan had last been in evidence at Le Carrousel eighteen months previously when he'd arrived with Lady Jane Vane-Tempest-Stewart (now Lady Rayne) who was escaping from the attentions of some man in England.

Now Duncan clapped his pink hands, wrote down my telephone number, and invited me to a buffet Sunday lunch in his house in St Leonard's Terrace, being given in honour of Vittorio De Sica (Vittorio was at the height of his social desirability, having won an Oscar the previous year for directing Sophia Loren in *Two Women*). Buffets were very much the vogue. They'd just been discovered. London was suddenly full of people walking about rooms with plates of food in their hands, whereas before they would have been bolted to tables. It was the beginning of the informality of the 1960s. Duncan gave so many parties, was such a generous host, that he was always running out of money, even though his wife left him all hers. The day she died Duncan took Viva King and Connie Mount out for a slap-up wake and spent, Viva said, more than she'd ever seen spent at a *dîner à trois*.

Everyone was there, serving themselves with gusto: Shirley Bassey, Fenella Fielding, Georgia Brown, Michael Rainey, Lucien Freud, Daphne Fielding, Lionel Bart and Frank Norman, Jane Vane-Tempest-Stewart, Muriel Belcher and the Maharani of Cooch Behar, Dorothy Donaldson-Hudson, Patrick Bashford, Christopher Sykes (the one who was known as the Prince of Chelsea, not the biographer of Evelyn Waugh), Carol Coombe (Lord Snowdon's stepmother) . . .

'Have you tried some of this?'

'No, but you must have some of that.'

'What is it?'

'Don't know – squid in cream?'

'Coleslaw!'

'Never heard of it.'

'I'm going to have heaps of these.'

'After you – if there are any left . . .'

It was so novel. Shirley Bassey threw a glass of red wine over an enemy – oh goodness, she's at it again and it's not my wish to give the impression that she was a violent person. Duncan was screaming, 'My walls! My walls!' because he'd recently had them covered with dove-grey silk.

One young male in particular kept me supplied with drinks. 'Are you an actor?' I asked, because although he had that massiveness of frame one associates with those handsome boys who eat well and have a drawer full of jockstraps, he was at the same time vervy, stylish, and wore a flowing neckscarf.

'No, I'm not, but come out to dinner anyway. My name's Tim.' He wished first to change, so we went to his house in Wilton Row, off Belgrave Square. A manservant opened the door and said, 'Good evening, m'Lord.'

'Good evening, George. We'll have a bottle of champagne in the garden, please.'

Lord Who? It was as if I had strayed into the pages of a Georgette Heyer.

'Do you like modern paintings?' he said. The walls were stacked with them, angry splodges in steel frames. 'Wander around and have a look while I take a shower.'

I stepped into a music room with a grand piano in the centre and daffodils blooming through the windows. Some writing-paper lay open on a desk and I tiptoed over. It was embossed in copperplate: *Lord Timothy Willoughby de Eresby*. All those exotic twirls of letters, those hanging 'y's' like licking tongues.

'Where do you want to eat?' He made me jump.

'I don't know,' I said.

'Well, I *do*.' What a confusing mixture of consideration and arrogance he was.

Where we ate I don't recall, but I did say 'Who *are* you?'

'You saw the writing paper on the escritoire.'

'Are you French?'

'God forbid! Actually I have some property there and some more in Corsica and a few bits elsewhere.'

'But you can't be more than twenty-three.'

'I'm twenty-five. My father is Lord Ancaster of Drummond Castle and Grimsthorpe, quondam Lord Great Chamberlain of England. It'll all be mine one day, so I should start now, shouldn't I? Let's go to the Stork Club, I'll get your coat.'

A slight yawn opened in the middle of his big oval face, revealing two rows of jagged carnivorous teeth. In quick succession restlessness, anxiety and despair followed each other into his eyes, which passed from animation to liverishness in a matter of seconds, and were as rapidly overtaken again by the brightness of the night and a teasing smile. In one evening Tim exposed me to the range of his emotions, including the melancholia which stalked him to distraction on occasions. For me it was like being dealt too many cards too quickly, very disconcerting and very exciting. A lesser man would have been contented with the mere privileges of his birth but Tim made you feel that peace of mind was something he never knew. This mercurial complexity, which amounted almost to an iridescence, attracted both men and women to him. They were enchanted by his frolicsomeness because of the intelligence and uneasy depths they rightly suspected behind it. He had all the makings of *le grand seigneur*, a love of pleasure made rich by his sense of tragedy.

Gloomsville! Let's get on with the story! He was fun to be with! Al Burnett's Stork Club was a popular retreat on Sundays because it was 'Amateur Night', when an assortment of the ill-advised made strenuous and hilarious attempts to break into show business. Because of the childish licensing laws, champagne was served illegally and, they hoped, anonymously in plain-glass water jugs to patrons such as Tim whom it would have been counter-productive to refuse. For all his fluctuations of mood, there wasn't a better escort to be had in London. The next morning my landlady, thoroughly vexed, mounted the stairs with a bouquet of yellow rosebuds bearing an inscription 'From Big Tim', the conceited ox. It was the beginning of a close and very dear friendship which endured until his final mysterious disappearance.

Sudden disappearances were one of his hobbies; and he would as abruptly rematerialise with tales of the South China Sea or Chichen Itza at sunrise or a fancy-dress ball on the Grand Canal in Venice. His skin seemed permanently tanned. It pleased him to take liberties with his wardrobe. Not only the flowing neckscarves (which were not taken up generally until the mid-1960s); sometimes he affected odd socks, one green, one black, or would arrive in full evening dress with fresh dandelions in his buttonhole. In 1959 he'd been among the two hundred or so guests who thronged a famous party on the Circle Line of London's Underground, which was a great success until broken up by the police at Farringdon Station. His professional activities included the ownership of Wips in Leicester Place, a club whose walls he covered in fake grey fur and which later became the Ad Lib. With Michael White he mounted a play called *The Connection* about the world of heroin. Many of the American actors were genuine addicts and the police raided it so often that it had to close.

Duncan told Tim my history and afterwards Tim called me his Bettina, a reference to the Aly Khan's mistress who, by staying in the background, outlasted all the wives. Debutantes were forever at Tim's heels. They approached me for advice: 'How can I catch him?'

'By just being yourself,' which is what I always say, but this presupposes that you know what you are, and none of them did. Tim was a bedroom nomad and stuck nowhere. He and I slept together often but we made love on only a handful of occasions.

We lunched at the Mirabelle more frequently than we made love: Beluga caviare, an iced bucket of it left in the middle of the table with a scoop, and champagne – perfectly simple, never anything else. In the evenings he took me greyhound-racing at the White City Stadium with Lord Clark's son Colin. It was his style often not to say where we were going. One night we turned up at a grand porch in Hyde Park Gardens. I was appalled to see the other guests arriving in tiaras and tails because I too had stunning things to parade in – luckily I'd thrown on a little black cocktail number which you could take anywhere.

At the top of the staircase Tim said, 'April, may I present you to the Earl and Countess of Perth.' I mumbled Sir and Madam, not knowing if it were the correct mode, but they seemed happy with it.

Butlers, footmen, dinner, cabaret, a small orchestra for waltzes and foxtrots. 'Just having a few friends in,' said Lady Perth. 'So glad you could join us.'

After dinner a group of men collected to smoke and drink in the library and I found myself among them. Lady Perth – Nancy Fincke from New York City – popped her head round the door and said, 'April, wouldn't you like to powder your nose?'

'Oh no, Lady Perth, I'd much rather stay with the men.'

I was quite taken aback when they all burst out laughing. Only Tim realised that I hadn't intentionally cracked a joke. What did I know of women withdrawing?

At the drop of another hat, I found myself racing along B-roads in Sussex until Tim turned through the gates of a Georgian manor house lit up with lanterns and fireworks bursting above it, two marquees, a dance band on the terrace doing the Chug-a-Lug. It must have been two in the morning, but Tim was often the last to arrive. There are those who always make a point of arriving late for parties, even if they have to sit at home staring at the clock until they are fashionably two-and-a-half hours behind schedule, just as there are those who pretend to forget one's name (but it doesn't happen to me any more – I often wish it did) in order to gain a bogus advantage. The implication is that they are late because they are in the thick of life and much in demand elsewhere; they pretend to forget your name, especially if you remember theirs, in order to imply that they happen to be more memorable than you are. But with Tim it was genuine. He was often late for engagements because he partook of so many. If he forgot names it was due to the fact that in the course of a week he encountered multitudes.

Though by and large I moved unsuspected through the saloons of wealth and rank, my voice was always noticed. It is the unintentional equivalent of my clashing scarf or wrong gloves in Paris days, something that doesn't quite fit and thereby attracts attention to the whole. Outside the loo at this party I tripped over a girl and the two of us went bumping down the stairs until we reached the bottom.

'Sorry,' I said when we regained consciousness.

'By Jove,' she growled, 'you can't possibly have a voice deeper than mine.'

'Oh yes, I can,' I replied, getting as low as possible in an attempt to out-husk her. But I don't think I could. Her voice was like a steamroller driving down an unmade road. She turned out to be Pauline Tennant, Hermione Baddeley's daughter by David Tennant, and we slung champagne down each other's throat for the rest of the night. Hermione Gingold of course has a voice deeper than mine but that is because as a girl her vocal cords sprouted nodules and she didn't have them scraped.

Tim invited me to spend the weekend with his mother and father at their great country seat, Grimsthorpe in Lincolnshire. He told me it was 'awfully nice to look at, thanks to Vanbrugh'. Never before had I been to a house party in a stately home and at the last moment I turned an uncharacteristic yellow. As I was packing my things I suddenly realised that, with however many brandies as lubrication, I was too terrified to face it. Guiltily, without even daring to ring and cancel, I drew the bedclothes up to my nose and stayed where I was all weekend. Tim was furious and assured me that I should not be invited to any of the family homes again. Apparently a reception party headed by the butler had been dispatched to meet me off the train and had stood on the platform for hours in the rain.

To make amends I asked him to travel with me to Paris for a weekend. A crowd of his hangers-on followed and some of them, including Marilyn Dent, turned up later while we were dining with Les Lee in St Germain. Hangers-on are always sad creatures but there was something about Tim's hangers-on which I found particularly distasteful. Part of me rebelled against these sprigs because they did nothing with life, they hadn't earned a right to the self-importance they flaunted. It was silly of me to disapprove of them in this way but I still had a puritan streak. I still have it unfortunately. Or fortunately if you prefer. I always think it unfortunate myself. Their humour was brittle and their behaviour trite. Above all they lacked intelligence, they simply weren't very bright – Tim easily dominated them all. And although some were aristocrats, they were not all by any means noble. The kind of nobleman who appeals to me is the 3rd Marquess of Hertford, who in 1848, the Year of Revolutions, could say without nuance, 'I have a place in Wales which I have never seen, but they tell me it's very fine. A dinner for twelve is served there every day . . . the butler eats it.'

Marilyn Dent took the lead in silly chatter. As for *her* voice, it was like the relentless fluttering of a copy of the *Horse and Hound* on a windy day. Then I couldn't believe my ears, she was saying to Les Lee, 'You are the most disgusting thing I've seen in all my life! You're the biggest phoney, the patheticest – '

'Phoney' coming from her was too much. I had to interpose. Or to be more exact, I came near to killing her with my mouth. Never before had I had the confidence to lose my temper with the upper-class English, but I had it now and I enjoyed myself. Finally, I told her to leave the table at once and take her trashy chums with her.

Timothy was drunk and looked sheepish. She looked at him. 'Marilyn, do as you're told,' he said.

When she started to argue I said, 'Do you want me to call the manager and have you physically removed from my table?' – because I was treating them and I certainly wasn't having her sitting on my bill.

Les Lee burst into tears. Under the *trompe-l'oeil* he was so easily damaged. 'Don't cry, darling, they're trash, I don't care what their families are. Tim, how dare you bring such muck to my dinner party?'

Since then I've never stood for it, for being patronised by those who imagine themselves superior. This was Sarah Churchill's tuition. She told me, 'Never be frightened of *anyone* because of what they are, only be careful of what they do.'

The following morning I had a phone call from Marilyn. 'I've fallen in love with you,' she said, 'and I want you to live with me.'

'Is there no stopping that silly bitch?' I thought. 'Marilyn, I didn't go through what I went through in Casablanca in order to shack up with you.'

The day after that she phoned again to say she'd now fallen out of love with me – so Marilyn turned out to have far more style and a deeper sense of humour than I'd given her credit for. She was always in and out of the gossip columns, like a Lady Charlotte Curzon of the early 1960s, really rather a terrific girl despite my unfortunate first impression.

When Tim had the blues, which was about once a week, he'd invite me round to Wilton Row to play psychiatrists and have a quiet cup of tea. It was here that I properly met his elder sister, Lady Jane Willoughby, herself very intense, and her boyfriend Lucien Freud, artist grandson of the Viennese genius. These afternoons were more precious to me than all the grand parties squashed together. Excepting Jane and Lucien, I asked Tim not to invite Marilyn or any of his more boisterous friends to our teas and he never did. Sometimes we'd go off for shepherd's pie round the corner at the Grenadier pub and watch the young guardsmen trading with the queens, which made him laugh and jollied him up.

The parties I enjoyed most were Brian Desmond Hurst's. They were like that one in *Breakfast at Tiffany's.* You never knew who would be there, Tennants and Guinnesses chatting up soldiers and sailors on leave. One moved in circles, the same people and places, so it was a thrill when the circle broke, as it did at Brian's, and one found oneself talking to . . . Hermione Gingold, for example. 'Don't expect me to be funny,' she said, 'because I'm the most lugubrious *dame*. I only know two jokes. I'm going to tell them to you now to get it over with. The first is about a lorry driver who was told to take some penguins to the Bronx Zoo. A few days later his boss was walking past the Radio City Music Hall when he saw the driver standing in the queue with the penguins. "I thought I told you to take these penguins to the Bronx Zoo," said the boss. "I did," said the driver, "and they liked it so much I thought I'd take them to the pictures as well." I can't remember what the other story is. It's not dirty either.'

Hermione was later engaged to a dashing young antiques dealer called Baudouin Mills. She was at London Airport waiting for a flight to New York when a reporter approached her and said, 'Is it true, Miss Gingold, that you're engaged to an antiques dealer?'

'Of course it is,' she said, 'because I know he'll appreciate me.'

Julia and Sarah I saw little of during this period. They were seriously involved with the theatre and moved in a completely different set when they moved at all. Julia did take me to see her mother's new house in Richmond – it was the first time I ever saw a mink bedspread, blue mink it was.

While all this nonsense was going on, I had a call from a friend of Les Lee called Louise. Although he had a woman's passport, Louise was a middle-aged male transvestite who had fathered children. He said that a friend of his was eager to meet me. I'd given up blind dates with weirdos but Louise was persistent and I agreed on condition that the appointment be for lunch, so that I could arrange an afternoon audition as a getaway, and that lunch be at the Caprice. I'd longed to eat at this famous restaurant ever since I'd seen Nubar Gulbenkian's car outside it. This car, NG 5, was a customised London taxi-cab with carriage lamps and wickerwork panels let into the bodywork. Gulbenkian had commissioned it because it would be tall enough for him to sit inside without removing his top hat. ('They tell me it turns on a sixpence, whatever that is,' was his standard line.) And logic told me that any man who was prepared to lunch at the Caprice couldn't be a complete lout. 'Don't worry about recognising him,' said Louise. 'I've given him dozens of photographs of you. He knows every hair on your head.'

Deliberately late, because I didn't want to be left standing there like a lemon, I went whizzing through the revolving doors on Arlington Street. I was immediately in a sea of expensive hats. The first person I recognised was Marjorie Proops, the Agony Aunt. Then I heard a voice.

'April? My name is Frank. What would you like to drink?' A tall thin man in his early forties had jumped to his feet and was being most considerate. I had a champagne cocktail, slotted in the small-talk cassette, had another, and we went to eat. 'This is pleasant,' I thought, dislodging a Sole Meunière from its skeleton, 'not at all loopy. And Frank – he has the same texture as Tim and that lot. The upper-class thing, quite at home in the Caprice. But why won't he give me his surname? He hasn't mentioned drag once but he sure knows all about *me*.' I focused on Jill Bennett at a nearby table. She was playing the hysterical actress part, going from Gwendolen Fairfax to Lady Macbeth and back again every few minutes.

Like Peter Finch, Frank was a natural charmer, skilful at putting one at one's ease. He wasn't my type but some would have called him handsome in a bony-faced way. Soon we were lunching once a week, then twice a week, then every other day, and always at the Caprice, always very politely. This couldn't be all. Eventually it came:

'I think I can trust you, April. I want to tell you something. If I don't tell somebody I'll go round the bend.' The bland well-bred expression fell from his face, the nose lengthened, the cheeks sank inwards, suddenly he looked awful, like something Ibsen might have dreamed up in a nightmare.

'You like dressing in women's clothes,' I said.

'How did you know?'

'I guessed.'

'For years I've been doing it. There's a male brothel, I pay the boys to dress me up, then . . . you-know-what.' The British, so squeamish, bad toilet-training they say. 'But now, here's the point, since I've been seeing you I haven't done it or wanted to. I think you've cured me. That's meant to be a compliment. It's something to do with knowing you were a boy, that you've had the operation, that it's a reality I can't compete with. You've stopped my pendulum swinging.'

It was the first time I'd heard about his pendulum. Frank explained that having been brought up in a world full of grandfather clocks it was the nearest he could come to describing the motion his personality sometimes took. Usually he was fairly normal, a job in the City, a healthy chauvinistic attitude towards the weaker sex, then out of the blue – SWING! He wanted to be a woman, to bind his hips in chiffon and sashay down to the boys in the brothel, 'those monsters' he called them. Such behaviour is not uncommon but Frank did seem to harbour an exceptional polarity in this respect – presumably the result of Dad's heavy hand. He was unable to resolve his conflict by surrendering to it and so make more tolerable his brief passage on this earth. Until he met me, he said.

'Go on,' I said, keeping my eyes on him while tilting back my head to sink an oyster.

'My name isn't Frank of course. It's Arthur.' Which sounded even more ridiculous. 'The Honourable Arthur Cameron Corbett actually.'

'Oh God, another one,' I thought.

'I want to tell you everything so that you'll understand my problem.' I positioned myself for an epic. 'My father's a Scotsman called Lord Rowallan. He used to be the Chief Scout. At the moment he's the Governor of Tasmania. I'm his heir. My elder brother was killed in action in 1944. You can imagine the dreadful pressure on me never to do anything untoward. Father would go bananas if he knew the real me. I went to Eton and to Balliol College, Oxford. My son Johnny is at Eton now. My wife's name is Eleanor. She's also from Scotland. We get on but it's not what you'd call a passionate marriage – she lets me once a week and that's my lot. I've three daughters too and we all live in Hampstead with a Nanny, a gardener, a maid . . . am I boring you?'

'Only a little bit.' He wasn't in the least, I was absolutely riveted, but I thought the kindest thing I could do was pretend that none of it was so very special. Arthur went on and on. It was like an enormous boil draining out through his mouth. The family's money came from Brown & Polson's Cornflour. Arthur's grandfather, Archibald, the 1st Baron, had married it in the form of Alice Polson. In consequence the 2nd Baron, Arthur's father, had been desperately straight. Arthur's mother, Gwyn, was the sister of Jo Grimond, the Liberal politician. The family house was Rowallan Castle, an ugly Victorian heap near Kilmarnock with 7,000 acres. He had three brothers and a sister but the only member of the family he could really talk to was his Aunt Elsie, a spinster of mannish appearance who was wont to distribute soup to the poor in gumboots.

In return I told him I was having an affair with Tim Willoughby. He was furious.

'Arthur, what a puritan you are suddenly.' He had a pedestal concept of women, even when trying to be one himself. 'There aren't many 26-year-old virgins around any more. What do you expect me to do?'

'Marry him.'

'Don't be foolish.' The admonitory tone I was later to adopt with him had already crept in. 'Tim doesn't want to marry me, he wants an heir.'

Their dislike was mutual. Tim thought Arthur an old croak and Arthur was annoyed by Tim's superior nobility and panache.

'What would you say if I said I've fallen in love with you?' he said.

Not long after, Arthur rang me in the evening which was unusual for him. Eleanor was having a fit.

'Why?'

'Because I've told her everything. I had to, darling.'

'But Arthur, what is "everything" exactly?' Because the only thing between Arthur and me had been the lunch table, the talk.

'I told her I've been seeing you and I've told her who you are. I've told her about the women's clothes and the brothel boys. Once I started there was no convenient place to stop, I had to go on.'

'Then I'm not surprised she's having a fit.' Eleanor knew of Arthur's transvestite idiosyncrasy. I discovered in court much later that in the early days of their marriage she'd even zipped him up a few times. But she thought it was all in the past.

'Anyway, she wants to meet you,' Arthur said.

This was something I hadn't expected. She obviously had guts and I admired her even before I met her. Eleanor, née Boyle, was a cousin of the Earl of Glasgow. Her mother was born Mary Mackie, daughter of Sir Peter Mackie, the Whisky Baronet, and Eleanor was very rich in her own right.

They were waiting for me at the Caprice. She was about my height, several years younger than Arthur, with masses of whisky-coloured hair, and far more beautiful than her photographs suggest – a faint resemblance to Virginia Woolf. She quivered like a violin string about to snap. I felt a sham trying to convince her that Arthur was only a friend with a problem, when in fact, without anyone wishing it, our lunches together had triggered in him something which augured disaster for her. She was an over-controlled woman and kept her passions hidden but when we went down to the Powder Room together she dissolved into tears and begged me to help save her marriage. 'Do go on seeing him if it stops him going off for the other thing. The thought of that, I can't bear it.'

Over lunch it was arranged that I should visit them in Hampstead on Sunday, and meet the children. The point of this was a hope that if I could be somehow built into the pattern of their life, albeit discreetly and to one side, it might prevent the collapse of the family. What an extraordinary idea that was!

The large undistinguished house in Wildwood Road overlooked Hampstead Heath. The interior exemplified good taste and lacked any sign of warmth or spontaneity, but the garden was full of flowers and a brook ran through it. Johnny was away at school. Eleanor and I took the girls for a walk on the Heath. Little Sarah ran along beside us saying, 'Oh Mummy, I love April – can she come and live with us?' Eleanor must have been havoc inside.

On a later visit I met Johnny, who didn't take to me very much. In fact I got the impression that he thoroughly detested me. Perhaps he understood what was going to happen. He suffered much at school later on, as did his sisters.

Tim was away for the summer so I spoke to no one about these developments. Eleanor went to Holland to stay with friends. She had given Arthur permission to take me out in the evening.

'So where do you want to go?' he asked.

'The 400.'

It was the most respectable club I could think of. Princess Margaret and Billy Wallace had made it smart in the 1950s but now it was coming to the end of its days. We talked. Inside I knew that this was where I should get off, wish him well, and hope that he would sort out his life in a way which didn't include me. But at the time I was going through acute anxieties of my own which clouded my judgment.

The chief bliss for a transsexual is to be regarded as a normal woman. The chief anxiety therefore is the fear of being exposed and ridiculed.

As I've already said, my true identity was not at this time generally known. Modelling London knew to some degree. One evening at Roter Models we had our feet up on the wall to reduce the swelling from walking up and down on carpet all day (carpet is the worst, concrete is much better, except that they say too much time standing on concrete gives you piles). All the models seemed to have problems. One was terribly in debt, living way beyond her means in order to keep up appearances which are so crucial to this profession. Two were undecided about artificial insemination (in the end they both had it and both had babies and lived happily ever after). One was hooked on pills, another on drink. Hildegard we already know about. Pauline Moore was beside me. Her boyfriend, Sid, was much older than she was and the age difference was a great worry to her, I can't think why but it was, so I decided to cheer her up.

'You think you've got it rough? Listen to me. I have terrible news.' Her feet immediately came down from the wall and she sat up. And I told her about my sex transformation.

She was staggered and said: 'It's the loveliest thing I ever heard.'

'Why do you say that?'

'I don't know, I don't know what to say.'

Parts of Society London and Bohemian London knew about me. But the press hadn't got hold of it and therefore it was possible, in that phlegmatic English way which is mistakenly called hypocrisy, for the fact to go unobserved on those occasions when it would cause inconvenience. Once the newspapers caught up, this would no longer be possible. And already there were hiccups.

Jobs would unaccountably be cancelled. I was due to fulfil a booking for a plain-chocolate television commercial with voice-over. They wanted a dark, husky voice to match the product. Then the client cancelled. It was the same with Hush Puppies. I was perfect – then not. A deb's delight invited me out for dinner. The boy arrived too early and pottered awhile. When I came out of the boudoir he'd vanished. There was a call from a phone box: 'You'll think me the most awful shit, and I am, but I saw a photo of you in your room and suddenly recognised you from Le Carrousel – I'm sorry but I can't take you out, oh Christ, I am a shit.' It upset me but I felt sorry for the wretch too because he'd suddenly been forced to face his own feebleness, that to be dissuaded from a heartfelt course of action by the disapproval of others is the most unmanly thing a man can do.

So the evening at the 400 was adding up to a monumentally depressing experience. It was saved by the arrival of Sir Iain Moncreiffe of that Ilk. He looked like a dapper little bookie and his humour prevented the evening from being a total flop. Arthur started to reminisce about Rosa Lewis and the Cavendish Hotel – how he'd been the first uniformed officer to go there at the beginning of the war, how she'd been particularly fond of him after he was awarded the Croix de Guerre, how he lived in terror of being landed with a bill for a case of champagne drunk by someone else because you never queried a bill from Rosa. If she made you pay for someone else's drink she had her reasons, although these reasons became increasingly inscrutable as her faculties slipped away.

But when Sir Iain left us, Arthur told me that he and Eleanor had in fact separated and he was moving into the Vanderbilt Hotel round the corner from my flat in Emperor's Gate. Divorce was set in motion soon after. Arthur hired 'an intervener' which was the way to do it before the reform of the law. They spent the night together at the Grosvenor Hotel at Victoria Station playing cards. Just before breakfast was wheeled in they hopped into bed so that the room-boy and the chambermaid could act as witnesses for 'adultery'.

It was late summer. Arthur wanted me to accompany him on a motoring tour of my old European haunts and I agreed. He grew more raffish with every mile that separated us from Wildwood Road. In Paris Le Carrousel had not yet moved to its new premises and we went to the 11 o'clock show. Little had changed. Still all that plush. They invited me onstage to take the finale with them. Arthur was horrified. Typically. His naughty side was always battling with his respectable side. Words passed between us, and we returned to our separate rooms in the Hôtel de la Paix in a sour mood.

We caught Peki's strip act in Milan – meeting the transsexuals and transvestites made Arthur volatile. In Juan I fell on to the neck of an old boyfriend, which led to an awful row – Arthur drove back to England by himself in a huff, writing contritely from Grenoble: *My most darling wife-to-be, First I ran over a sheep which caused quite a stir and lost me a whole hour. Secondly I was immediately behind a car which crashed killing one and badly wounding two others, and lastly I met with a bicycle race!*

With hindsight I see the whole ghastly mess in these few weeks abroad with him . . . but we made it up in London and he flew to Spain to view some property.

It was a weekend and Della was away – she usually was. There was an unexpected knock at the door. I opened it ajar and, as a man applied pressure from the other side, slammed it shut.

'My name's Roy East!' he shouted from the landing.

'And so?'

'I'm a reporter for the *People* newspaper.'

Silence.

'Is it true you used to be a boy?'

My stomach hit the floor, blood flew to my head, my ears sang and my mouth dried up. I sat down and tried to work out what to do next. Taking a very long breath and moistening my lips with an adjacent Tio Pepe *frappé*, I yelled, 'Go to hell!'

'We know all about you.'

Silence.

'We're going to publish the story anyway.'

'I'll call the police!'

'Open up and make sure we get it right.'

'Whichever way you do it, you'll ruin me.'

When all my pleadings failed I let him in and spoke as fully as I could. I also discovered that the paper had been tipped off by someone from Nevern Square days, he wouldn't say who, but he or she had been paid a paltry fiver for it.

It was only when he left that panic hit me. Tim was away, so I turned to Arthur. That was the secret of his success with me – he was *always* there. On Monday he went to see the Editor. This made it worse. Barbara Back, a friend of his working on the *People*, tried to have the story spiked but now they were doubly convinced they were on to something fruity. It appeared the following Sunday under a banner headline: 'The Extraordinary Case Of Top Model April Ashley – Her Secret Is Out'.

The next day I called Signon and went in. 'Those bastards! I'm sorry, darling, all your bookings have been cancelled. And there have been a lot of abusive calls from people who've used you in the past. I don't know why they bother. You realise you're finished, darling. You can forget England.'

I was in the middle of a season for Roter Models but went home to hide. Marcel's 'You'll be back' kept running through my head. Then the dirty phone calls started which, until recently, were to be a feature of my life. Sarah and Julia rang and tried to raise my spirits. I felt like a criminal and was frightened to go out.

Mrs Schroter rang. 'Where are you, April? We're missing our lovely girl. It's not like you to be late.'

'Mrs Schroter . . . you must know why.'

'I don't care about silly newspapers, my dear. For me you are just late for work. So I hope you won't be late tomorrow.'

The next day I forced myself to go in. There was an embarrassed silence. 'Good morning, everyone.' They broke ranks and gave me their sympathy in the best way of all – by hugging me. Even Mrs Schroter, normally so practical, joined in the mood. The door burst open and the Spanish and Greek women trooped forward to add their comfort. But it was impossible. Beyond the dressing-room was a carnival of gawpers. I was the centre of ridicule and terrible insults and cruelties. For me London had collapsed overnight.

While in Spain Arthur had bought the Jacaranda nightclub in Marbella. There were many things about him which fascinated me. For a start, his intellect – he could add up columns of figures like a computer. There was hardly a subject on which he did not have an informed opinion. But what appealed to me most of all – he was genuinely kind, not only to me but to many others. So, when he asked me to go and help him run this nightclub, I didn't refuse.

When the film was released they had even removed my credit from *The Road to Hong Kong*, the bastards.

7 Spain

As we grow older, there comes a time when we are obliged to acknowledge the limits of what is possible in one short life, to strike a balance between the behest of one's dreams and the chastening douche of cold fact, and perhaps come to understand that the only real peace on this earth lies not in the gratification of what one wants for oneself but in the sympathetic contemplation of the follies of others. But I hadn't yet reached this stage, I didn't yet have one foot in the grave. I still wanted to change the world. None the less I had suffered a serious reverse and it was advisable for the time being to withdraw with my shattered expectations.

December 1961: numbness was my most positive sensation on departure. Arthur collected me from Emperor's Gate in the morning, in a white Zephyr convertible he'd recently bought. With my Great Dane puppy, Mr Blue, half-asleep under my arm, we set off. Arthur was very chatty, excessively so. This was probably because he was taking a brave – most people said insane – step into a new life. Something inedible aboard the Channel ferry – France – an overnight stop – where? – the hearse moved south.

Madrid. They wouldn't take dogs at the Ritz, nor at the Castilliana Hilton. But the Palace Hotel was charming to Mr Blue, poor lamb. Apart from a little flatulence as we passed through the Home Counties, he had behaved like an angel throughout. Arthur and I had separate rooms of course.

We went to the Patio Andaluz nightclub: flamenco cabaret, a mixed bunch of the international set gossiping among smoke and shrouded table lights, plus Arthur and I against a wall drinking champagne and growing more festive, I felt. I was walking briskly towards the Ladies when there was a yelp behind me. It was Paco, a Spanish dancer who'd worked at Le Carrousel years before. We must have been chattering longer than I realised because suddenly the figure of Arthur appeared, looking murderous.

'Whore!' he screamed. It was a word he often used when angry. It gave him a *frisson*. He threw my mink at me, followed at high speed by my handbag. 'Whore!' He dragged me out by the arm and hailed a taxi. I let him get in first. Then I slammed the door and told the cabby to drive off, which he did, thank goodness.

I jumped into another cab. The driver told me – once he'd unravelled my meaning from the three Spanish words I knew (*sí, non* and *definidamente*, but they get you everywhere in combinations) – that the real place for flamenco, where the Spaniards themselves go, was called El Duende. The flamenco is a marvellous dance when one is in a rage. Later, while in Marbella, a local ancient monument called Ana de Pombo (at whose house Jean Cocteau would stay until he was barred from Spain because of the boys) used to come to the Jacaranda in the afternoons to give me lessons. I became quite good at it in the flagrant style with a rose between my teeth.

The next thing I remember is Arthur standing over my bed waving his shirtsleeves about, ranting while my eyelashes slowly unstuck, how he'd been out of his mind with worry, what a mad thing it was for me to go wandering by myself around a strange city at night. I said I didn't care, I'd often wandered by myself around strange cities at night, I wanted to go back to England, I didn't want to go on to Marbella to do his bloody nightclub effort, would he please shut the door, there were people in the corridor, that it all seemed pointless, dreadful, draining, my nerves, my headache, oh God, etc. By now I was trailing round the room throwing bits and pieces into a suitcase, madly uncrisp.

The twelve-hour drive to Málaga was very quiet. The only incident was that we ran out of petrol in the middle of nowhere, barren rocks wherever you looked. Luckily we were able to free-wheel down-and-along, down-and-along to the next human settlement where the petrol had to be pumped up from an underground tank by hand. It took Arthur an eternity of physical jerks to fill the tank and all but finished him off. When we entered Marbella it was dark and pouring with rain.

In 1961 Marbella was still only a fishing village of whitewashed houses with geranium window-boxes, climbing up the slopes of La Concha mountain which sheltered the town and gave it its agreeable climate. In the centre was a square of orange trees where the guitarists plucked their tragic folk-songs and the widows sat in black. Fishing boats were pulled up on the beach as if immobilised for ever in a postcard. The main street was full of cafés, bars and shops where at the hour of *paseo* (6 o'clock on) the town would parade up and down in fresh clothes, checking itself out. It was at one end of this street, in the direction of Málaga, that the Jacaranda Club opened its doors at 9 p.m.

There are many fishing villages like this in Spain. What certified Marbella as *the* spot was the Marbella Club, then going through its most fashionable period. Several years earlier Prince Max von Hohenlohe-Langenburg had made over a seaside property to his son, Prince Alfonse. In 1955, at the age of thirty-one, Alfonse was married in fairy-tale, even outrageous, circumstances to Clark Gable's friend, the fifteen-year-old Fiat heiress Princess Ira von Fürstenburg. After bearing him two sons she hopped off with a Brazilian playboy called Pignatari, tried to go into films, and flopped. Alfonse turned to work and opened the property as a resort club for his rich and aristocratic connections, which he ran with the help of his cousin Rudi (Count Rudolf von Schönburg). Stocky and looking somewhat like a Turkish-carpet dealer, Alfonse also had an unGermanic flair for the business of letting people lounge around at great cost to themselves and soon established his *casa* in the calendar of the jet set.

Visitors who came for longer periods rented villas. Crops of these had sprung up on the outskirts of the town on the sites of old farms and were known as *fincas*. Arthur had rented a new villa on the *Finca el Capricho*. '*Capricho*' means 'caprice' or 'whim' – and didn't we know it in the end! When we arrived the house was damp and surrounded by mud and the log fire wouldn't catch. Rogelia, the wife of Pepe (the *finca*'s caretaker), brought us some supper. As usual Arthur and I had separate rooms, which delighted her. For the Spanish peasant 'separate bedrooms' is the last word in gentility. I had insisted on it, wishing for as much independence as possible. Arthur agreed, not being a rapist by nature. In fact he was curiously prim, given to making remarks like, 'You will never be my mistress, only my wife.' He once wrote to me in London: *I have already said to my father and to Aunt Elsie that you would make the best and most beautiful Mrs Corbett and eventually Lady Rowallan. Of this I am sure and it is my life's work to convince you of it!* He wanted me on a pedestal, not on a barstool. My inability to remain on any such thing – on either thing – was the cause of many conflagrations between us.

The next day the sun was shining and it was almost hot. We went down to explore the Jacaranda: zany tropical décor with a cool marble floor. Outside through sliding glass doors were orange and lemon trees and a plant called *Dama de Noche* which blooms on only one night of the year. Arthur always kept this flower for me by putting it in the fridge. Also in the garden was the jacaranda tree from which the club took its name. In the spring this tree turned into a large mauve cloud.

Mark and Min, the previous owners, called in to wish us well. Naturally the staff were curious about me, especially when Arthur introduced me as his fiancée, but my notoriety was excellent for business. Jaime Parlade, who owned a local antiques shop, was the leader of the young fast set. Gerald Brenan, lover of the painter Carrington, headed the older 'I remember Andalucia when' crowd. Bill and Doreen Godwin were Reuters correspondents for the region and became good friends, of Arthur's especially.

My drinking partners were Sarah Skinner, an English girl living with a Spanish count; Rosemary Strachey who lived in a tiny cottage with no electricity, was madly in love with Jaime, and was a very good painter of cats; and Evelyn Locke, one of those dogged English women from Crawley in Sussex whom nothing daunts. My intake of alcohol increased. Customers came to the club in the hope of witnessing a scene. Sometimes they were lucky. Certainly I was unpredictable. This bewildered Arthur who was both distressed and mesmerised by it. For the first year he had terrible eczema.

Not long after our arrival he bought the villa, which I named 'Antoinette'. This he ostensibly gave to me, minus the relevant documents. Neither the telephone nor the postman quite reached us at first. The villa was plonked in the middle of a field and looked almost unseemly, like a virgin at a party. I soon threw up a low wall, Arthur planted a few trees and shrubs and put a palm tree on either side of the front gate. The outside of the villa, though nothing grandiose, thus acquired presence.

The inside needed a firm hand too. All the rooms were different colours. I had the lot whitewashed. However, my experience at the

Ormskirk Hospital told me that matters could not rest here. Inspired by the Robinson Crusoe tomfooleries of the Jacaranda, I went bamboo. With wild junglified prints for upholstery and rugs rioting on the floor.

Soon Rogelia was established as our cook, Pepe as the gardener, and their son José-Luis who was at school did odd jobs like splitting figs in the sun or delivering secret notes or swimming with me in the pool at the old farmhouse where his parents lived.

The only problem now was Arthur.

I was twenty-six, he was forty-two. There was much about him that I genuinely adored. If sometimes I sound patronising it is because he lived, breathed and dreamed 'April Ashley'. Whereas this often led him to treat me with great tenderness and generosity, it could also become horribly claustrophobic. I made strenuous efforts to understand the complexity of his feelings but my own nature – impulsive and romantic too but with a strong, qualifying dose of self-preservation and Liverpudlian common sense – repeatedly rebelled against his attempts to contrive me as the miraculous resolution of his inner conflicts. If the advantages of birth, education, influence and property were his, I believe that in the end the inner strengths were mine. I think he knew it, which is why he both worshipped and resented me with a pathetic vehemence. Arthur often needed uncloying. My disappearance now and again on one of the roads out of Marbella, in the company of a beautiful young man nearer my age, sometimes below it, usually did the trick. Not that I was unduly promiscuous. That came later.

Life at the Villa Antoinette was no chocolate-box affair. 'She' began to make unwelcome and unnerving visits. A sidelong look would slither into Arthur's eyes. The spine would stiffen and the legs suddenly cross. The inevitable cigarette, normally wedged down firmly between his first two nicotined fingers, would slide up and perch effetely between the outstretched extremities. He would take short petulant puffs, cupping the elbow in the palm of his free hand, then with forearm upright the cigarette would twitch round to point backwards over his shoulder. A bitchy accusing edge came into his voice, the mouth pursed, his bottom squirming among cushions . . . When 'she' had gone, his line would be: 'If only you'd marry me, I'd be cured!'

To escape I went for walks with Peter Townend, a young writer tinkering around Marbella in a state of post-Cambridge oatsiness. He lived with Menchu, a scarlet woman with wild eyes who was openly flouting her strict Spanish upbringing. They were always having fights. Often I went swimming naked and alone in a natural pool on La Concha (until I discovered a shepherd boy had been peeping at me through the bushes like a satyr – it was the whiteness of his teeth which gave him away).

But when Arthur slipped into grotesque parody of myself, I rebelled. It was approaching spring and my spirits were inflamed. Fortunately Sarah Churchill was at hand in her dark glasses and slacks and flat shoes. She had popped in on her way to see Henry Audley (Lord Audley had a house on the other side of the *finca* from mine).

'Sweetheart, come and stay with me for a while,' she intoned, pushing back her hairband, 'until your nerves slacken.' Marbella had attracted Sarah too. She had moved into the Villa Santa Cecilia beyond Los Monteros, bang on the sea. I spent several weeks there, walking up and down the terrace with a glass in my hand. Occasionally I paused to ogle the Pillars of Hercules (the twin rocks of Ceuta and Gibraltar which Sarah christened Bally-Hai and Bally-Hoo) and dream.

She wrote most of the time at the opposite end of the house. Sarah loved to write but I believe her greatest talent was for acting. She could have become a great actress if she'd concentrated on it instead of letting her energies seep out in so many different directions. She had trained for the ballet as a girl and would often get up on her toes after a few drinks. Arthur went out one day and changed all the Jacaranda tabletops from wood to glass because of Sarah's tendency, and mine, to dance on them.

Henry called frequently. He had been crippled by a stroke. Sarah prised him out of his wheelchair, made him throw away his sticks, and take up motoring. It was a remarkable transformation, accompanied by growing affection and furious rows. Soon they were married.

Meanwhile Arthur had been asking me to return. Sarah bumped into him in the village sucking his teeth and scratching his arms, talking April this, April that. She suggested that since he claimed to have given me the house as a grand gesture, he should do the chivalrous thing, move out and stay out until I chose to invite him back. This wasn't impossible since there was a small unused flat available for him at the Jacaranda. He acted on her advice and covered the walls there with photographs of me. I returned to the villa and planted a hedge. I urged it to grow quickly because by now I was becoming one of the tourist attractions of the region. Strangers would drive up the dust track and leer at me.

Relations warmed between Arthur and I. We took to dining regularly at the Marbella Club . . . where one evening we met the Duke and Duchess del Infantado.

The Infantados had been very influential ever since the fifteenth century. The Duke was grim – as befitted a man descended from the Borgias. He had three sons. My eye fell on the eldest, Inigo, the heir, but not before his eye had fallen on me, both his eyes, the biggest I'd ever seen, too big to fit in his head. He was twenty years old, slender, solemn, sensual. The head was like Humphrey Bogart's. I asked him to visit us at the Jacaranda. He did. We foxtroted and faintly smooched. A little rock 'n' roll and the Twist which had just come in and was considered very lubricious. Arthur told me to lay off or else the family would be down on us like a delivery of coal, close the club, have us deported – his imagination ran away with him, although the Spanish aristocracy can be desperately parochial compared to the English. He accused me of sleeping with Inigo. Incorrect. But not for long.

After the holiday Inigo had to return to Madrid with his family. Every day he telephoned me at the Golf Hotel where I waited for his calls. Sarah used to run me out there because she loved the place – and glamorous intrigue besides. Suddenly he called from Seville, from another family *palacio*. Officially it was closed except during the *feria*. He said we should be alone there to make *amor* . . . apart from the usual servants . . . Surely it is no accident that the Spanish, French and Italian words for love, *amor*, *amour*, *amore* begin with a long sigh on the 'a'; involve on the 'm' pushing the lips together and thrusting them forwards in blatant imitation of a kiss (especially so with the French 'mou'); and end with an 'r' sound in which the lips are curled back to reveal both upper and lower teeth while the tongue is fluttered hungrily within the mouth. Why, the very word amounts almost to an act of rape. By contrast, the English 'love' begins by withdrawing the tongue in an arc as far away as possible from the action; then just as the tongue begins to emerge, the mouth has second thoughts, the upper teeth are bared and champ down sharply on the lower lip as if it were being told to stop it at once.

'Where are you off to?' said Arthur.

'Seville.'

'What for?'

'Sight-seeing.'

'How long are you going for?'

'I don't know, Arthur, a few days.'

'Then why are you taking seven suitcases and the Great Dane?'

It was true. I was full of hope.

Latin noblemen christen everything, the flimsiest bungalow, a palace. But this one was genuine. There was an avenue of them, all in glowing golden stone set in their own grounds. Inigo drove me through high wrought-iron gates, up a short drive flanked by birds and love-seats sculpted from yew to the house, where a retainer took the car away. Inside was a magical world of decaying smells, dark, gilded, shuttered. Mr Blue was led downstairs and I upstairs.

Inigo was a very old-fashioned young man. He hardly spoke at all. When we did, it was in French. Love-making, as opposed to sex merely, is a mysterious, frown-filled, incessant business for Spanish males. All that I learned of his other affections was that he was mad about flying. Our passion was secretive and moody and exciting.

And brief. Papa telephoned. *El duque*. He threatened to have me deported if Inigo didn't return at once to the capital. Inigo suggested we flee to North Africa where he had a *hacienda*. But I was older and wiser and couldn't place my future in the infatuation of a boy with very noble prospects. He took the plane to Madrid. I booked into the Alfonso XIII Hotel (King Alfonso's old Andalucian *palacio*, next door to the tobacco factory where Bizet's Carmen supposedly had her fits). Throughout this period I was attempting not very effectively to come to grips with the home truths about myself. For example, could I ever have a straightforward affair? Or a straightforward job? And to what extent did the answer depend on the fact of my sex-change or my own basic nature? When it all became too oppressive I forced my mind and my emotions to go blank. To others this made me appear capricious.

Each day I made the trek to the palace to visit Mr Blue, who was being cared for by one of the Duke's gardeners. I'd prepare his meals and place the bowl on bricks. Young Great Danes have to be fed in this way. If the food is placed on the ground they splay their legs giraffe-fashion and can grow up permanently disfigured.

Arthur rang. He was extremely sweet at exactly the right moment and met me at Málaga Airport in the white Zephyr. As usual when I returned from one of my crazy escapades, he had filled the Villa Antoinette with flowers. But I was angry and set fire to the curtains with a brand pulled from the fire.

Inigo I saw only once again, at the Marbella Club, firmly locked within his family group, eyes down, hands under the table as if handcuffed. Where are you now, young man with the high forehead? Are you the Duke yet? I must say, your papa seemed indestructible, a heart of leather. I remember you for your nut-brown hair and sensitive spirit. You will remember me only as a youthful folly, but you will not forget me.

The biggest boost was the offer of employment, a season of fashion shows for the House of Rango. Mr Blue and I flew to Madrid and checked into the Palace Hotel for six weeks. I spent my free time in the Museo del Prado, or at the cinema improving my Spanish, or chatting with the ex-Queen of Albania at Carita's Hair Salon – 'How's King Zog, dear?'

The Rango shows were a success. The Duchess of Alba, who traditionally came on the last day, paid me the compliment of altering her appointment to the first day. Spanish noblewomen are far more powerful than those elsewhere because all titles can pass through women and they confer their titles on their husbands too. The Duke of Alba was a comparatively bourgeois figure, aggrandised by marriage. Before the Spanish Restoration, the Duchess had been the first lady of Spain. Doña Maria has sixty-seven titles. One is the Duchess of Berwick dating from 1707 and she includes 'Fitzjames Stuart' among her many surnames. In Spain only Doña Maria, Duchess of Medinaceli, is more 'handled'. Small, fair and shy, the Duchess of Alba cropped up again at the Seville *feria* where each year tradition required her to affix an expensive piece of jewellery to the Festival Madonna as an offering to the Church.

The Jacaranda was now doing excellently. Arthur had established a travel agency and an estate agency on the premises, and continued to supervise the English Subscription Library set up by Mark and Min for the English colony.

The English residents, living in Spain to stretch their pensions, were not exactly me. Many had been in the Colonial Service and separation from the Motherland had exacerbated not only their snobbery but also their belief in a kind of P. G. Wodehouse fantasy which England could no longer justify. I was not prepared to meet this set much more than halfway after my experience of Sir Ronald and Lady Cross.

He was the 1st Baronet (and the last) and had not long retired as the Governor of Tasmania. Since Lord Rowallan was the current Governor of Tasmania, Arthur presumably thought we should all be thick together. The Crosses were down there at the bottom of Europe trying to marry off their nervous daughters among the minor aristocracy, the German princelings, anything foreign with a handle, anything English at all, and Arthur pressed me to lunch at their villa.

'How's the Tasmanian Situation?' asked Sir Ronald.

'Ah,' said Arthur.

'Improved, I hope,' said Sir Ronald.

'Is there a Tasmanian Situation?' tried Arthur, 'I mean, is it worrying?'

'Could be tricky,' said Sir Ronald.

Stumped by the Tasmanian Situation, Arthur began to expatiate on my O.K.-ness, how I knew Lord X, Lady Y, Count Z. I found myself yawning and was also annoyed by his cringeing. So, as a livener, and as a way of saying 'Take it all with a pinch of salt', I started to give Lady Cross smacking great winks behind Arthur's back. Nothing happened at the time but later Arthur came stamping up to my villa in a fury.

'Lady Cross says she'll never receive you again!'

'Receive?'

'She won't because you were making passes at her!'

'What? That little fart from the Colonies? Passes?'

'She said she'll never receive you again because you kept winking at her over the luncheon table.'

'The woman must be mad! I don't give a damn about Lady Cross or about the Tasmanian Situation and I won't receive *her*, at the Jacaranda, here, or anywhere else. Now run back and tell her so!'

This social touchiness even crept into the Marbella Club, an establishment usually far more *mondain* than the Villa Cross. The scraping and slobbering that went on from the Hohenlohes downwards whenever the Princess Bismarck, for example, turned up was unbelievable – it's always so much more frantic in these Court circles that no longer exist. I love protocol and grandeur when it's authentic, but when the show's been over for fifty-odd years . . . I got into awfully bad odour because I refused to stand for the Princess Bismarck.

'Princess Bismarck,' I explained, 'I refused to stand for you because I was told that the Hohenlohes refused to bow to the Duchess of Windsor.' The Windsors were often in and out of Marbella.

The Princess Bismarck was the most gracious of all the Germans. 'I quite agree, my dear,' she said. 'It was ill-mannered of them to try and hurt the Duke in that way.'

One aspect of all this made me howl, however – the English widows. They were immensely respectable in rose-print frocks that were skin-tight from a tendency to excess weight rather than from a desire to be bold. They came to the Jacaranda for their Gimlets and ended up dancing with the local bloods. These lads, constantly frustrated by their own girls, would make up to the English women by asking them to dance, very close, and a young Spaniard doesn't have to press against much to get an erection. One always knew when this had happened – the Spanish hit of the moment was 'Burroom Boom Boom' so it happened all the time – because the trotting matron would suddenly go bright red, become confused and girlish, and rush to the table to swallow off what remained of her Gimlet. They often made assignations with these boys – who weren't gigolos incidentally, they only wanted somewhere to put themselves – in a covert sign-language that was so elaborate in its attempts to go unnoticed that they might just as well have used a loud hailer.

At home, one damp evening, relaxing in a batik sarong and creaming my face to the whirr of crickets in the garden, I heard the sound of a car thrumming in the drive. I'd had a slightly draining stint at the Jac. Peter and Menchu had been throwing mud at each other and I didn't want to be sucked in – Menchu was very good at sucking people in and I wasn't feeling sufficiently innocent to survive it. Only the week before she'd come elbowing up to the house and very nearly caught Peter in my bed – he'd had the wit to jump out of the window. Avoiding them at the club I'd got myself jammed between some real Gibraltarian horrors.

Carmen – my divine Carmen who replaced Conchita who stole things – said that the car was for me. Kevin McClory and Bobo Sigrist had sent it to collect me for an impromptu party.

Now Kevin I had originally met somewhere in London. Later he made a fortune out of *Thunderball*. And Bobo was, well . . . Bobo, the aeroplane heiress. In those days she was hiding from the press and her estranged husband, Greg Juarez, an American whom nobody had heard of until Bobo eloped with him in 1957. Juarez was trying to gain custody of their daughter Bianca. Kevin and Bobo had rented outside Marbella a property with lots of locks and alarms belonging to General Franco's daughter, Carmen, Marquesa de Villaverde (incidentally, when Carmen married the Marques, the Generalissimo had the Cortes pass a special law preserving the name 'Franco' in the couple's children).

I threw on some slap, slacks, a silk top, and jumped in. The Villa Verde was a tremendous clifftop pile inhabited by a mad gang. Typical Bobo, playing the recluse in style. I was handed a vase of cocktail topped with fruit and sat down beside a thin blond male.

'Haven't we met before?' I gurgled through the fruit (everyone was laps ahead of me).

'Have we? I'm Peter O'Toole.'

He wasn't famous then. I had first met him at Duncan Melvin's in London.

'You've changed,' I said. Where was his big nose? The mousey hair?

'I'm doing this David Lean thing about Lawrence of Arabia. I'm playing Lawrence.'

'Is that why they've straightened and dyed your hair?'

'Yes, and a nose job as well. It was in the contract.'

'Peter, you look divine.'

'Do you know Omar? We call him Cairo Fred.' Peter lolloped over and dragged the man back. Omar Sharif was then at the height of his beauty, powerful and delicate with stunning eyes. He was also the most sober man in the room, cast straight from Egypt and on his first international picture. More than a smudge of bewilderment clinched his appeal.

The party went zing-zing until dawnish. Peter's studio car, one of those long black American ones suddenly to be seen rolling all round the unmade roads of Spain, took the three of us back to the Villa Antoinette, where Peter and Omar decided to spend the remainder of their leave. We went bananas. Peter especially. Whenever he had time off he'd dive headfirst into a bottle. He doesn't drink these days because he recently had half his guts removed. He and Finchie were two of a kind.

King Saud of Saudi Arabia, who was hanging round the vicinity of the film to check out whether Arabia was being maligned or not, invited Peter to dinner. Peter refused to go, saying he had better things to do than be quizzed about T. E. Lawrence's inscrutable motives. The following day Omar and I saw the King at the Málaga bullfight, creating an extremely good impression by distributing gold wristwatches to all the *toreros*. That evening we came across a clutch of royal princes in a nightclub. Peter forbade pranks, knowing how funny they are about women (they only recognise two varieties, the tart and the nun). One of the princes told me he was a motoring enthusiast – he would buy a Cadillac, drive it into the desert and leave it there when the petrol ran out, return by camel, and buy another one. He was thoroughly put out when I explained that these machines are designed to be refilled with petrol.

When Peter and Omar returned to the location in Seville, they invited me along and I put up at the Alfonso XIII with its rotten memories of Inigo. Many of the cast were living there. So was Orson Welles, up to something secret – or possibly nothing at all, which was usually the case with him.

With a few wood and cardboard minarets Seville had been turned into a convincing pastiche of Cairo. The Military H.Q. scenes were being shot either at the Military Academy or at the Duchess of Medinaceli's palace. During the shooting at the palace a cable snapped, swung down, and demolished an important-looking statue. How could they tell the Duchess? Since she had a pash for Jack Hawkins, he was delegated to break the appalling news. 'Don't worry,' she said, 'it's only Roman.'

I was introduced to Peter's stand-in, John Fulton Short. All the stand-in does is get lit because he is of a physical type similar to the star's. But John was a personality in his own right, being the first American to achieve full matador status. Peter took me to John's flat hung with his paintings done in bull's blood. John explained why in the ring bullfighters do not wear underpants. Since the male genitalia are substantially composed of gristle, there is in the event of being gored a greater chance of those vitals sliding aside undamaged if they are unconfined.

Pedro, the Marqués de Domecq d'Usquain, was opening a new *bodega* in Jerez de la Frontera. It was my last night with the actors and

I made a drop-dead entrance in emerald satin, Peter O'Toole giggling on one arm, Omar Sharif smouldering on the other, flashbulbs popping about us.

Pedro had laid on a gruelling feast, a different sherry with each course, followed by cabaret, dancing and mixing. How many Don Pepes can you meet and recall? This was always the problem, a river of new faces streaming past one's eyes. After an hour or so of flirting with the grandees, a footman said that Mr O'Toole was howling for me at one of the bars.

'Peter, what on earth is it?'

'Oh, darling!' he wailed and hugged me. 'How can you bear the pain?'

'What pain? I haven't got a pain.'

'You know, the pain . . . of it.'

During the evening about half-a-dozen people had tried to enlighten him about me. Nothing he didn't already know but he was always upset by it on my behalf. By now he was sozzled and maudlin. I suggested we leave. On the way out I hit one man in the face, he'd made some lewd remark. Peter took a swing at another. Back at the Swan Hotel, undressing in my room, I heard a nearby door slam – Peter was heading for the lift. Naked except for my coat, and clattering along in mules, I flew after him into the rain. He'd almost made it back to the *bodega* when I caught up. It wasn't easy to turn him round. Incoherent, fighting drunk, he was obviously looking for a brawl – I shared a bed with him to prevent him from making a klutz of himself.

Next morning three wrecks sat in the bar of the Swan. Peter's face was like a sucked gumdrop. He was getting down to the serious business of drinking off his hangover. Omar and I had a spot of lunch. Then they returned to their exciting work in Seville. And Peter's driver took me back to Marbella – and to a big surprise.

The *News of the World* wanted to buy my story. They weren't the first but they were the most organised. I flew to London and took on as my manager a friend of Ronnie Cogan's. This was my first disastrous contract – but not my last. The paper offered £3,000. I demanded £15,000. They retired, returned, and suggested £10,000 which I accepted. My manager took £3,000 of it, an exaggerated percentage which didn't exactly endear him to me.

Noyes Thomas did the story. It was the classic, six-part sensationalisation of a short ragged life. My aristocratic associations gave it piquancy. England was unbelievably ho-ho in those days and I was often pilloried for having the nerve to make friendships among the upper classes. The series, via sex and drugs and violence, but no names, ended with a reference to my liaison with Arthur.

His divorce had finally come through and before leaving Spain I had agreed to a formal engagement. Don't ask me why. I'd been fighting him physically and mentally the entire time. But his extraordinary insistence may have led me to believe there was solid ground in the idea. I was well aware, because Arthur kept reminding me, of the position and fortune (something between four and five million pounds) he had surrendered to be with me. His father had cut him off, entailing everything on Johnny. And could it conceivably be fun to be Lady Rowallan? Did it promise some kind of security of identity? I insisted on a long, amorphous engagement, even as the family's jeweller, Mr Hardwick at Asprey's, helped me choose a ring.

While the story was appearing (May–June 1962) the *News of the World* gave me a bodyguard. Not that I really needed him. Being treated like a movie star by one person, like shit by another, there was no inducement to go out. If I did, it was late, I got blasted, came home. Lying low seemed the best course . . . until my manager announced that he'd committed me to a cabaret tour to capitalise on it all.

One week's rehearsal, a few singing and dancing lessons; quite inadequate. Originally Des O'Connor was going to prepare the show, advise on material and so on. But when he asked for £3,000 we dropped him like a box of concrete.

The Astor Club (black tie and full of tarts) off Berkeley Square offered a contract for a one-week trial with a five-week option. Arthur wanted to come over and see me but, he wrote, *I must stay here and work at this club, to make lots and lots of filthy money. I can't for a second time have a wife much richer than me! . . . P.S. More old family friends in the club last night! The Marquess and Marchioness of Reading and Lord and Lady Kindersley!!* (him and his exclamation marks!!).

My manager signed up some small support acts for the provinces while I came down the stairs at the Astor to the theme tune 'April Love' on to a stage adrift with dry ice, the chorus stretching their arms towards me in supplication. Pretty corny. The songs they'd exhumed were no better. 'A Good Man Is Hard To Find,' 'An Old-Fashioned Millionaire', 'Lola Lola' was the level of it. I did my week and broke all Astor attendance records. But I loathed it. Mistaking the nature of a five-week option, I had already bought my ticket for Spain.

When it was explained to me that the option was theirs, not mine, I was forced to stagger on; but after another three weeks I went to the manager and said, 'Listen, darling, this is a crappy show. Let's ditch the last two weeks. It's so *bad*. I'll do ten damn weeks if you want but at least give me a chance to get something presentable rehearsed.'

'But you're pulling more people than Shirley Bassey!'

'I know. I'm the biggest freak in town. But I don't like what I'm doing to myself.'

'Miss Ashley, do you realise that if you went out there and said "Shit" they'd still come to see you?'

The next night I went on and said, 'Ladies and gentlemen, I hear from the management that even if I only said "Shit" you'd still come to see me, so – SHIT!' And I walked off.

There was a sound as of a wave sucking back just before it breaks forward on to the shore, a short interval of absolute silence, followed by booing and cheering. The management were horrified, the cast delighted.

'I've been wanting to say that to them all my life,' said Jacki, one of the chorus. She was a sexy creature who'd worked on *Summer Holiday* with Cliff Richard. She'd been trying and trying and trying to have an affair with him, but he didn't go in for sleeping with girls, so she went off and married Adam Faith. The Astor season came to an abrupt end.

As a result of the newspaper series I had a monstrous postbag, hundreds of people wanting sex changes, wanting help, all with terrifying problems, plus the familiar quota of abuse. Arthur was writing daily with news from Spain:

> . . . the Westmorelands have arrived here and I had a letter from the Angleseys so we really are in the midst of the British snob world! Kevin was in the other night and said he had seen your act at the Astor and enjoyed it . . . I've also seen Sarah and Henry who cut me twice deader than ice!! I should worry. From the swimming pool today I could hear her shouting and yelling and speechifying and breaking all the glasses . . . Russ and Patsy, Rosemary, Rudi, and Ana de Pombo were all in last night and sent you their best love. Menchu and Peter are still fighting like cat

and dog . . . Enid Riddle has been fined 60,000 pesetas for smuggled whisky . . .

Smuggling was second nature to most people. In Gibraltar one could easily pick up 5lb. tins of caviare from the Indian shopkeepers who exchanged them for Western goods with the Russian fishermen. Arthur told me that smugglers trained dogs to swim across from North Africa to southern Spain wearing saddles of cannabis.

My manager had signed me to appear in Manchester, Dudley and Weston-super-Mare. We were tied by contract and he was beginning to get on my nerves. I didn't even have proper stage costumes and was professional enough to know that they are not the same as ordinary clothes. For example, one has to be able to move about in them without falling over.

'It's so tacky. "A Good Man Is Hard To Find" – that's every drag queen's number. I'm not going to do these shows!'

He threw the songsheet in my face and said that if I didn't he'd sue me for everything I had. By now Ina Barton and I had moved into a flat in Queen's Gate Terrace opposite the big hostel for young sailors (who used to slip over for drinks) and I didn't want to be thrown on to the streets.

June 1962, Manchester: the Northern Sporting Club, cabaret then bingo then cabaret then bingo. I looked a dream and sang like murder, it was awful. On to the Dudley Hippodrome where they billed me as 'The Sensation of the Year'. For this show they had signed up a stripper called Miss Fifi. During the finale she upstaged me by letting her left tit drop out as I came down the stairs. It was very effective because in 1962 tits were rare. After two nights of this I'd had enough. 'Fifi dearest, I may not be very good but I'm good enough to know when someone's upstaging me. That's two nights you've dropped your tit. I don't want to see it again. If I do, you'll have to take the consequences.'

On the third night I sashayed down the staircase. Plop. There was that tit! I leant over and sank my teeth into it. There was a short scream, followed by a sound beyond the footlights as of a wave sucking back just before . . . ah well, we didn't see that tit again. Actually, it looked much worse than it was because the wound was embellished with lipstick (stage lipstick is very dark and heavy because the lights eat it).

Next the Arena Club, Weston, where I was billed as 'The Most

Talked About Woman in the World' – one week, twice nightly. We digged in a boarding house. The landlady refused to send up my breakfast so I went down to find out what was going on. The cast had rampaged the previous night and were still drunk, swearing, fighting each other, being sick. I was blamed for leading them astray. We moved into an hotel but it could only sleep us for one night. Eventually we ended up in a couple of caravans between the abattoir and the gasworks.

By now I wasn't even speaking to my manager but when it was over I announced I was returning to Spain to recover from the ordeal. 'Well, you can't go for long,' he said, 'I've signed you for shows in South Africa and Australia. And I'm cooking something in Las Vegas.' Lunatic!

Ina returned with me to Spain. She'd visited once before, with her boyfriend Brian McDermott. The three of us had gone to dinner with Renton Fontana and Brian, high on champagne, was going on about the advantages of Communism. The atmosphere had become prickly. Ina was drunk and wanted to drive back.

'No, you're not, Ina. You'll smash up Arthur's car.'

'Are you suggesting I'm unfit? Heave off, sister, I'm driving.'

'No, you're not, you – you goose!'

'Yes, I am!'

She pushed me aside. I smacked her face. She smacked mine. This reciprocal slapping went on for a while and I thought, 'This is boring – we'll be slapping all week if someone doesn't put a stop to it.' So I threw my fist into the centre of her face and she went flying. When I realised what I'd done, I begged forgiveness because I'd broken her nose and knocked out several teeth. She and Brian packed and left directly.

I hoped this time Ina's visit would be less physical because she looked as though she needed a thorough rest. Pauline Moore and Sue Pratt came over too. Kevin invited the four of us up to the Villa Verde for post-prandial drinks with Shirley MacLaine. We'd already had quite a hen party ourselves – Rob Roys and Rusty Nails followed by wine followed by *fundador*.

It was decided to take Sue's hired Morris Minor and, knowing the roads better than the others, I decided to take the wheel before Ina (who was even more sloshed than I was) started laying claims to it. Driving came naturally to me. Although I'd had no lessons, taken no test and had no licence, I often went for spins along the coast roads of the Costa del Sol or through the *montañas* of Granada.

Everything went swimmingly until halfway up the mountain. When in the course of chatting away the miles I happened to mention my lack of authorisation, Pauline started to scream. She lost her grip, became hysterical. I turned round to reassure her (this seemed to make her worse) that licences weren't the be-all and end-all of life, that they were only the outward symbols of a knowledge which might be possessed without them – at that moment we shot over a cliff –

Thank goodness the car landed on a narrow ledge fifteen feet below, albeit on its side and with a bone-breaking crunch. If I had been driving at my favourite speed we should have been dead. I once drove Peter Townend at over 100 m.p.h. along the Torremolinos road. He was so anguished he made a grab for the car keys and I said, 'Peter, be sensible, if you pull out the key there really will be trouble.'

From here on events became hazy. I heard Pauline sobbing. Ina was so distraught she urinated over me while trying to clamber out. Sue followed her. I crawled up the bank and set off down the hill. An American found me sprawling senseless in the road. He delivered me to the Villa Antoinette where my automatic pilot sprang into action. Thinking he was up to no good I threw the man out and made for the bathroom to remove my make-up. 'Good heavens,' I mused, 'where is all this blood coming from?' The sight that bounced back at me from the mirror was of the sort with which meat cleavers are familiar. Blood was spouting from my neck and hitting the glass. I looked down at my arm. Bone poked through the skin at the elbow.

In a trice I remembered it all. Pauline was still in the car! What if it blew up? Or tipped over the cliff . . . There was a tattoo on the front door; Arthur, the girls and five doctors jabbering on the doorstep. Breaking into a feverish sweat I admitted the girls, the youngest and best-looking of the doctors, and sent everyone else away. The girls had been treated for shock and were as high as kittens. But I was the only one requiring stitches and clamps. The doctor was going to fix me with a local anaesthetic until I explained that I was already full of it. He had to trim the flesh and set the bones. I gripped Ina's hand. 'Endeavour, darling, endeavour!' she urged. Then she turned green and vomited all over my junglified rugs.

The only other damage was to Sue. She had been asking me for years whether she should cap her front teeth. They were black and downgraded her smile. The question was now settled because they had vanished. She went on to become Miss England and might well have become Miss Universe too, but the day before the competition she was knocked down by a car and her leg was snapped in two.

The following day the authorities arrived. I had distributed flimsy négligés for the occasion and four scantily clad beauties faced them *en bloc*. The *policía* were helpless. I was fined only 1,000 pesetas, about £6 then. Apart from my suicide attempts and my heart attacks, this was I think the nearest I've come to death. The best thing to come out of it was that I didn't have to do the cabaret in South Africa and Australia. Nor did I see my manager again.

In the summer of 1963 Tim Willoughby called from his house in Torremolinos. He owned a nightclub there called 'Lalli Lalli' (which he said was Polynesian for 'Penis Penis'). His call didn't surprise me. He was a talented drifter, always popping in and out of the blue. But he sounded in the pits of despair and asked me to accompany him and his valet Jorgen to Tangier for a week or so.

I'd last been to Tangier with Arthur to visit Marguerite McBey, the Red Indian princess with a huge house in London's Holland Park which she never uses. She was the widow of James McBey whose portraits of Allenby and Lawrence had been printed in *Seven Pillars of Wisdom*. That weekend had come about as a result of Marguerite having received a poison-pen letter from someone posing as April Ashley. Arthur was very upset because she was an old family friend. 'Take me to see her, Arthur. I have nothing to fear.' This was the Sarah Churchill coming out in me. Tangier had been fun. The leadership of the English colony was being enthusiastically contested between David Edge and David Herbert, Henry Pembroke's uncle, while Barbara Hutton slowly shrivelled up at the top of the Casbah. We met the legendary Mr Dean in whose bar the spies and stars had gathered during Tangier's heydey (which lasted until 1956, when it ceased to be a free port). His real name was Donald Kimfull, I believe, and he'd been a gigolo in London before the Great War. He was very old and died not long afterwards. And we saw the famous dancing boys with bells on their fingers and kohl on their eyes. They retire at fifteen and do something else, like work in banks.

So I looked forward to a second visit. Tim became wildly romantic on the ferry across and lifted the ban on my visiting the family homes. We plunged straight into the Casbah and stopped at the door of an Arab house. It was opened by Hetty-on-the-Jetty McGee who'd gone ethnic in a big way (she had picked up her nickname years before on the jetty of Ibiza harbour where it was her living to concoct mammoth cauldrons of stew and sell it for 25 pesetas a bowl).

The house was typically Moroccan, inward-looking, a large room on each floor. Tim's depression returned; he and Jorgen sat all day long on cushions listening to tinny Moroccan pop music on the radio and smoking hashish. They gave me some and I was sick. As a child Father had caught me with a cigarette and forced me to finish the whole packet, creating an aversion which has endured. However, I have since learned to accommodate myself to a little hashish.

The days passed, Hetty kept us fat with her cooking, but there were no visitors. We didn't go out at all and I was bored, bored, bored. So I decided not to stay on. Tim saw me off in a daze and said he was planning to visit Corsica and would I go with him? It was left that he would collect me on his return through Spain to France.

But he didn't. I have no idea what his subsequent movements were. Some weeks later, in the middle of August, I heard that he was missing. Apparently he'd been drinking in Cap Ferrat with a chum called Bill and against advice decided to put out for Corsica in bad weather in a small motorboat. Bill was a sailor but they never arrived. No trace of either of them was found. The speculation in Marbella was that Tim had arranged his own disappearance and dropped out to Tahiti. He'd visited it during the filming of *Mutiny On The Bounty* and often said how he wanted to buy an island in the South Pacific and populate it with his offspring. Tim's adored sister Jane hired a plane and spent days flying low over the area. Nothing. He'd simply vanished.

It was a bizarre and tragic end to a dynamic personality. Tim could be very haughty at times – what he called the 'Nancy' coming out in him because Nancy Astor was his maternal grandmother. But his loss was keenly felt by all sorts of people everywhere. The absolute lack of physical remains must have been doubly distressing to his family, who were plagued by sightings of Tim for years afterwards. And now there was no heir to the £15 million Ancaster heritage. Jane has never married and shows no likelihood of doing so. Tim's father has therefore founded a multi-million-pound trust to maintain Grimsthorpe and Drummond Castle for the general public. On his death Jane will inherit the Willoughby de Eresby title, which dates from 1313, and with her it will die.

Around the time of Tim's exit from this life, Alfonse Hohenlohe disappeared with his two sons, Christoff and Hubertus. He'd been fighting Ira for custody and lifted them from a yacht she was staying on. And then the Profumo scandal had broken. I'd been spotted in Madrid with Noyes Thomas and Kim Proctor, the third Profumo girl. The press laid siege to the Villa Antoinette in pursuit of any details on these three stories. I was even thought to have harboured Christine Keeler when she vanished somewhere along the Costa del Sol. Day and night, reporters would pop up from behind bushes when I least expected it and start ranting at me.

So when I was woken up one night by a rumpus in the garden I was inclined to dismiss it as journalism. But the clock said 4 a.m., a time when any self-respecting reporter is tucked up in bed in a drunken stupor. I thought, 'So it must be the gypsies.' They migrated through Marbella to the Romany gathering in the caves of Granada and at night often stole the undies from my line as they passed through, if Carmen forgot to bring them in. Then I made out singing voices. 'I've got a dog, his name is Blue.' Peter and Omar, at the time unquestionably the world's two most beautiful men, had come to stay.

Peter and I often slept together on these occasions, on the divan in the sitting-room in front of the log fire, chastely. He didn't like my bedrooms. He had his quirks. He didn't like daylight much. He loathed sunlight and writhed out of chairs whenever it struck him. Apart from his face, neck and forearms, which were deeply tanned from filming, he was a deathly colour. His flesh looked blue with cold, like an emaciated El Greco. Another thing he didn't like – there was such a list of them – was the sight of blood, so I was seconded into taking his father to the bullfight in Málaga. Blood I knew about.

Sian Phillips, Peter's wife and pretty emaciated herself, came over to the house with their daughter Katie on the girl's second birthday. Sian spent most of the time on the floor to ease her back. She knew of my association with Peter but wasn't disturbed by it. Nor had she any reason to be.

With Omar, however, there *is* a little carnal knowledge to report. At lunch *à deux* he mentioned the word 'desire'. When Omar raises the subject of desire it's not like the price of eggs or the Tasmanian Situation. It's like a meat hook which catches you under the ribs and curves up into the brain, causing wild haemorrhages of the imagination and acute fluctuations of body temperature. The air about us took on a pinkish hue in which sparks and fireflies danced. A tingling sensation, like an electric centipede, crawled up my right arm, across my shoulders, and down the left arm. An understanding had taken place.

That night I waited in front of the fire for Peter to pass out. He seemed to take for ever. Finally he slumped and I tiptoed away, opened Omar's bedroom door, and discerned immediately his eyes because they were much much blacker than the surrounding darkness which he thereby, in contrast, caused to be pervaded by a sultry light. In due course this light enabled me to make out his body which lay like a massive stain on the bed.

Omar lived up to all my exotic expectations. I hope I lived up to some of his. To my very great surprise I later discovered that he knew nothing of my sex-change. Peter hadn't bothered to mention it! After our brief encounter, with my head resting on his damp brown chest, we chatted until the sun came up and then I crept back to Peter. As I slipped between the sheets and lay back feeling pleased with myself, Peter stirred. 'Traitor,' he said and we fell asleep laughing. Before we leave them, I must say that, with all the alcohol, I never understood how Peter could make it to work, but he always did. It was an endless fascination to his colleagues that he never once forgot his lines. Maybe this love of drink explains why Peter is best in feverish roles.

Inspired by their company, I decided to become an actress and lent the villa to Lionel Bart and Lionel Blair for a month while I stayed in London with Caroline Stocker (an out-and-out English rose with a smart languid style, she and Michael Stocker had spent their honeymoon with me). Sarah Churchill had introduced me to the actress Ellen Pollock, who agreed to prepare me for an audition at the Webber-Douglas Academy of Dramatic Art. Her husband, the painter James Proudfoot, gave me his portrait of the young Peter Ustinov which I still possess – for years it was hung in the spare bedroom and was the first thing guests saw on waking, but there were so many complaints that it has now been supplanted by an Augustus John portrait, 'Young Viva King Naked and Masturbating', which Viva herself left me in her will.

I also made contact with Signon. She tried to help but eventually had to explain, in the nicest possible way, that people thought me too weird. Signon herself came to an unfortunate end. She fell heavily in love with Barbara Back's son Patrick. Barbara was set against it and Patrick wasn't over the moon either, so Signon finished her life off with the bottle.

At my audition I did two pieces, Lady Macbeth's 'Unsex me here . . .' and a snatch from *The Seagull*. They stopped me halfway through and said they'd let me know. I got the message and flew back to Mr Blue, the club, Sarah and Henry, the villa full of flowers, and of course Arthur, beaming with a present. He was always buying me bits. This time it was pearl earrings, very pretty actually. But I used to get so mad with him. 'For God's sake, Arthur, stop buying me these scraps! Wait until Christmas and buy me something really *big*.' I also had visions of breeding and to this end had a bitch puppy (Zoë) flown out for Mr Blue from his old kennels.

The visions didn't last long because while I was in Madrid doing another season for Rango, Arthur telephoned to inform me that Zoë had been shot dead by a shepherd on La Concha. And sadder still – Henry Audley had died from a cerebral haemorrhage at the Alhambra Palace in Granada in the middle of a motoring tour with Sarah. He always said that his time with Sarah was by far the happiest and most exciting of his life.

It was in Madrid that I became friendly with Simon Munro-Kerr, great-grandson of the Father of Gynaecology. The first night, Simon, I couldn't believe a man could be so golden, so handsome . . . we made love violently. Then we picked up a friend of his and drove to the *feria* in Seville. Such noise, so many people showing off on horseback. The Duchess of Alba sped from palace to bullring to palace in her landau pulled by six Arab greys. Ahead, attached to the leading pair by only a slender cord tied to his mane, ran a naked white stallion. The Duchess was the *prima donna* of the season and very uncomfortable she looked too.

Back in Marbella, Arthur was going through a bad spell, threatening to drown himself. At such times he would hand over to me his keys and his will. One morning he appeared with these at my bedroom window.

'Arthur, if you are going to put an end to yourself, why are you carrying a weekend case?'

Sarah showed up with him a few hours later. She'd found him

wandering along the Gibraltar road looking wretched. I shouted, 'If you want to go down to the sea and submerge yourself, as you keep saying, then just go there and walk in! The Mediterranean can handle it, it's full of trash.' Then I brewed some tea, returned the keys and the will, and the incident was buried. But Sarah was angry with me. She thought I was being cruel, so I went to a drawer and produced several suicide notes which I had kept instead of throwing them on the fire as they deserved. She was sensitive on the subject of suicide. That year, 1963, her sister Diana had killed herself, unable to cope with the disintegration of her twenty-five year marriage to Duncan Sandys.

It was all too much. I jumped into a taxi and yelled 'Madrid!' The driver was struck dumb. A thirteen-hour fare. My longest-ever taxi ride. Quite accidentally I bumped into Simon in the Calle San Geronimo and went off with him to another *feria*, this time at Pamplona, the Basque capital. None of us had ever been to the Pamplona *feria* before. Hemingway made it notorious in *The Sun Also Rises*. It has been called the last Bacchic orgy in Europe. The town was awash with liquor, and of course there was nowhere to stay. Simon found a closet in a back street that cost galore.

After the first day I hardly dared go out. Foul-breathed men kept lurching into me with '¡*Que guapa*!' which means 'What a beauty!' but sounded revolting. To find a whole town behaving like one did oneself at one's worst was a most unattractive experience. I hit the bottle directly, then scrambled back to Marbella. We didn't even see the famous bull-run through the streets.

Spain was getting jagged. I was going from pillar to post and fast. So when Arthur caught me in a particularly gregarious mood over dinner at the Marbella Club and asked me to name a date for the marriage, I agreed. 10 September 1963.

Soon it was across the English papers. The telephone at the Jacaranda hopped up and down twenty-four hours a day. Lord Rowallan wrote from hospital, where he was having treatment for throat cancer, and pleaded with Arthur to come to his senses. Bobby Corbett sent a wire: *Congratulations – can I be bridesmaid?* All my friends were disgusted with me. They knew I didn't love Arthur and saw it as a cold act of self-advancement. Peter Townend thought it a farce. Sarah didn't mention it at all. Arthur and I fought as usual. Right up to the day itself I wanted to back out but lacked the decisiveness. And what was the legal position? My birth certificate had not been altered. Arthur's lawyer in Gibraltar said that my passport was sufficient for a licence.

The morning of the 10th my nerves were at their worst, spitting like bacon fat, while my head swam and I fought against attacks of breathlessness. On top of it all had descended influenza. We were so late in getting to the Register Office in Gibraltar that the registrar had given up and gone to lunch. Evelyn Locke, Nicolette Meirs, and Bill and Doreen Godwin (who were killed in a car crash soon after) were the witnesses and we all drank whisky until the registrar came back. I went through the ceremony anaesthetised. Coming out of the building with sneezes and hiccups, I was amazed by the size of the crowd which had gathered. Sarah, who'd been married by the same man in the same place, warned me that this tended to happen, Gibraltar being so small and having a very efficient bush telegraph. As if by second nature, I started to give royal waves, the white glove fluttering like a bird then going up and down on a pivot. We went straight back to Marbella and I was feeling so foul I went straight to bed. The reception at the Jacaranda for which invitations had been printed had to be cancelled.

Arthur and I had one wedding present. It was from Maxine Baird, an Australian/American friend of his from Scotland. She had been a famous New York beauty and had married Robert Baird of Lennox-love Castle before the war. But East Lothian drove her ever more to the drink. She used to hide bottles of gin in the suits of armour. She and Robert were divorced in 1960. When later I met her in London she was living with the Earl Sondes at Lees Court in Kent. Life seemed to be looking up for her. She would show allcomers a picture of herself with Princess Margaret at a fling in the West Indies. It was her hobby to cover herself in diamonds, approach one of the big London estate agents, and view property in the Rolls-Royce they would lay on, believing her to be a rich customer. Since it was never Maxine's intention to buy anything, she would always choose the most opulent mansions where her imagination could wander until tea-time. But the Earl Sondes's son disliked her. 'Maxine,' I would say, 'surely you realise that the first thing one does is enchant the children.' But after the death of Sondes the new earl had no time for her and she died in alcoholic confusion. She was always threatening suicide. I remember getting an emergency phone call from her and dashing across Marbella to the Apartimentos Fuerte. When I arrived she was in the ground-floor bar drinking, flirting with the barman. 'April, you mustn't believe all you hear on the telephone,' she said. Her present was for Arthur really, matching cigarette-box, lighter and ashtray.

Now Arthur moved into the Villa Antoinette, which development gave me the creeps. Despite all the peculiarity, I was under the impression that four things had been fully understood:

1 I should not stay on in Marbella, which for me had become like living in a glass coffin. I should commute to Spain from London and Arthur would do the reverse.
2 We should adopt children.
3 He would grant me an allowance of £2,000 per annum.
4 He would be fitted with a new set of false teeth. The ones he had were old and green and he had a maddening habit of sucking on them to keep them in because his gums had shrunk.

The first understanding I now put into practice. I flew to London and stayed with the Stockers until I'd found a super flat in Cheyne Walk. Arthur wrote several times a week. *Poor Sarah is in dire trouble again but I haven't seen any mention of it in the English papers. She has been fined 5000 pesetas and recommended by the Governor for deportation from Spain for being 'drunk and disorderly' in Malaga and also because she nearly killed two workmen who were on top of a wall she knocked down with her car!*

Arthur decided to sell the club after an impressive offer from the developers (the site is now occupied by the Apartimentos Jacaranda). He wrote in October: *Well, this is it, the last day of the Jacaranda! What a life it has been for me here and how much I have loved it and hated it, cursed it and thanked God for it!*

Carmen came to London with Arthur at the end of the month. Belatedly we exchanged wedding gifts. From him an oyster mink coat. From me gold cufflinks set with pearls. But our relationship nosedived. Love-making was not a success. For three years Arthur had been gearing himself up for the great moment and his fantasy collapsed in bed. Then everything else began to turn into thin air. It was nobody's fault. Just the truth at last. After a week of shilly-shallying Arthur left for Spain and I moved on to a flat in Lennox Gardens where I was burgled of my jewellery.

In December Carmen and I flew over. Her father was ill and I had promised to spend Christmas with Arthur. With no club to go to he was smoking more than ever. Rogelia and Pepe had been thrown out of their farmhouse by the owners and were living in a wooden ranch-house with rain pouring through the roof (Pepe eventually surmounted his problems and became the local Chief of Police). Bickering broke out between Arthur and myself. Recriminations followed. Suddenly his spine stiffened, he petulantly crossed his legs, the cigarette shot up to his fingertips . . . This time something detached itself and fell away inside me. I told Carmen to pack my bags and call a cab. At the airport I waited all day long for an empty seat to London. I had plenty of time to think. It was dark, wet and freezing cold when I fell into Lennox Gardens. I saw down and wrote to him:

> A letter from me. A none too happy one, I'm afraid. I have thought and thought, not slept for days. But from all the pain and torture in my mind, I see one thing very very clearly. That is, I will not ever be coming back to you. I don't know what I will do, I don't know how I will live. But I know I won't be back . . .
>
> I am paying dearly for my sin of marrying you. The worry and the anguish I have felt in the past three years is making me ill. So the only thing I can do is try to cut you out of my life completely. Then all I have are my earthly problems. A job, a less expensive place to live. Arthur, don't think I expect money from you. I don't. Because I know I should never have married you . . .
>
> It's so funny but I felt so much more (although I never really did) secure before I married you than I did after. Then you denying what you had promised made me feel so sick in the stomach, I could never have stood myself, let alone you, afterwards. Then I seem to remember you trying to convince me of other lies of yours in the past. I don't want to sound bitter, but I suppose I am a little. At the moment my life seems a wreck all over again. I hope this time I have a little more strength . . .
>
> I hope you sell your land. In brief, Arthur, I hope one day you find happiness. Although my heart is breaking I think you had better have Mr Blue. Give my kindest thoughts to Rogelia and Pepe and José-Luis.
>
> God bless you,
>
> April

8 Rome

Isn't it strange? Marriage, I mean. This locking up of people in pairs, this elimination of individuality. Presumably it has evolved as a way of preventing the community from being overrun by unwanted children; but also as a method of organising the compulsion for the nourishment of an adjacent soul, the yearning for a sense of belonging to the heaving mass of humanity at its fundamental level. Is this what marriage is about? If so, it's a very haphazard way of going about it. People marry for so many different reasons and the more they've seen of life the more *ad hoc* their reasons become. Yet nearly always the reasons centre on the fight against loneliness, the fact that life acquires meaning only in its relationships, however awkward, transient or intolerable these may be.

So in theory, in my romantic theory, marriage seemed a desirable state because it fixed you in the fellowship of the world. It was also one of the accoutrements of womanhood at that time. And a marriage of companionship to an older man is still something I should like to consider. But as far as fellowship of the world is concerned – I should have known better. Marriage is no short cut to that. You acquire such fellowship the day you are born, no matter how often the world appears to drive you into a corner where you ache and weep alone.

I've had more than my share of ostracism and ridicule, more than the usual inducement to imagine that God has singled me out for the special horrors. Each time an obstacle presents itself you must steel yourself, harden, toughen, in order to endure it. But endurance is a passive virtue, though not a meagre one. And obstacles have to be overcome, not merely endured. And in order to overcome, you must extend yourself. It is necessary to cultivate a certain ruthlessness, a certain rigour with regard to yourself as well as to others. And when the obstacle has been negotiated, it is equally important to allow yourself to soften again. This is possible, because through the exertion you will have discovered unexpected strengths in yourself and therefore have a little more confidence.

This process of toughening, extending, softening is inner growth. It may not enlarge your wisdom but it does enlarge capacity – and capacity is a kind of wisdom. The softening is vital. If you do not soften you will come to find the world a cold and malevolent place, with yourself the coldest thing in it. And experience will turn you into a coward or a bully. Cowards and bullies have an identical view of life as an arena filled with threat. Always to be on your guard against attack does not make for a lovely existence.

The world has slapped me in the face so many times – and I say this not out of self-pity but purely by way of observation – that sometimes I find I have to toughen then soften very rapidly, an accelerated procedure which has contributed to the apparent volatility of my behaviour. I think I can explain it by saying that whereas I'm determined not to take these slaps lying down, I am just as determined not to become an embittered old bat.

Also, I'm a natural optimist, I have a terrific zest for life that frightens even me sometimes. And perhaps suffering is the consequence of this. It doesn't have to be, but usually it is. The more roads you cross, the greater the risk of being hit by cars.

Being single can be such a responsibility day after day, year after year. People imagine that to be single and childless is to be free and unaccountable. Superficially this is true. But it is also another test of endurance, not so much of loneliness, since marriage itself can raise loneliness to harrowing levels in much the same way as the crowded environment of a city can. The test of endurance comes about because as a single person you always have to bear the full weight of your own existence, can never relax into the abiding presence of another, or allow your identity to lighten and blur through the sharing of it.

The burden of individuality for single people is exhausting. It requires you to employ stratagems and draw on reserves of energy you never thought you had. As a result single people are exceptionally strong and to choose the unmarried life can give a person great power. To be lumbered with it however can be painful.

With me loneliness was never an acute problem. I'm never bored when I'm present. I like my own company and indeed seek it out. It helps maintain my orientation. Some people become very jittery when left to their own devices. Sarah Churchill was rather like this, always needing the proximity of a male, although she was too much of an individual ever to find marriage an easy ride. So was Arthur in the end. A genuine eccentric he turned out to be. Looking back, I cannot see how on earth he and I could ever have made a go of it or how we ever imagined we could. All told, we spent no more than fourteen days together as man and wife.

While sweating it out in that bed in Casablanca, I was convinced that after the operation life could only be a shower of diamonds and almond blossom. But isn't it maddening? You move one mountain only to find yourself at the foot of another. Maybe some don't live like this, maybe for some life is just a frolic among molehills, but I always seem to pass from crisis to crisis. What made me able to survive these abrupt switches of fortune (although finally the emotional strain did get to me and I was very ill) was an underlying wonderment at my own transformation. No worldly distemper could obliterate my sense of the mysterious alchemical nature of the world, its ravishing possibilities, the chances for turning an idea into a fact.

Whenever I looked at myself in the mirror it was not in self-admiration or self-congratulation but in disbelief. Yes, I looked beautiful. I was told this so many times that it ceased to affect me. This is not quite the same as saying it was unimportant. One may cease to be sensitive to such flattery only to find oneself sensitive to the absence of it. Many people, including Viva, felt that my chief weakness was an excessive pride in my looks and Viva said so in her autobiography, *The Weeping and the Laughter*. If it is true, I have always felt it to be a relatively ludicrous failing, comparable to eating too many chocolates.

The great gift is to *feel* beautiful. I never felt beautiful before the operation. And after it? Hardly a day passes without my being astonished and exalted by what was possible for me. I resist the temptation to thank God, just as I resisted the temptation to deify Dr Burou (too many sex-changes develop God-fixations on their surgeon). None the less, the fact of my transformation is a continuing source of strength.

I am letting my thoughts circulate around these subjects because I am about to take off again, and I wanted a breather before I do – as I'm sure you did. Feeling cooler now? Have you poured yourself a little something? Right, let's go.

Arthur's reply to my letter told me to stop being silly and return to be his wife. It suggested that he understood little about himself and nothing about me. During those long first nights at Lennox Gardens I developed a habit of ringing the Caprice at one in the morning and asking them to send round two-dozen oysters in a taxi. They arrived on a silver platter covered with wedges of lemon and one of the things that dawned on me as they slid down my throat was that I should have to develop less expensive tastes and find a cheaper place to live.

While in Spain I had become friends with a girl called Cecilia Johnson. She had been born in Shanghai and during the Second World War she had been interned there with her family in a concentration camp. This had permanently damaged her health, she was prone to internal haemorrhages, but she looked like Elizabeth Taylor and was very brainy too. Cecilia needed a flat-mate and I put myself forward. She told me years later that she wasn't at all happy at the prospect because when she and her boyfriend Peter West had first met me in Seville she'd assumed I was a raging lesbian.

The flat was small, in the basement of a house in Shawfield Street, off Chelsea's King's Road, owned by a Mrs Guppy whose son Nicholas was married to the Persian singer Shusha. Mrs Guppy had a high trilling voice and wore twin-sets. Every Wednesday Cecilia and I took tea with her and her sister upstairs, salmon-paste sandwiches and angel cake, and we'd come out of the parlour bloated and feeling dreadfully guilty because we were both fighting the flab.

And the reason we were fighting the flab was that we were always being taken out to dinner. Cecilia and I got on frightfully well with each other and had turned into a couple of playgirls. I shouldn't want to speak for Cecilia on this (although she did say Oliver Reed was a wonderful lover) but I certainly found myself being extremely promiscuous. Cecilia loved gambling, I loved clubbing, and we both loved parties. While she was seeing Anthony Haden-Guest, I had a crush on Sir Peter Osborne, Jenny Little's brother; so much so that I used to drag myself out of bed at the dot of dawn in order to go riding with him in Richmond Park: the closest we came to congress. I don't jump but I do ride quite well. All the same, one morning I was badly thrown. As I flew through the air I stretched my hands out in front of me to break the fall. Ten very long fingernails went driving into the ground like stakes and then they all broke off.

'Peter darling, I know you're not as mad about me as I am about you, and all this getting up at 6 a.m. and now I've lost all my fingernails, well, shall we call it a day?'

For a rest I would go to Wips, Tim's old club at the top of Charles House in Leicester Place. Its best feature was a veranda running all the way round, overlooking London. It was very quiet there after he died, a ghost club, and I'd feed strips of my steak to a tank of piranha fish and think of Tim.

I met two couples at this time who were to be important to me. First – Denny Daviss and Al Mancini at the Establishment Club. Denny was the daughter of a South African shipping magnate and was an opera singer, golden-haired, a cornucopia of Rubens curves, large breasts and wide hips, a tiny waist, long elegant legs. Second – Carol Coombe, who had divorced Ronald Armstrong-Jones and married Pepe Lopez, an Italian lawyer. Carol and Pepe divided their time between London and Italy.

Cecilia and I had been putting ourselves about so much that we decided to call a halt in order to analyse the situation. Not only were we getting fat, we also concluded that we had become wastrels, flibbertigibbets, we were not Real People. Men we were using as meal tickets and so we decided to ditch them. Instead of saying yes to any man who phoned, we agreed to accept the invitation only if we genuinely liked him. But in our current mood we didn't like any of them and after you say no for the third time a man stops ringing. We ended up sitting it out in the local, the Chelsea Potter, which Cecilia hated. She didn't like pubs at all because she didn't have the art of tittle-tattle and was accustomed to arranged meetings during which she would be able to thrash out her various hobby-horses. Eventually the phone stopped ringing altogether. We rented a television to occupy our evenings. Now I became hooked on TV, which has been a companion and tranquilliser ever since. But TV or the Chelsea Potter – it was hardly grabbing life by the horns. It was so boring that when at long last the phone did ring we made a lunge for it. It was a man whom we both *loathed*, a right gawky groper, but we'd landed ourselves in such a cul-de-sac that we said, 'Oh yes please, we'd love to go out.' Which was the end of our trying to be Real People.

Ina had finally completed her sex-change at the Charing Cross Hospital and as a present I decided to take her to Jersey for a week. I was still fighting the flab, and Ina was no string bean, so we hired bicycles to transport ourselves round the island. On the second day we were pedalling down a steep hill towards Gorey Castle when Ina slipped and fell heavily on the cross-bar. She seemed to have hurt herself so we dumped the bikes and cabbed it back to the hotel for an inspection. Her twat had ballooned. She looked like an orang-utan on heat. We phoned the gynaecologist in London who told her to go to the nearest doctor right away, but she refused.

'Don't be silly, Ina. It's probably nothing serious but it might be. And they'd love to see a sex-change. I bet you'd be the first in Jersey.'

But she wouldn't and insisted on flying back the same day to her doctor in London. I was furious with her for being so sensitive. I always feel that if you've had this operation you should try to be, as far as the outside world is concerned, as down-to-earth about it as possible. If one wants the world to treat one matter-of-factly, one must start by treating oneself in this way – which means getting in the queue with the in-growing toenails and the alopecia and the haemorrhoids.

I stayed on at the hotel and went to the pictures. Coming out I heard a call: 'Hey, April, what are you doing here?'

It was Joey and Eunice, dammit.

All the old cogs and flywheels flew into top gear. When had I last seen him? Four years before? Eunice looked the same, Joey if anything fresher and more boyish but the seaside usually does that to men. They invited me out to dinner. There was a wide chasm between us but of course underneath none at all. Which level should one play? Eunice looked equally uncertain. Joey of course loved to be the centre of other people's emotions, he positively crackled. And when Eunice went to the Ladies, he said, 'I'm thinking of taking off for Canada. I'm at the boatyard again. I virtually run the place. I want to open my own. How about coming with me?'

'Oh Joey, don't start, please . . .'

'I'm serious.'

'You're never serious.'

'You're wrong. It's just that I can't be serious about staying in one place for ever and doing the washing-up.'

'Then you'd find me too possessive.'

'You're not really, you know. You like to think you are but you're not really. Only when it suits you. You're like me, you like to take off at a moment's notice, without a second thought.'

'That isn't true!'

We weren't exactly seeing eye to eye. He came to the hotel. He was very firm and very vigorous, warm, simply and completely male. The London playboys were never like this.

On Monday I went to the boatyard where he was working. 'I've come to say goodbye. I'm flying to England. The taxi's outside. Don't stop me.'

He followed me to the airport in a second cab. Eunice – I don't know how she found out – followed him in a third. I flew through the checkpoint, turned and blew him a kiss. He stood there with a strange expression, a mixture of impetuosity and bewilderment, with his hair in his eyes.

Maggie, Countess of Kimberley, said, 'Molly Neville and I are starting up a model agency. Will you come on to our books?'

'Honestly, Maggie, I don't think there's any point.'

'We disagree. It's been years since the story broke. And now you've got this Honourable bit. We'll get you heaps of work.'

However, there was no reaction at all. I answered a newspaper advertisement placed by Simpson's of Piccadilly. 'Wanted: to sell men's ties, a girl with personality.' That was me. Back came the letter: *We regret to inform you that the post has already been filled* . . . This happened with Fortnum & Mason, Harrods, Harvey Nichols. I suppose it was understandable. You don't want a celebrity selling ties. It causes disturbances. The ties don't flow smoothly over the counter. You see, I was terribly well-known, my picture was always popping up in the papers. It's fun at first and can even be beneficial if you're an actor. But when you don't have a profession it is a great discouragement to prospective employers.

My only job at this time came about through Sarah who put me up for the position of Assistant Stage Manager in a revival of *Fata Morgana* at the Ashcroft Theatre, Croydon, in April 1964. The play is about a *femme fatale* (Sarah of course) who seduces a young man (David Hemmings before *Blow-Up*) on a hot Hungarian plain famous for its mirages. David was half-naked most of the time and when he wasn't rehearsing he played the guitar and wrote verses. Such a poetical young man.

Sarah said, 'We'll try to keep you anonymous, tone down the slap, keep it low. I'll introduce you as Jane (as in Plain) Spencer (as in Churchill) and I'm sure there'll be no problems.'

On the first day of rehearsals David Hemmings came bowling through the door and said, 'Christ, April, you were pissed last night.'

'Was I? Where?'

'At the Establishment.'

'Extraordinary, I don't remember being there at all, I mean, no, my name's Jane Spencer.' But it was no good.

Ellen Pollock directed it – she often came to Shawfield Street and had palpitations watching the Saturday-afternoon wrestling on television. Also in the cast were Tony Singleton, Edina Ronay (Egon Ronay's daughter who was living with Michael Caine), and a beautiful young actress called Lyn Ashcroft. She was being tipped for stardom but alas had a tragic disease which was eating away the bones in her neck. Eventually her head collapsed on to her shoulders and she died in her early twenties. We rehearsed in Soho and my job was to dish out coffee, take people for lines, tidy up, brush their wigs . . .

Sir Winston and Lady Churchill came for the last matinée. They sat in the front row flanked by detectives and the press, accompanied by their grand-daughter Edwina Dixon and her husband Piers. Each time Sarah had an exit one could hear Sir Winston's voice booming, 'Where's she gone? What's Sarah up to now? Why has she walked off?' Or if an episode took his fancy, 'That was a jolly amusing bit, yes, very good.' The audience waited for his remarks.

After the show he came on to the stage. Sarah had put a table and chairs there, a large glass of his favourite brandy and a fat cigar, and everyone was presented. It was too much for me, I ran and hid, but Sarah pulled me out. Then as Churchill got up to leave, the two bodyguards went to support him under each arm, but he pushed them away, and this vast, grandiose accumulation of history, this ancient and overpowering spherical presence alone in his magnitude and about whom hung a delicate bluish mist of sadness, or maybe it was just solitariness, shuffled out on a stick, leaving behind an equally vast hole which we quickly – desperately – filled with trivialities. He died the following year.

When a protégé of Francis Bacon's, a New Zealander called Peter, invited me to spend a week in his studio in Positano I accepted. Bacon I had first met with Tim Willoughby at Muriel Belcher's

Colony Room Club in Dean Street, lair of bohemian alcoholics (Murial's mouth was so obscene that every time I think of her I want to give up swearing; Francis has painted her in full screech). Bacon had a boyishly good-looking face topped by short dark curls. If he'd been shot through gauze he'd have looked eighteen, but shot through reality his features were already blitzed by the booze. My first impression was that he was drunk and it has been my first impression of him every time since.

Anyway, five weeks later I was still in Positano. It is built vertically on to a cliff face. You have to walk up and down everywhere. The whole town is permanently purple-faced. Peter's friends were an arty lot but fortunately included Jessica Mason, whose husband had written *The World of Suzy Wong*. Jessica had no ankles. Her feet were stuck straight on to the ends of her legs, but from the knees up she was exactly like Joyce Grenfell.

On the beach was an open-air nightclub full of stone lions. Everyone seemed to have boyfriends except me. Then I spotted a prospect. Dark-blue eyes, fair wavy hair, a pink mouth made for peaches, teeth like glory.

He said, 'Will you dance?' I shook my gaudy earrings and joined him. We stopped in the middle of our Mashed Potato. I said the first thing that came into my head: 'What's your name?'

'Niccolo.'

'And what do you do?'

'I'm a gigolo.'

'How much do you charge?'

'Depends.'

'Come and have a drink.'

'April, how could you?' whispered Peter; 'he's a gigolo.'

'I know – isn't it fun?'

After a few drinks I said, 'Niccolo, can I hire you for the night?'

'For you a special rate. Nothing.'

'Done!'

He came from Naples – quite a lot of Neapolitans are blond. He wanted me to meet his family, so I hired a car and we drove there. Papa was a doctor and I felt that Niccolo's being a gigolo was not from necessity but a delicious wantonness. We dined with the Baron de la Tour in the Baron's labyrinthine palace overlooking the Bay of Naples. The three of us sat at one end of a long banqueting table in deep candlelit silence made more sombre still by the sound of gold cutlery on porcelain plates. A butler and footmen served us in white gloves under a painted ceiling. The Baron was very young and very weary, with heavy parchment-coloured eyelids which were usually lowered. Occasionally he drew them up with an unsteady deliberation which seemed to enlist all his strength, so that when fully opened his eyes shone for a moment or two with a tremulous intensity until the effort became too great and the eyelids fluttered and fell to their original position. 'I am all alone in this big palace and I'm very lonely too,' he said in English and plucked a small bunch of grapes and turned them in the candlelight. So far as I remember, he didn't speak again that evening.

Naples is a city of extremes, all squalor and glamour. You tingle on a knife-edge as if anything could happen at any time. The Neapolitans cannot resist a beautiful woman. They fall apart at the seams, they become like children, they sigh and they swoon. In the streets they shout and whistle – you turn round – they melt, sink to their knees and start singing. Naples is so romantic it is unreal. But I had to return to London. Niccolo begged me to take him with me because Naples was unreal for him too. London was where things were happening. But I couldn't afford him.

Back in Shawfield Street I said to Cecilia, 'I've made a few discoveries while I've been away. The Italian fashion industry is booming. There's this place in Rome called Cinecittà where they make films – that's booming too. I'll never get any work in London and I've got to keep trying, haven't I? Well, I've done Paris, London, Madrid . . . perhaps I'll click in Rome.'

The Hotel d'Inghilterra off the Via Condotti, which Jessica Mason had recommended, is in a part of Rome packed with palaces where only by walking through the gates do you discover the fountains and noble courtyards.

I arrived with a long string of luggage and several candy-striped hatboxes, so the hotel treated me well. The Italians go for display. Unlike the English who delight in hiding wealth and distinction under an old darned pullover, the Italians like to give it all out in the first act. They lack mystery but their freedom of emotion makes short work of diffidence, as so many English men and women have discovered. A Roman holiday is the finest cure I know for a tight arse.

The first night, I couldn't wait, I felt the city's invitation pouring through the windows, and walked along to the Spanish Steps. I had no idea about Roman men but I knew where I wanted to go – Piazza di Spagna, Piazza del Popolo, Piazza Navona, all those piazzas. I walked along the Via Sistina, where I began to feel somewhat harrassed. It is a narrow street lined with tarts and the men were impinging horribly. So I hopped into a cab and said, '*Trastevere, per favore.*' Trastevere is the equivalent of Paris's Left Bank except that it's got the Vatican City too. Deciding to fall in love with the Piazza Santa Maria I sat down at a café in it and ate a seafood supper alfresco. I'd hardly dug in my fork when the *ragazzi* began to hover round. I thought that if this was how it was to be, I might as well go the whole hog and see what all this *dolce vita* was about up on the Via Veneto. Ever since 1959 Fellini's film had been a byword for all that was most interesting in the Latin temperament.

Outside the Café de Paris on the Veneto, sipping an Irish coffee chased by a bottle of Guinness, I did my best to be grand but it was hopeless, it was like trying to fight off the weather, so I went back to bed to rethink how a lady does Rome on foot.

Next morning I telephoned Jessica and she said, 'Come over and meet Ginny Campbell-Becker, the puppeteer.' These were the sort of people one would meet. Another was Jill St Amant, who married a painter in the Campidoglio and asked me to be matron of honour. She was a fast girl and when her mother arrived in Rome for the wedding she said, 'Jill, don't tell me – what weirdoes are coming to the wedding?'

'Well, Mummy, the only well-known one is April Ashley.'

'Oh dear, she's got such large hands.'

And when I met the mother she said to me, 'I've read in the newspaper that you have huge hands – where are they?'

Jill had warned me and I'd worn white gloves to make them look as large as possible.

'But they aren't huge,' she said; 'why did they describe them as huge?'

My hands aren't petite but they're no larger than many other women's. If you are a sex-change this is the sort of thing you must go through at least five times a week. And even if people don't say it, you know they're thinking it. It is one of the main bores, constantly to be the object of scrutiny for the tell-tale signs. It can make you awfully self-conscious if you don't hit it on the head. What might, for example, be a perfectly normal fluffiness on the face of an ordinary woman suddenly becomes, in the case of oneself, the revelation of a morbid fact. It is very annoying and some sex-changes try to overcome it by turning themselves into parodies of feminity which of course makes their predicament worse. One can only be oneself and try to bear in mind that men and women have far more in common with each other than otherwise. When not long ago a television company came to my house in Hay-on-Wye to film me for a documentary on transsexuals, they said, 'Just go about your normal business and we'll film you.'

'Well, I'm going to mow the lawn now.'

'Oh. Can't you do something more feminine like wash the pots?'

'But I don't wash the pots. I hate washing pots. I get someone else to wash the pots. I'm going to mow the lawn.'

'Like that?'

'Like what?'

'In jeans? Couldn't you wear a dress or something?'

'But I don't wear a dress to mow the lawn. It's a crazy idea. I wear jeans and Wellington boots to do that. Now get your cameras ready. We can do the glamorous bit afterwards if you like. But if you want to film me going about my normal day then I'm afraid it's mowing the lawn in jeans and boots.'

You see, although they were supposed to be researching a documentary, they had all these preconceived ideas which they wanted me to exemplify. Sex-changes, like everyone else, have to be human beings first and their label-group second. In fact I dislike being asked to be a representative transsexual, although I suppose it's unavoidable.

Apart from Jessica Mason's, my other number in Rome was Carol and Pepe Lopez's. 'Would you like to drive out to Fregene tomorrow for a picnic?' Carol said. This was their favourite seaside jaunt. They had a magnificent apartment occupying a whole floor of a *palazzo* on the Piazza Santa Maria in Trastevere, one golden room opening into another into another. Carol said that she kept her hips trim by rolling back the carpets and bicycling up and down. She'd become *persona non grata* with the Royal Family because Tony had married Margaret in 1960 and Carol had sold her memoirs to the press, the ultimate sin if you are connected with royalty.

She had fine blonde hair and even in middle-age looked staggering in a bikini. Pepe was big, burly and Latin, very cocksure, always making passes at the girls. I'd never known a man with a bigger collection of pornography, concealed behind a false wall in the library. Carol wasn't interested in the pornography but she made no objection because she was passionately in love with him and a little older too, and gladly put up with any naughtiness for the sublime pleasure of having him attached to her. She had been an actress and retained that edgy actressy quality, that air of alarm so many of them have when required to be merely themselves.

It was at one of their *soirées* that I first met a most extraordinary man. I'd come on from having dinner with the journalist Julian Pettifer and an ex-priest called Richard Bagley, and Carol said to me, 'April, I want you to meet Captain Lenny Plugge.' He was short and tubby, wearing thick round spectacles through which he peered at you as if trying to descry a mountaintop a great way off. Though in his mid-seventies he was bursting with eagerness so that this, along with his attempts to catch sight of the top of one's head, conspired every few moments to lift him off the ground in little hops.

'I've rented a tower in the middle of Rome because I've decided to become a sculptor,' he announced.

Basically he was an inventor. Born in 1889, he had invented Two-Way Car Radio (the basis of his fortune – it went into every police car), as well as Television Glasses and the Stereoscopic Cinematograph – I never grasped what those two were. He had been the Member of Parliament for Chatham in Kent. Though rich, he spent recklessly. The club Les Ambassadeurs off Park Lane had once been his town house, run by a staff of thirty footmen in powdered wigs. He'd had a house in the country, a flat in New York, a yacht in Cannes, but by the time I met him all this had shrunk disastrously to a house in Lowndes Square, two flats in Dolphin Square, and his tower in Rome. His wife Anna he adored but they hardly ever lived together, their recipe for a successful marriage. Besides, he was something of a philanderer – at least, he loved the company of beautiful women. Lenny had a son, and a twin son and daughter. The twin son was killed in a car crash. The daughter, Gale Benson, was murdered by Michael X in the West Indies.

Lenny and I saw a great deal of each other in Rome. He adored fancy-dress balls and would dress up as a cardinal because he said it was such a thrill to bless all the women who rushed the car whenever it stopped at traffic lights. We would meet for squid lunches at the

Piccolo Mondo, where he always began by explaining that he was working on another invention which would again make him a multi-millionaire. It was at the Piccolo Mondo that I introduced Sarah to him. He said, 'Everyone, just everyone, says I remind them of your father.' She tore him to bits.

I kept up with Lenny later on in London. By then his entry in *Who's Who* read 'Politician, scientist, writer, inventor, painter and sculptor', and listed among his inventions the Plugge Patent Auto Circuit. He would write from the Carlton Club, inviting me to performances of *Carmen* over and over again. It was his favourite opera. Lenny also took me to the last night of the Bolshoi Ballet at Covent Garden. When the curtain calls came he began pulling flowers out of a carrier-bag and flinging them at the stage. He'd pulled them up by the roots from the garden in Lowndes Square but hadn't removed the clods of earth. 'I find a little weight helps them to travel,' he said, as the ballerinas tried to avoid these dangerous missiles.

By the time Sarah arrived in Rome I'd moved from the Hotel d'Inghilterra into my own flat. I'd become chummy with a group of English people working for the F.A.O., especially Bob and Anne Tannock. She came to my hotel room and burst into tears. 'Life has passed me by, I've done nothing with my life, I've got no talent, no furs,' she sobbed into my mink. The upshot was that the Tannocks were leaving Rome for a while and did I want to rent their flat? It was in the Via della Chiesa Nuova around the corner from the Piazza Navona where so much went on, and right at the top of the building with a roof terrace so of course I took to it immediately. Five large comfortable rooms, £36 per month.

'The only problem', said Anne, 'is that a young man called Geoffrey Aquilina Ross goes with it.'

I took a look at him. Not stunning but personable. Good. To have been shoved in with a stunner would have posed too many problems. At this moment in my search for equilibrium I needed to pick and choose my men, with plenty of turnover, to be in a position to show them the door if necessary – like every morning. I didn't want a deep and complex relationship deranging my brains. Rome was the city where I was going to establish a modest little life for myself. A nice little flat, a nice little job, nice little bills to pay, nice little dinner parties, very simple, very straightforward. Geoffrey would come in handy as an escort. It would be possible to go out in the evening without being savaged.

I'd hardly unpacked my shoes and was doing a spot of ironing when Sarah turned up.

'Oh Spain, S-p-a-i-n, one doesn't deliberately drive into walls, does one? . . . but they don't want me around.' (She eventually sorted out her affairs there in order to erect a public bench to the Memory of Lord Audley in Málaga Cemetery.)

The friendly thing to have done would have been to invite her to move in with me. But we knew it would be disastrous. We were both big personalities now, with big cardboard egos strapped on to our shoulders. We'd have been crashing into each other morning, noon and night. So Sarah moved into the Hotel Sistina or if she went on special binges she'd invariably end up at the Hilton, miles away, and I'd get a call in the morning: 'April darling, be a brick and bring me over some day clothes – I'm at the Hilton again – my evening dress is a write-off.' I'd travel out to the Hilton on its hill with an extra blouse and a pair of slacks and join her for breakfast – Bloody Marys followed by a sauna bath. This was my introduction to saunas. Sarah said, 'Don't cop out, we'll try it together, they say it's very good for you.' Once inside I got the giggles.

'I know you're laughing at me.'

'I'm not, Sarah, I'm just a bit nervous.'

'No, you're not, you're laughing at me.' It was because she had a typical redhead's complexion and went brilliant purple in the plunge pool with a little ginger muff.

The press were on to us directly. 'Sarah Churchill and April Ashley have brought back the *dolce vita* to the Via Veneto' said the *Daily American*. Which was idiotic because Sarah detested the Via Veneto. We hung out mostly at the little restaurants of Trastevere where an old lady trailed us playing Offenbach's *Barcarolle* on her fiddle.

The press kept getting it wrong. 'Lady April Corbet *ex-capitano di marina*.' Another claimed I was born Edward Ashley and underlined it with a photograph of the Eton Wall Game and the putative me arrowed among the scrum. 'Mandy Rice-Davies *si è esibita per qualche sera in un night all'aperto alla presenza di* Sarah Churchill *e dell'ex-marinaio* Lady April Corbett.' The Profumo scandal had naturally been vast in Italy and Mandy was taking round a cabaret act while the iron was hot. The press kept asking me if I were the son of Lord

Rowallan and it became so irritating that I gave the full story to *Gente* magazine and they still got it wrong.

Carol Lopez had accompanied me to the Max Factor Studios to try for a job which they wouldn't give me and we were being served trays of Guinness at lunchtime on the pavement of the Café de Paris, watching the summer visitors sweating up and down the Via Veneto. Carol had to dash but I lingered and, looking up, saw moving towards me through the heat-haze Denny Daviss and Al Mancini. She was looking as voluptuously baroque as ever. 'We're on our way to see Fellini. He's casting a new film. *Giulietta degli Spiriti*. Why don't you come along?'

The casting girl Paola recognised me right away from one of Jessica Mason's parties. The maestro arrived in an extravagant manner, bellowing and smiling and winking and twirling his fingers in the air like an elephant who'd had ballet lessons. I saw Paola whisper the low-down on me. He clapped the other portfolios shut and came across. Taking my face in his warm capacious hands, he gave me a smacking kiss on each cheek and said, 'You must be in my film.'

Denny, Al and myself went off to celebrate. After a long, long dinner we decided to do Rome by *carrozza*. At one in the morning we climbed into Michelangelo's Piazza del Campidoglio. It was a perfect night, moon and stars, and I asked Denny to sing something from *La Bohème*. She chose '*Sì, mi chiamano Mimi*' and as her clear soprano lifted across the square like a silver ribbon the carriage driver shook his grey head and began to cry. I started too. Then Al. But Denny didn't waver. Her lovely voice went on and on, she standing like a goddess with one hand against the plinth of Marcus Aurelius.

While I waited for news of the film, Billy Wantage arrived from London with his girlfriend Sonya – I'm not sure what was going on there because she'd become engaged to a policeman the previous week. From the moment they plonked down their suitcases they were screaming at each other, squabbling over a randy little Turk called Aggie they'd picked up on the plane. Aggie had exceptional stomach muscles and was happy to cover all the angles but the arguments raged on. As a way of earthing the atmosphere I suggested taking everyone except Aggie to Capri for the Assumption of the Virgin August bank holiday. But the atmosphere didn't earth and I was relieved to bump into Niccolo, even though he threatened to leap off a cliff if I didn't become his lifelong partner. I said fine but

I'd love to meet him for a drink the following day on the terrace of the Quisisana Hotel.

When I arrived there, Niccolo was late. I ordered a cocktail and began to flick through a magazine. Being a bank holiday the island was jammed with tourists and some of them began to gather round me. I was used to this by now, but even so, whole families seemed to be stopping and staring at me. I flicked ever faster. Then someone must have identified me because a loud buzz ran through the crowd. Before my eyes groups of ordinary Italian holidaymakers were ceasing to go about their ordinary affairs and were turning into a mob. The thoroughfare was completely blocked. I was on my feet, everywhere I turned faces were babbling at me, and when they smelt my fear I began to be jostled. This was dangerous. I was in a panic. A waiter saw what was happening, grabbed me by the arm and ran towards the dining-room. We scrambled inside and he threw across the plate-glass door and locked it on them. I turned round to see the glass completely covered with faces and hands pressed against it, more pushing from behind, all yelling for me to come out. It was horrifying. What did they want from me? What could I give them?

I thought the glass was going to give way. '*Signora, sbrigati!*' said the waiter and led me along an underground tunnel which debouched near my hotel. I was in a desperate state, having cast aside my shoes for a speedier passage, when I heard behind me in the street, 'April, is that you?' I reeled about like Anna Magnani having a convulsion – it was Shirley MacLaine and her husband Steve – 'Oh, Shirley, every time our paths cross something dreadful happens. Last time it was a car crash, this time I've nearly been torn to pieces by an hysterical mob – do excuse me, I'm going to bed.'

But there was no sleep for me until I'd jettisoned that island and regained Rome, where I phoned Paola. 'Don't worry, April – Fellini always takes ages – he's so creative, you can't rush these things. We'll be in touch.' I knew that if Fellini used me the ice would be broken and I'd be saved, saved! By this time I'd discovered Sonia's good side – she'd been superb on the train back to Rome, teasing all the soldier boys with her luncheon salami – so when she and Billy started quarrelling again I said, 'Right, Sonia. I'm sick of the men too. They never take us anywhere. Let's go off for the weekend by ourselves. I haven't the foggiest idea where but I've got a map and I've got a pin, so here goes.'

The pin embedded itself in Santa Marinella, a village on the coast north-west of Rome. It sounded gorgeous and looked a mess. We booked into an hotel on the ugly rocky seafront and went to watch the dancing in an open-air café next door. Two strangers walked in, one wildly good-looking in the Mediterranean way, the other studious in horn-rimmed spectacles. I was irritable with my pin and told them to get lost, refused the drinks they sent to our table, but they persisted all evening as only the Continentals will. Sonia succumbed at midnight. The dishy one, Alberto, whisked her on to the dance floor and I thought, 'Hell, now I'm going to be landed with Spectacles.' The first thing he said, in excellent English, was, 'I've never heard a woman say "fuck off" before.'

'Go away, you drip.'

'But I think you're the most wonderful woman I've ever met.'

'Drop dead.'

'You're magnificent – you must know that. I want to tell you how magnificent you are.'

'Piss off, Four Eyes.'

'You drive me crazy! What's the matter with you?'

'Look, I don't want anything to do with you. Go and chat up that one over there, she looks your type, the one with the knickers round her knees already.'

'*Mama mia*, I love you! At least let me buy you a drink, yes?'

He sat down and I thought, right, you greasy pig, we'll have champagne. But I still refused to dance with him. He grew huffier and more aggressive, casting looks at Alberto who was doing very well by comparison, escorting Sonia round seventh heaven on the dancefloor with his hands all over her bum.

Then Massimo – that was his name – did the loveliest thing. He began to pelt me very gently with geranium petals, making a light popping sound with his lips. The gesture was so ravishing, I had to respond and so removed his spectacles – he was transformed.

The boys came back with us to Rome. One look at Billy and Geoffrey was enough to persuade me to accept Massimo's invitation to drive to Milan where he lived and worked as an industrial manager. The first few days were a great pleasure. We played houses. But everyone in Milan wanted to know who I was, where I'd come from. I held back on the truth because the anonymity, the ordinariness was such an adventure. But Massimo started to tell me to wear less make-up. And he rang from the office to say, 'I've some business colleagues in town – will you cook dinner for eight tonight?' I went to the grocer and bought all the goodies and began chopping in the kitchen. Then he rang again, cancelled dinner at home, we'd be going out to eat, he'd be home to collect me in twenty minutes, would I be ready please.

Would I be ready please! Is this what it means to be married to an Italian? Cock all night, shit all day? What would be next? His laundry? I left a note and flew back to Rome. When I walked into the flat Geoffrey said, 'Hi, love. We were wondering how long you'd be. He's phoned of course.'

He phoned again: 'What are you doing? Why aren't you here with me?' Italian men are accustomed to wives and mothers who are chained to the ironing-board. The vanity of Italian males demands vast amounts of perfect laundry each day.

'I'm not cut out to be an Italian Momma, Massimo, so there was no point in staying.'

'But I love you. Isn't that enough?'

Almost. I'd become emotionally entangled with him in a very short time and made flying visits to Milan afterwards. But when the ironing began to loom I fled. Suddenly his phone calls stopped. I was dying to ring him but he'd succeeded in making me bourgeois, the girl who waits for the man to call. A few weeks later he did.

'Hullo, stranger, I thought you'd given me up.'

'April . . . I don't know how to say it. Look, I was told the most incredible story about you. *Stupefacente*! I wasn't going to ring. But I must know if it's true.'

'I can guess what it is.'

'Is it true? Were you?'

'Yes.'

'I don't know what to say, I'm astonished.'

He was very upset. And his *machismo* had been hurt. I don't think it was the fact of my sex-change exactly. When it comes to sex most Latin men are capable of going 360°. It was that he felt he'd been hoodwinked not only in his own eyes but in the eyes of others too.

'I know, Massimo, I should have told you. I don't want to hurt you, so I'm going to put the phone down. Call me later or don't call me, whatever you decide, I'll understand.'

I should have told him. I don't tell every man I meet but I do when it begins to get serious. Very often they already know of course. But if one is abroad, in comparatively unsophisticated parts, very often they don't realise. It was such a luxury to have that man love me for myself, without the intrusion of all the other business. Telling him, I'd put it off and put it off. This is always such a dilemma for me. Today the greatest joy in going abroad is to find myself free of notoriety, to encounter others without the weight of history twisting it all up. I'm not an escapist but just for a few weeks, to leave all the rubbish behind, you can't imagine how invigorating it is.

Cecilia Johnson dropped by on her way back from holiday in Sardinia.

'Rome's heaven, isn't it?' said Cecilia.

'Darling, nothing happens here, absolutely zilch, but yes, it is.'

'I think I want to come and live here like you. What about sharing this flat?'

'I'd adore it. But the Tannocks are returning soon. How about sharing a new place?'

I phoned Mimi Capparoni who knew all about flats (her brother owned my London *poste restante*, Alexander's Restaurant in the King's Road). 'It must be cheap, amusing and, Mimi, it must be Trastevere.' She came up with a gem in a peasant enclave which stank gloriously behind the Piazza Santa Maria.

Cecilia, as always, was quick off the mark. She packed up in London, waved goodbye to Mrs Guppy, and in Rome immediately met a man who said he wanted to copy the swinging new idea from London of getting girls to man the petrol pumps. In London they wore hot-pants. This was far too *oltraggioso* for Rome but he thought they could get away with jeans and a shirt tied at the waist. Cecilia arose enthusiastically at five o'clock every morning to sell her petrol and soon had them queueing round the block. The drivers would see the station, screech to a halt and reverse to the back of the queue where they would wait patiently for the big moment, Cecilia's smile and nozzle. The local proletariat were frightfully shocked when they saw her going off in her uniform. They were even more shocked when the customers started knocking on the front door.

Selling petrol was no good for me – the girls had to be young and innocent-looking. Monica Vitti said she wanted to check me out for a part in a film about things from outer space. I was collected and driven out to a Renaissance palace in the country, ushered into a *salon*, Miss Vitti stood up, walked round me, snorted, and I was led out again like a borzoi. I had the distinct impression that she only wanted to satisfy her curiosity about the sex-change, to see if I looked better than she did.

Peter Dragadzi, *Time & Life* opera critic, took me to the Caracalla Baths for a performance of Verdi's *Un Ballo in Maschera*. During the first interval I asked Peter, 'Who's that man over there in the curly red wig and the giant diamond knuckledusters?'

'That's the King of Constantinople. I'll introduce you.'

The King was of sallow complexion and an ample girth buttoned into dog-tooth English cloth with a *foulard* in the breast pocket and a *fichu* at the neck. This sartorial fastidiousness was violated by the ostentation of his rings. He was in two minds about them, at one moment flaunting generously, then suddenly thinking better of it, and stuffing his hands hurriedly into side pockets from which, by and by, they would again flash out to forestall some disaster in the set of his *perruque*, or to grasp – or indeed grab – a goblet of champagne presented by a massive aide-de-camp (who seemed to combine the functions of bodyguard and teddy-bear). The King's whole manner was timid and unsettled as if he had long experience of public assault and expected the fur to fly at any second.

During the second interval he said, 'You've been so very charming and kind – I create you duchess.' It seemed to be a present for not having hit him, but duchess of what he didn't say. According to Peter he was descended directly from the Emperors of Constantinople with endless scrolls to prove it. There was no money left, the rings were his last gasp. If you phoned him up, his mother would pretend to be the housekeeper and say, 'Sorry, His Majesty's busy with his affairs.'

Although I saw less of Sarah now because she was living with a black painter called Lobo whom I didn't like, I was socialising frantically, splashing through the fountains of Rome until the early hours of the morning. A policeman pulled me out of one in the Piazza del Popolo, but I explained I was English and intolerably hot and he let me climb back in again. But now the *polizia* were to show up in less agreeable fashion.

It was on a roustabout with two Englishmen, both called Tony. As the car turned into the Via Veneto, the driving Tony put his foot down and we shot forward. Police cars were soon jangling on our tail and I hollered to be let out, arranging to meet them in Dave Crowley's Bar. I'd walked only a little way when I was swung round so violently I thought I was being attacked. I found myself confronted by yet another good-looking, pint-sized Italian. I wasted no time and slapped his face.

'You're drunk!' he shouted.

I swore.

Alas, he was a *poliziotto*. Soon they had surrounded me and glancing down the street I saw that the two Tonys had been similarly ambushed. At the police station a little hand-in-pocket went on and the problem appeared to have been resolved. But the young man whom I'd struck demanded a public apology in front of his fellow officers.

'He attacked me first,' I said. 'But I'll be happy to apologise to him if he apologises to me.'

He wouldn't. The two Tonys begged me not to be stubborn but I was stinging with indignation and saw no reason for abandoning my principles in a crisis.

'If you don't apologise, you'll have to go to prison.'

'Right – let's go!'

There was the question of which prison. One of them said, 'This one's famous because she's a man really.'

'When you cart me off,' I said, 'can we go out the back way? Because I know the *paparazzi* will be waiting out front.'

They took me out the front way, where the photographers clicked to their heart's content and I yelled '*Stronzi! Stronzi!*' The two Tonys went free.

The prison was headed by an unpleasant governor with a sarcastic tongue, and the women's section, where after a prostitute had examined me I was to be lodged, was run by nuns (which always spells horror). I was on remand, so they couldn't force me to wear the uniform and I clung to my sleeveless gold-lamé dress and mink stole. The sanitary arrangements were disgusting. I couldn't bring myself to use the lavatory, apart from a little urination, and so ate nothing, deliberately constipating myself. This wasn't difficult because the food was inedible pasta slops. I kept myself going with a few sips of water every half-hour.

Behind the cells was a collection of zoo-like pens giving air. While pacing my pen I heard a hissing. The arrangements of bricks and bars was such as to prevent even visual contact but if one pressed one's face against the bars it was just possible to glimpse the face of one's neighbour, provided she did the same. She was gabbling away in street Italian and I was saying '*Sì, sì, sì*' by way of being accommodating. Suddenly the penny dropped, she was saying, 'You must be very expensive, you must be Via Veneto stuff, I bet you charge a lot.'

'*Non, non, non*!' I replied, but couldn't be bothered with the complexities of my story. When it is such a wearisome business to explain what one really is, it is often more convenient to remain a mystery.

A nun asked me if I wanted to do some work. Anything to stretch one's legs, meet people, defeat the monotony, get some other air. I was escorted by the Governor and his officers to a larger pen, where I burst out laughing. Half-a-dozen women were sitting in the sunshine sewing labels on to mailbags. I had thought that this sort of thing happened only in cartoons. When the Governor had gone the women turned peculiar. They started to touch me, feel my clothes, wanted to try on my hand-made satin shoes. I thought I was going to be assaulted again. But I sat down and started sewing the mailbags, as I had seen them do, and the tension cleared. Soon I had all their stories. Most of them were prostitutes and petty thieves and were being fed by their relatives because the prison diet was so bad. One thief had been in there nine months without trial. How can she have endured it? The not-knowing which is so frightening, the claustrophobia. And the monotony and solitariness which force you too deeply into your own wandering imagination.

On the fifth day my possessions were returned and I was told I was leaving for the lawcourts. As I went out through the prison doors into the police van, I was overjoyed to see Pepe waiting. 'April, this is terrible,' he said, 'so pointless. Anyway – it's exactly like England. We have to go before a magistrate. The policeman will explain his side of the case, we shall explain yours, but I do warn you, this is Italy, you are a visitor, they are not keen on finding the local *polizia* guilty at the hands of a foreigner.'

My evidence was given through an interpreter. I didn't understand a word of the proceedings. Pepe said nothing as we came out and brushed past the flashbulbs. But in the car he explained that I could either leave Italy within three days and remain banned from the country for five years or I could pay a massive fine and do a stretch in gaol. The only chance for appeal was if Fellini would give me a contract.

Paola said, 'Can't really help there. Fellini doesn't give out contracts. Sometimes not even to the big stars.'

I had to go. Cecilia said she would very likely follow me because selling petrol was no career.

As we were about to take my suitcases down to the car, there was a great honking outside. I ran to the window. It was Massimo in the Alfa Giulietta. '*Mia cara*, I wanted to surprise you!'

'Darling Massimo, I've got a much bigger surprise for you. I've been thrown out of Italy. And I must rush because the *polizia* will be arriving any second to escort me to the airport.' It was like the departure of a head of state minus the brass band.

Arrivederci Massimo, *arrivederci* Italy, so magical, so fruitless. Special goodbyes to Carol and Pepe who'd given me such happy times beside the sea and were such a support during that final week. It was the last time I saw them. Not long afterwards, driving back from Fregene along our favourite route, they were killed in a pile-up.

9 In Which I Meet Just About Everybody

'Let's fight till six, and then have dinner,' said Tweedledum.

Lewis Carroll, *Through the Looking-glass*

When I landed from Rome, the *News of the World* was waiting in a black limousine. Noyes Thomas was inside it. I was eager to find out if Mrs Guppy was of a mind to reroof me. She fussed around, throwing open windows, making up the bed, and while she did so I gave Noyes the story of my incarceration and expulsion.

Next morning I awoke early and took out the basket to gather some provisions. As I veered into the King's Road it was as if I were seeing it for the first time . . . Quorum . . . Alvaro's . . . Mary Quant . . . the Casserole . . . Hung On You . . . the Pheasantry . . . Were they all there on that morning? Mini-skirts, op-art dresses, geometric haircuts (Vidal Sassoon), men with hair over their ears wearing striped blazers, chiffon scarves, white shoes, purple trousers . . . The Picasso Café was full of Mods, boys like dolls, girls with orange lips, white faces, black Dusty Springfield eyes, the Beatles were singing out of boutique doorways and there was an ozone zing that was new, alert – it was the beginning of winter and felt like spring. Diving into the Chelsea Potter – Joan and Shura Shivarg, Charlotte Rampling and Jeremy Lloyd, Ozzie Clark; David Bailey lunching with Jean Shrimpton at Alvaro's; Sir Mark Palmer and Catherine Tennant in silver shoes, pea-green stockings; Tara and Nicky Browne chatting to Michael Fish in the middle of the road and handing out sweets to strangers. Anthony Haden-Guest was writing about them, Michael Rainey was selling clothes to them at his shop where, if you knew him, he'd go down into the basement, pull out a brick and roll a marijuana cigarette (later he married Jane Ormsby-Gore and left World's End in a gypsy caravan to look for the Holy Grail in the West Country). It was *à la mode* to go to the opera on the arm of your hairdresser, interior decorator, fashion designer, photographer, plumber. Hairdressers had the shortest vogue of the lot – it lasted about three months – plumbers the longest . . . 'The Avengers' on TV, Harold Wilson in Downing Street, young boys driving Rolls-Royces, groovy, with it, too much, fab. Lord Snowdon had discovered Carnaby Street, and the King's Road gossiped in its favourite haunt, the Aretusa Club, which heiress was thrown out of the Royal Enclosure at Ascot for wearing trousers, which heiress had eloped with a road-sweeper.

Sarah rang from Rome wanting to know if anything had appeared in the English papers about her and Lobo. Yes, in one of the 'evenings'. Mary (Lady Soames) rang, saying, 'We're all very worried about Sarah.' I told her I didn't like Lobo a bit. There must have been a family tiff soon after because Sarah got it into her head that I'd rung her mother and ratted on her. I'd no more ring Lady Churchill than I would the Queen of England. But the rift didn't heal. In fact I began to see more of her sister-in-law, June Churchill, Randolph's wife.

A new generation of clubs. Annabel's. Sybilla's. The Pickwick in Great Newport Street, where I swapped sweaters with Kim Novak and stuck an electric back-scratcher up Hermione Gingold's skirt. The big question about 'Ging' was: what did she do with her money? I asked her. 'It's so expensive being a star,' she said. Tiny flat in New York, cheap wigs, buses instead of taxis? So the question remains.

Wips had been taken over by Brian Morris, rechristened the Ad Lib, and became the most fashionable club in London, all the new gush went there, the Bedfords, Sandie Shaw, Rollo Fielding, Patrick Lichfield, Anita Pallenberg, Terence Stamp, Chris Stamp, P. J. Proby, Marianne Faithfull, that Sixties lot. I adopted a table near the doorway where one could see everything without being crowded by it. One night I went and my place was occupied by a bunch of boys.

'What are you doing in my place?'

Brian Morris took me aside and said, 'But they're the Beatles. Do you mind? Just for once?'

A few nights afterwards they were in it again. We had to come to some arrangement. First come first served was no good. They were such early birds. We agreed to alternate. As a result John Lennon dubbed me 'Duchess'. Always the most open of the group, he invited me to join them for a drink.

'Duchess, this is Mick Jagger.'

'Who?'

'C'mon, April, you know Mick Jagger.'

'What?'

'Of the Rolling Stones.'

'The Rolling Pins?'

You see, I couldn't hear a thing, it was like Regent's Park Zoo on a bank holiday in there, and I'd been away, was out of touch, but they thought it was a put-on and Mick Jagger never took to me after that. He was very tiny, I remember, with fantastic skin. The Ad Lib was succeeded by the Revolution, which was succeeded by Tramp, and so it goes on.

Diana Dors (née Fluck) was more my era. I'd first seen her when working for Rowland Sales in the 1950s. She would turn up in a powder-blue Cadillac with 'DD' monogrammed on the doors (the 1950s was the age of The Car. Lady Docker had a cream-and-gold Daimler upholstered with the skins of six zebras 'because mink is too hot to sit on,' she said.) Diana had a flat in the King's Road above Safeways supermarket. It was here that Linda Christian said to a friend of mine, 'Roger, why don't you give April presents? It's the kind of thing a gentleman should do.' Linda was a true cosmopolitan. I'd first met her with Edmund Purdom at the Buchanan-Michaelsons' home – Edmund said he was more interested in music than acting and had recently found the finish of Schubert's Unfinished Symphony in an old shop in Naples, but nobody would acknowledge it.

Roger was Roger Dawson-Denver, one of my favourite youngsters, living on social security (just coming into fashion) in Leinster Square with a starving wife and kids. He frequented the Chelsea Potter and was always staring at me so I said, 'If you're going to stare at me like that, you might as well speak to me.' Roger was the first man in the King's Road to wear a flowered tie – he'd run it up himself. He once tore his tropical curtains down in order to make costumes so that we could run off to Tahiti together.

'I want to see a doctor about changing my sex,' he said. 'Will you dress me up?'

By the time we'd finished he looked very becoming and tottered off to Dr Geoffrey Grey's. When he came out the mascara was running down his face where he'd been crying with laughter.

'What did he say then?'

'He said, "What can I do for you, miss?" And I said, "I'm not a miss, I'm a boy, but I want to become a miss." And Dr Grey said, "Well, you're the best one I've seen all day."'

Chelsea was such a mixture. It's been pretty thoroughly gentrified since, but in those days you could look down Shawfield Street and see a Court limousine drop Princess Margaret off for tea at a house on the end, while in a council house opposite lived the MacNamara kids sleeping in one damp room. The four of them, Terry, Rita, Gary, Little Jed, would spy on me through the railings, and one afternoon I overheard the girl saying to her friend, '. . . but she's a witch. My mum said she changed from a man into a woman so she must be a witch.' The father was Irish, the mother half-Indian, and the house had no electricity. The racial combination made them fabulous to look at, but to begin with my favourite was Gary because he was the naughtiest and had a slight squint. I took him to Polperro for a short holiday and he wouldn't eat anything except fish and chips four times a day.

Mrs Guppy approved of my foster-mothering enormously. She was less taken by a red lamp I'd put in the window. It made the sitting-room very cosy but Mrs Guppy had other ideas. 'Apreel,' she fluted, 'don't you think you might risk possibly giving the wrong impression with that lamp?' This was her phlegmatic English way of controlling the roost. When Roger and I were sitting out on the pavement one very hot afternoon in the pouring rain, he in under-pants, me in bra and panties and sombrero, she said, 'I really do think there's a chance, Apreel dear, of your catching a chill if you sit outside the house with no clothes on.'

Peki turned up in London. We'd kept in touch by post and phone. She'd been working with Ricky Renée at the Chez Nous Club in Berlin, billed as *Ein Märchen aus Tahiti*, a fairy-tale from Tahiti. Peki went through terrible indecisions about 'the Operation Pussycat' as she called it. I offered to pay for her to go to Casablanca in the early 1960s but she said no, a German baron was courting her, money wasn't the problem. I don't know exactly what course her treatment took, she was very secretive about it, and the details may have been dissimilar to mine, but by the time she arrived in England she was living as a woman and wanted to build a new life.

Peki's ambition was to be an English lady with a British passport. She loved its air of distinction beside which all other passports look like dog licences, its size, the board binding, the Royal Coat of Arms in gold on dark blue. *Her Britannic Majesty's Principal Secretary of State for Foreign and Commonwealth Affairs Requests and Requires* . . . well, we all love that, so I expect they'll be doing away with it soon. Meanwhile Peki began her quest for English respectability at Raymond's Revue Bar doing a whips 'n' leather act, and changed her name to Amanda.

'The neatest way for you to get a British passport', I suggested, 'is to marry an Englishman.'

We went to the Chepstow in Notting Hill, a very 'mixed' pub. After a drink and a reconnoitre, we spotted a stranger looking suitably innocuous and impoverished. For this sort of business you don't want anyone with too big an ego or too high a standard of living.

'Hullo, what's your name then?'

'Lear.'

'You're English, Mr Lear?'

'Scottish.'

'He's Scottish, Amanda.'

'What a shame.'

'Scottish still counts, they have the same passports. Mr Lear, do you want to earn £50? Would you marry my girlfriend here – Amanda, where are you? – who wants to stay in the country?'

The following Saturday, we drove off to the Chelsea Register Office. I'd telephoned a friend called Rosemary and borrowed her open white Mercedes as a nuptial wagon. After the ceremony we were travelling down the King's Road in it towards Sloane Square when I began to feel sentimental.

'Oh, marriage, it's always so romantic – don't you feel somehow different, Amanda?' She scowled at me. 'Since I'm already paying for this spree, let me treat you newlyweds to a wedding breakfast at the café in Peter Jones Department Store.'

'A wedding breakfast?' Amanda's eyes unslanted. I'd never seen them go like that before. 'Give him the money and tell him to fook off!'

'Sorry, Mr Lear – no buns for you today.' We dumped him

among the shoppers clutching his banknotes. We all understood the arrangment but I still think it rather humourless of her.

Immediately she applied for the passport and was henceforth 'Amanda Lear'. When changing one's identity, a new passport gives one a tremendous sense of security out of all proportion to the document's legal significance. When I received mine in the name of 'April Ashley' it seemed finally to seal matters.

Amanda moved into the Hotel Constantine, a curious establishment near South Kensington Underground station which had some pretension to being London's equivalent of New York's Chelsea Hotel. To her Eurasian beauty and mystery was now added a voguish sense of style. She became one of Ozzie Clark's favourite models and gravitated towards the pop-music world, especially towards Brian Jones of the Rolling Stones.

Amanda was a quick-witted girl with a sly humour veiling her iron determination to 'make it'. She always knew how to sell herself, which I never did, and always learned from her mistakes, which I never did. At the same time there was a brittleness in her which disappointed me. She began to move into a younger, more superficial set, I into an older, more established one. In the end she telephoned only when she wanted an address or was depressed.

Rosemary, from whom I'd borrowed the white Mercedes, was getting married to Aubrey Wallace, whose sister Pauline ran a gambling club to which Cecilia had often taken me. The reception was at the Hyde Park Hotel and halfway through it Pauline marched in with a portable television set so that she wouldn't miss the afternoon racing. I was introduced to Clive Raphael, gregarious, Jewish, overweight, middle-aged. He owned a string of garages in the Midlands and offered me a lift home. A few nights later he called in his Bentley, a massive cigar sticking out of his face and in his buttonhole a red carnation the size of a cricket ball. We ate at the 21 Club and went on to Annabel's. He said he was twenty-eight years old. 'But you look forty-five!' I couldn't help it. And I was rather irritated by his constant efforts to impress – not me especially, but the world, and most of all himself. Underneath the playboy act he was so insecure that he began to interest me. I decided to educate him, give him the Sarah Churchill.

'Don't be overfamiliar with waiters. Be friendly by all means but don't talk as if you were related to them – they don't respect it. And if we're not given the best table, don't feel so crushed. It's not necessarily a deliberate slight on the part of the management. And stop handing them fivers every two minutes. Waiters are the biggest snobs around and despise a grovelling nature. And Clive, yes, I'd love to go out again. But the Bentley, the cigar, the carnation – two of them must go and I don't care which two.'

Fortunately he kept the car and we became a couple, usually at Shawfield Street, because his own house, in a mews behind Harley Street, looked like a nightclub in Tel Aviv. 'When we come to furnishing, the thing to remember is quality. Things should be beautiful and useful at the same time. Old or new, it doesn't matter. Any good old piece will automatically go with any good new piece. To have all new stuff is cold and impersonal, as if you're ashamed of your past, or worse – as if you don't have one. And all old stuff, unless it's the finest, is just dreary nostalgia. A mixture is best. And don't call your sitting-room "the lounge" – it's a dead giveaway, like "serviette" for napkin. And nylon plush, orange wallpaper, ormolu kitchen cupboards, musical cocktail cabinets – are out! Remember – the picture should always be more valuable than the frame.'

We used his house only to give dinner parties for his business friends. Clive's commercial interests were wide and murky. He called himself a 'wheeler dealer' with a smirk. I never understood what this meant, but it seemed to be the maverick's equivalent of the gentleman's 'something in the City'. I daresay they both amount to the same thing, exploiting other people's money. One of his friends made a fortune by illegally introducing the pill into Mexico. Another claimed to be a boar-hunting Sardinian duke. When we went out they spent money like water, a definite breed of capitalist cowboys with appalling taste. Money ruled their lives because it was the only thing they had. I'd end up saying, 'Clive, let's go somewhere really smart. We don't *have* to go to the White Elephant, Les Ambassadeurs, the Hilton, those gaudy joints.' But he was never comfortable in places like the Caprice. His favourite recreation was flying, he had a pilot's licence, and I believe he found peace up there alone, away from all his social paranoia.

Clive took me on holiday to Beirut, a very prosperous city before it blew itself to bits. Aubrey Wallace had moved there to sell encyclopaedias to the Arabs. He and Rosemary were living in a rough hotel while a house was being prepared for them. We stayed at the Phoenicia. You could ski in the mountains in the morning, swim in the Mediterranean in the afternoon. But the Wallaces weren't getting along. They were so broke they couldn't pay the hotel bill and had to stay on until they could. When I saw their house I wasn't surprised. It was a sultan's palace and must have soaked them dry. Every five minutes one of them was in our room character-assassinating the other.

'I can't stand him! He's driving me nuts!'

'What's wrong with her? I love her so much but she's always running away!'

After ten days I'd had enough and announced my return to London. Rosemary became contrite and asked me if there were anything I'd like to do before I left.

'Yes, there is. I'd like to go to Damascus, find Jane Digby's tomb, and put a flower on it.'

The Honourable Jane Digby El Mezrab is a heroine of mine. She was born in 1807, the daughter of Admiral Digby, and at the age of sixteen her parents married her off to Lord Ellenborough. In London she fell in love with Prince Felix Schwarzenberg of Austria, followed him to Paris, had two daughters by him, and Ellenborough divorced her. In Paris she had an affair with Balzac, who described her passions as 'African' and her hair as 'soft tan'. In 1831 she went to Munich and took two more lovers: King Ludwig of Bavaria, and the future Emperor Napoleon III, who was in penniless exile. It is thought that Ludwig interceded with the Vatican to obtain a dispensation so that, as a divorced woman, she could marry the Catholic Baron Venninger, which she did, giving him a son and daughter. Ludwig's son had recently become Otho I of Greece. She went there, had an affair with him, but fell in love with Count Spyridon Theotoky, was baptised into the Orthodox faith, divorced the Baron and married the Count. She was in the prime of her beauty and conquered Athens as she had London, Paris and Munich. But when her Greek son fell to his death at her feet from a balustrade she went to live in the mountains with Hadji Petros, an Albanian bandit. On a horse-buying trip to Syria she was swept off to a Bedouin tent by Shekh Salih. She fell in love with him and with the desert, returned to Athens for another divorce, returned to Syria and met another Sheikh, Medjuel El Mezrab, whom she married.

Jane built a house on the outskirts of Damascus where they lived six months of the year *à l'Européenne*, the other six months in the desert *à la Bedouine*. Contemporary travellers such as Sir Richard and Lady Burton, Wilfred Scawen Blunt and the Emperor of Brazil would call on her. Edward Lear wrote: 'Lady Ellenborough in a crimson velvet pelisse and green satin riding habit, going up to complicate the absurdities of Jerusalem.' Jane was faithful to El Mezrab for nearly thirty years. She died from cholera in 1881 and insisted on being buried according to Christian rites. El Mezrab refused to attend the funeral in Damascus but after her burial he rode up on her favourite Arab mare and trampled the grave in anger and grief and rode off into the desert.

'Have you got the papers, Rosemary? Are you sure?' Her car needed papers of ownership to be presented at the border. The Syrian government was trying to stamp out illegal car-trading. At the border we were turned back. She'd forgotten the papers! The Middle East never really gave . . .

Clive and I ventured more modestly after this. I'd go along when he went up to collect the money from his garages. We stayed many times at the Château Impney Hotel, a mass of turrets and finials near Kidderminster, with a beastly parrot in the hall and a Siamese cat which spat at you on the staircase. It had been built in the nineteenth century at enormous expense by John Corbett, the Droitwich Salt King, for his wife Anna who refused to live in it. Here I made Clive ride because he was petrified of horses, and take long walks, until he had lost weight and looked more his age.

In Leeds he asked me to marry him and suggested we fly to Mexico for a licence. Legally I didn't know how things stood with Arthur, no one did, so I suggested we go to Manchester instead to visit Mother. Crossing the moors in a cold winter mist we passed small police huts and policemen digging. They were exhuming the corpses of children tortured and murdered by the Moors murderers, Ian Brady and Myra Hindley.

I hadn't seen Mother since the *News of the World* had arranged a rather silly reconciliation and for some gummy photographs to be taken. When I telephoned she said, 'What do you want?'

'To see if you want to go out for lunch.'

'Just a minute and I'll ask Bernie. Hey, Bernie, can I go out to lunch with our April? . . . he says it's all right if I'm not long.'

We collected her at one o'clock. Mother was wearing a beaverskin coat down to her ankles. Since she was tiny it made her look like a molehill travelling on white high-heels.

'Clothes are getting shorter these days, Mother. Have you heard of the mini?'

'But this is genuine beaver. I couldn't cut it.' She snuggled into the back of the Bentley and all but disappeared. 'Aren't these American cars big!' she said.

'Where do you want to go for lunch?'

'Once a week Bernie and I go for a Chinese. I'd like to go there. It's very posh – we'll get good service. They know me there.'

'Hullo, Mrs Cartmel. We have a nice table for you and your friends.'

'I told you they knew us, Bernie and me,' and with a big smile of false teeth she started to tuck into her Woodbines. Mother never introduced me as her daughter.

Clive's parents lived in north London and he was very close to them. His father was an excellent pianist. With all these family introductions, Clive said, 'Go and find a flat for us and I'll buy it.' I found a new block behind Belgrave Square called Montrose House. Except for two or three, they were all untaken. He bought the lot and started to remodel them inside. The penthouse floor was to be ours.

This sounds much cosier than it was. There were sinister undercurrents in him which from time to time spouted poisonously to the surface. Clive beat me up one night at the Château Impney. Afterwards he burst into tears, said he didn't know why he'd done it, bought me a jeep as a peace offering, and suggested we go shark fishing in Cornwall. We went with Jamie Granger (Stewart Granger's son). Jamie and I hooked the same shark simultaneously. The beautiful beast became hopelessly entangled and had to be clubbed to death on the deck. Clive didn't enjoy it either. He spent the whole time in dark glasses.

We tried Majorca for a week. I took him over to lunch with Bob and Janie Buchanan-Michaelson at the Felix Hotel. Bob and Janie I'd been seeing much of since Cecilia first introduced me. Their house in the Vale had the largest private swimming-pool in Chelsea. Ducks gathered there in winter and Janie would feed them caviar on biscuits, which they adored. When we returned to our villa, Clive beat me up again, and again said later that he didn't know why. I thought it was something to do with his inferiority complex and suggested he visit a psychiatrist. But it was the end. I didn't want a man who knocked me about. Some women accept it, even like it. I

Above: As Eliza Doolittle at Le Carrousel, Paris, 1959

July 1960, just after the operation, with a friend in Juan

1961, with Mother after April's engagement to Arthur Corbett

With Arthur in the pool, Finca el Capricho, Marbella, 1961

With Peter O'Toole at the Domecq party in Jerez de la Frontera, 1962

Opposite: Modelling days, 1961

At the première of Valentino's *Blood and Sand*, re-released in May 1973

With Edward Madok, 1968

Opposite: The blind leading the blind: in Rome with Sarah Churchill, 1964

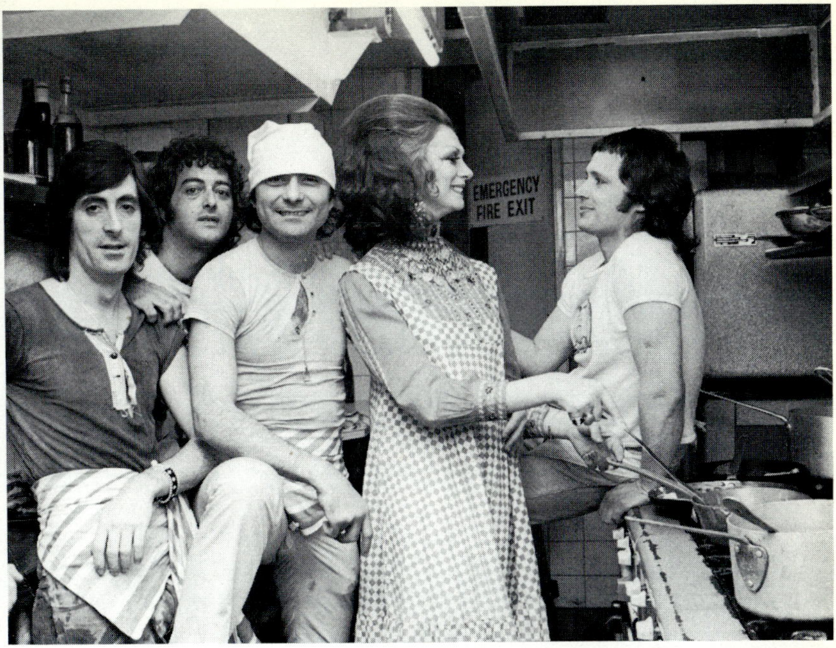

Above: The kitchen staff at AD8; Pepe (*to April's left*) and Alonso, 1974

Right: As Countess Dracula at the Collegiate Theatre, 1974

Opposite: Modelling Thea Porter for the *Sunday Times*, photographed by David Bailey, 1969

Studio Portrait, 1975

Below: The Sphinx on the Sphinx, Châeau Croix des Gardes, 1976

don't. It's so claustrophobic, like an explosion of in-growing toenails.

Clive married Penny Brahms soon after, a very young model, but didn't find contentment there either. I saw him shopping in Beauchamp Place. 'My wife's left me. Will you have dinner? Come up to the flat.' It was the Montrose penthouse. Like his previous habitation, it looked like a clip joint, with purple walls and gold fringes on everything. He was alone and unhappy with two Dobermans for company and panoramic views across London. Without speaking he began to play a grand piano. I sat at the opposite end of the room on a long dark sofa until I couldn't stand it any longer and left. He had forgotten about dinner, thank goodness.

I heard nothing more of him until 1972 or 1973 when, while piloting his parents and girlfriend across France, the aeroplane exploded, killing all four of them. It was rumoured that the explosion was the result of a planted device, that he had caused offence while gun-running (which was one of his ambitions) to the Middle East. But far more bizarre than his death was his will. In it he left £500,000, but to Penny Brahms only one shilling and four nude photographs of herself. She challenged it in the courts where the will was discovered to have been a fraud cooked up by Clive's lawyer and the Sardinian boar-hunting duke.

Finishing with Clive threw me back on to my own financial resources and thus I discovered that I had none. I sold the mink. In the Chelsea Potter an American G.I. said he was driving down to Ibiza and would happily give me a lift. If Majorca were anything to go by, Ibiza would be cheap. By now Cecilia was Mrs Richard Lewis and living in New York and, although Mrs Guppy offered to drop the rent, I could no longer afford Shawfield Street.

Ibiza is a red and rocky island. But its primitive days were coming to an end. First the film people discovered it. Then the bohemians. Then Society. Then the general public. By the time I got there Ibiza was somewhere between 'bohemian' and 'Society' in its evolution. The first person I made friends with was Major Teddy Sinclair, who took a great pride in his figure and marched up and down the beach every day in shorts, eyeing the girls. 'I've been offered a house in Talamanca, just across the bay,' he said. 'Why don't you share it? £9 a month.'

There was no electricity and the water had to be drawn from a well but it was right on the sea. When we arrived the cottage was carpeted with a thick layer of dead black beetles. But Teddy and I didn't crowd each other. He liked the English Bar and I preferred Arlene's Bronx Bar. He had a stream of girls passing through and I had Klaus Schmidt.

Klaus was a German painter whom I'd met at Ivor Spence's gallery in the town. He had learnt English on the slopes of Mount Snowdon so language wasn't a problem. He had also been a pupil of Kokoschka and taught art outside Nuremberg. Tall and dark, he loved cracking jokes and he cracked them in the English style because 'a German joke is no laughing matter!' Though the middle of summer, he insisted on wearing a black suit, shoes and tie, and a white shirt, just like an undertaker. He also detested the sun and the sea. To put himself through it in this way was part of his theory of art. Another part of his theory was that in order to be a great artist one had to be celibate for long periods, to drive the energy up into the imagination 'so there will be no hankie-pankies please.' Teddy said, 'I don't approve of Krauts as a rule, but your Schmidt's O.K.'

We didn't do much, lazed around, ate paella, drank red wine thinned with *gaseosa*. We couldn't afford to do more. Even so, I was forced to sell some more jewellery. At the end of August Klaus had to return to Nuremberg. When the boat goes out there's hardly a loo-roll left in Ibiza. We waved until we could no longer see each other. I suddenly felt immensely lonely and burst into tears.

But his departure forced me to be more adventurous. Sandy Pratt's Bar at Santa Eulalia del Rio was the hub of a show-business colony whose loudest mouth was Terry-Thomas's. Diana Rigg turned up with David Warner. He was rehearsing *Hamlet* – the Prince of Denmark as '60s dropout – and spent his time running around with his head in the text, reciting it at anyone he bumped into.

Polly Drysdale had a large *finca* on the island. She gave only intimate dinner parties, not cocktail parties. Polly I'd first met with Arthur in Marbella when she had floated into town on her yacht, the 365-ton *Hiniesta*, with her first husband (the Comte de Mun), her current husband (the Hon. John North) and her future husband (Stephen Drysdale) all on board at the same time. Polly was American and always had plenty of money. Her mother was Caresse Crosby who invented the brassière and who married the handsome multi-millionaire poet-murderer-suicide Harry Crosby, founder of the Black Sun Press in Paris in the 1920s. Her mother left her, among other things, a huge cinquecento castle in the Sabine Hills, Rocca Sinibalda, built in the shape of an eagle, including beak.

The house of the Baron and Baroness van Pallandt (better known as singing duo Nina and Frederick) was by far the most beautiful on Ibiza, an old farmhouse carefully restored and lit completely by candles. When they gave a party it was like going into a cathedral. I went with a friend of mine, Shura, and during the party asked him to play the piano. Everyone groaned and carried on talking. But one by one they stopped because he was the world-famous concert pianist Shura Cherkassky. Shura is a methodical man and does everything by numbers – just *four* prawns, just *two* potatoes, just *six* strawberries, just *seven* hours' sleep. Sometimes the numbers are quite arbitrary but he sticks to them as an exercise in self-discipline, so much so that his wife divorced him for mental cruelty.

Ibiza became a regular summer stop for me in the second half of the '60s. When I first visited it, the lion of the island was Elmyr de Hory, the art faker. He was a tiny, precious Hungarian who painted forgeries of Matisse, Renoir, Chagall and Modigliani. These sold for fortunes in Europe and America through the dealers Fernand Legros and Real Lessard. Elmyr was quite shameless. He would go down to the harbour to meet the boats, holding a big bag of money in one hand and a big bag of dope in the other, and ask the young men if they needed a place to stay. I ran into him in the Bronx Bar.

'I have ze Viscount Maugham coming to stay and he'll be staying viz me for some time I sink.'

'Robin! How lovely.'

'You know zis Viscount?'

'I met Robin years ago when he was Mr Maugham and I was – oh, years ago.'

'Then I sink you must come up for a drink.'

Elmyr loved titles. He was a monumental snob until he was exposed (after which he improved no end. Although fame often ruins people, there are a sizeable number who regard it as their rightful state and when they achieve it all the bitterness goes and all the pettiness and they acquire large and generous spirits.)

Robin Maugham so fell in love with the island that he asked Sandy Pratt to find him a house on it. This was Casa Cala Pada, not large but it lent itself to glamour, overlooking gardens of pine, palm and oleander which spread down to the sea. He later added another floor and, thinking it too big, sold it, to his subsequent regret.

Going up to Elmyr's one night, Robin and I were stopped by policemen with machine guns. Fernand had rung Elmyr to say he was coming over to murder him. We were allowed through only after the police had telephoned the house. When Robin was asked, 'Do you think it's true that Elmyr painted all those forgeries?' he replied, 'Good God, no, the man can't even paint his face properly.' Which was true. Elmyr went out in far too much rouge and powder. He also dyed his hair.

The scandal broke in 1968 with Elmyr shouting, 'I've been framed!' The thing he dreaded most about his imprisonment in Barcelona was that he'd be unable to dye his hair. When he was released it had grown through grey, but he decided this was immensely distinguished and didn't dye it again. He went free on a technicality. Although he had painted the pictures, someone else in the conspiracy had signed them.

Clifford Irving was living in Ibiza at this time, a failed Jewish novelist in sandals. He persuaded Elmyr to collaborate on his story *Fake*! This had the side-effect of drawing out from retirement Orson Welles, who made an appalling art documentary of it. But Clifford made his name with a fake of his own, the bogus 'authorised' biography of Howard Hughes. The most brilliant literary hoax of this century, it forced even Howard Hughes out of hiding in order to refute it – but not before Irving had hoodwinked everyone else.

When Robin moved to the island he displaced Elmyr as its leading social figure. He was the son of the 1st Viscount Maugham, the Lord Chancellor, and qualified in law himself but had no appetite for it. His uncle, Somerset Maugham, advised him to marry a rich woman and go into politics so that he could end up as Governor-General of a remote island. But Robin wanted to become a man of letters and began to model himself on Willie. His only major success was *The Servant* and that largely through the success of the film made of it. Perhaps the proximity of Somerset Maugham had the same numbing effect as Sir Winston's had on the Churchill children. But the title went down very well on Ibiza and he was a grand host. I hostessed many of his parties there, one a month in the summer. His guests included Alan Searle, his uncle's secretary. When Somerset Maugham died in 1965, Alan lost whatever stuffing remained in him. Fat, friendless, alcoholic, his hypochondria turning increasingly into genuine diseases, but with skin as fresh and pink as the belly of a sow thanks to Dr Niehans's Rejuvenation Therapy, he wandered purposelessly through the old haunts looking for someone who might acknowledge him, around his neck an old Etonian tie he was not entitled to wear, a gruesome warning to all kept boys.

Robin told me many stories about people I was later to meet, especially Sir Michael Duff. He was the Lord Lieutenant of Caernarvonshire and Lord Snowdon's godfather. One day he suddenly remembered this fact and sent the boy a teddy-bear. But Michael had forgotten about Time and the thank-you letter was written from Cambridge where Tony Snowdon was an undergraduate. There was an occasion when he had to give a dinner to the local dignitaries of Caernarvon and decided to start with liqueurs, fruit and meringues and end up with soup and rolls, the entire meal being served in reverse. So intimidated were they by Sir Michael's aristocratic mien that not one of the councillors made a single reference to it. But I never thought of him as eccentric. His effects were too calculated for that. He was more of a practical joker. One of his favourite pranks was to dress up as Queen Mary and pay surprise visits in a royal car – until he bumped into her in a neighbour's hall.

Robin wanted to write my life story. We met at the Ivy Restaurant where I often went with 'Daddy Pat' Dolin, and it was arranged that I go out to Ibiza to discuss it. When I arrived his first question on the subject was unbelievably tactless.

'Mind your own bloody business!' I replied.

He flew into a tantrum and I was banished to the back of the house. Robin often threw tantrums, especially after drinking too much. 'I'm the Viscount Maugham! How dare you *speak* to me like that!' He had an outstanding war record, had been terribly brave against Rommel in the desert, but had survived with a piece of shrapnel in the brain and this could well have had something to do with his ill-assorted humours and bouts of amnesia.

Viva King entered my life at a party given by the painter Martin Newall. At this gathering two people stood out. One was Simon Fleet, endlessly tall, about fifty years old in a chocolate wig and tight leather boots going all the way up his long legs to the tops of his thighs so that he looked like a giant locust. His features were very fine, with a touch of Frankenstein's monster (up close you could work out where his face had been lifted, especially around the eyes).

Simon's real name was Kahn and he had a brother who was the Anglican Bishop of Haiti. Juliet Duff, Michael's mother, had taken him up when he was in the Merchant Navy and rechristened him 'Fleet'. Simon inherited a house in Fulham from his friend Sophie Fedorovitch who had been killed there by a leaking gas pipe. It was called the Gothic Box because it was small, crenellated, and apparently cursed. It was the first place where I encountered imitation grass, a tiny lawn of bright-green plastic, and Simon entertained there as best he could, titles clashing with the hit parade and the armed services. Alas, one day he tripped in his thigh boots at the top of the stairs and was found at the bottom dead with a broken neck.

The other was Viva King, who totally monopolised me, perhaps because she was being flustered by a new man in her life, Matt, whom she'd met only minutes before.

'Take your hat off,' was the first thing she said.

'I can't take my hat off, my hair's in a bun, it's full of pins.'

'I won't pay any attention to you until you take your hat off.'

All my hair fell down and she said, 'That's better. Now we can talk.'

From the beginning I detected something delicate and complex in her which was immensely attractive and I was determined to make friends. Viva was born in Argentina in 1893, the daughter of an English railway manager. Her exploits in 'upper bohemia' began in the 1920s when she was secretary to Augustus John and went into the study one morning to find him beating the desk with an erection, shouting 'No, no, no, no, no!'

I never knew her husband, Willie King. He died in 1963, just before I met Viva, leaving her a handsome house, full of Victorian paintings and signed first editions, in Thurloe Square opposite the Victoria and Albert Museum where he had been the Keeper of Ceramics.

They had no children. Viva said that she had had an abortion when young, the baby of a great celebrity, and led me to believe that she couldn't or wouldn't become pregnant again. She and her friend Nancy Cunard were the first women in London to have public affairs with black men, Nancy with the pianist Harry Crowder, Viva with the musician Hutch (who was rumoured to have had most of the peeresses in the kingdom). But the only man she ever really loved was Philip Heseltine who composed under the name Peter Warlock. He had gassed himself to death in 1930.

After Willie's death, his friend Gerry Wellington (the 7th Duke) proposed to her three times.

'Gerry says being a duke is like having a birthday every day.'

'So why don't you accept him? I'm dying to say, "My friend the Duchess of Wellington". You're mad to refuse him.'

'I'm not mad at all. You've no idea what I had to put up with from Willie all those years. I don't want to marry ever again. I've got my freedom and I'm enjoying it.'

Besides, she was having a full-blown affair with a man fifty years her junior – Matt.

'It's a great tragedy,' she said, 'for a woman to discover sex at the end of her life. I don't mean banging. I mean proper sex.'

'It's better than never discovering it at all.'

'Do you think so? It's made me terribly fretful over my lost opportunities. I'd have had a much happier life if I'd cottoned on to sex at the beginning instead of at the end. Willie was hopeless. He preferred the boys of course. I've always been a passionate woman but now that I'm no longer ashamed, it's too late.' Sadly Matt indulged in petty theft, which pained her terribly because she adored him so.

Viva was the epitome of the elderly English lady: white hair, china-blue eyes, the skin of a young girl, the house with eighteenth-century furniture, the stick, the memories, the sharp tongue which would suddenly melt into intimacies and good nature. She had her 'Sundays'. Among those who came were (off the top of my head): Violet Wyndham (daughter of Ada Leverson, the Sphynx, Oscar Wilde's friend), Patrick Kinross, Michael Holroyd, Philippe Jullian, Richard Buckle, Heywood Hill, Gladys Calthrop ('Blackie', Noël Coward's designer), Lady Aberconway, Bumble Dawson, Connie Mount, Anthony Blond, Lady Charlotte Bonham-Carter, James Pope-Hennessy, Iris Tree (who conversed in four languages simultaneously), various Stracheys, Bentley Bridgewater, Angus Wilson, Viola Hall, Viva's nephew Richard Booth, Lady Diana Cooper. From 1964 to 1974 Viva's birthday present to me was a party in her house. Diana Cooper came to one in a cream trouser-suit and an enormous cream stetson with a rolled brim. While chatting she nonchalantly raised her arm and retrieved from behind the brim a cream chihuahua which had been hidden there, and continued to talk while tickling its neck.

At the first birthday party, a miniature Humpty Dumpty with

nervously fluttering hands toddled up and said, 'Hullo, my name is James Bailey. Happy Birthday.' Then he fell over in an alcoholic coma and had to be carried up to one of the bedrooms.

'Who's he, Viva?'

'A lovable little dipsomaniac – rich – neurotic – a stage designer and painter.'

He became my great opera partner. Very tiny, very fat, very effeminate, James none the less had the knack of commanding people's respect. But I don't know what his family could have made of him. His father was a Lieutenant-Colonel and his mother a daughter of the Earl of Inchcape. Actually he got on very well with his sister, Lady Felicity Rumbold, who shared his interest in clothes – she introduced Queen Sirikit of Thailand to Balmain and ever after those gorgeous Oriental creations were designed and made in Paris. As a young man James had come under the influence of Oliver Messel, Tony Snowdon's uncle, and had designed for La Scala and Covent Garden. But he was ruined by the drink – he would check into a clinic and have himself put to sleep for three days solid in order to give his liver a holiday. His other vice was uniformed policemen. He tended to importune them while they were on duty. He also suffered from absent-mindedness. Having inherited a house in Scotland, he forgot he was having one of the bedroom floors replaced, walked in and fell through it to the floor below, breaking his nose, of which he was very proud, and precipitating another period of neurotic seclusion.

James's moods were utterly unpredictable. He would either be overjoyed to see one or simply aghast. So I always waited for invitations to his flat. A huge golden buddha flanked by candles stared at you in the hall. Going through to the candlelit drawing-room you were astonished to discover that the walls were hidden by enormous banks of artificial flowers, hillsides of them. James changed them four times a year to correspond with the seasons. But the hours of the day he did not follow. The windows and heavy silk curtains were never opened. James lived in an eternal evening of lavender light. When he lit all the candles in the middle of the day it was stifling in there. About three times a year (and once as we drove away from Connie Mount's funeral) he would clap his little plump hands together and say, 'Isn't it time I bought you a frock?', and he'd go off to Thea Porter or Yuki or Bill Gibb to choose one. If exceptionally lucky I'd be given something from his collection of pre-war theatre and evening clothes. One mouth-watering jacket of cream ostrich feathers I idiotically gave to Liza Minnelli in Tramp discothèque in a fit of drunken generosity.

James Bailey's oils, especially his pictures of Venice, were magnificent, I thought: haunted compositions in greys, purples, greens, blues, filled with a mysterious sadness and behind that something more threatening. They were the perfect expression of his own unhappiness and refinement. And he was the unhappiest of men. One Christmas Eve he invited me for a drink and when I arrived he'd gashed his throat. The wound had opened up like a flower. He was drunk, gurgling inanities while the blood bubbled from his neck. Fortunately I was with two strong men who carried him to a car. He said he had fallen. I stayed behind to tidy up and thought, 'Fallen? There's nowhere he could fall and hurt himself like that.' The only place I found blood was in the bathroom and on a blade.

When we went to the opera, he would hire a limousine and we'd both dress up. One evening in 1965 the car called at my flat to take us to Verdi's *Don Carlos*. We were about to go down when the phone rang. 'Mrs Corbett? This is the Fazakerly Hospital calling. Your father is here. He's dying.'

'Thank you for letting me know.' I said nothing whatsoever to James, the opera went ahead as planned (a macabre and depressing show about the Inquisition – there is an *auto de fe* in it), but the next morning I caught the train to Liverpool. I hadn't seen Father since 1961. It was in the same hospital and he had said, 'I always knew, darling. I'm proud of you.'

At the hospital my sister Tess said, 'You won't recognise him. He certainly won't recognise you.'

Father had shrunk to nothing but I took him by the hand and said, 'Hullo, Dad.' He gave me the most wonderful smile. He recognised me. Three days later he died. Tuberculosis.

I phoned Mother who said there was an insurance policy to cover the funeral expenses. With help from the hospital, I managed the arrangements. Tess was furious that I'd called Mother. She hated her and they hadn't spoken for ages. Now Tess said that after the burial she wouldn't speak to me either. And she didn't for twelve years! Apart from me, the mourners were Aunty Frances (his sister-in-law) and Aunty May (his sister) – she was sweet, I liked her. The boys could not be found.

At the funeral parlour I said, 'Make it the cheapest coffin you've got.' I've never been sentimental about death, just like Father.

The man came through and said, 'Does anyone want to see him?' Aunty Frances jumped up and said, 'Yes, I'd love to.' But I put my foot down. 'None of that nonsense – let's get this thing done.'

Between Fazakerly Hospital and the Catholic cemetery there's a hump-back bridge. As the funeral car approached this bridge Aunty May said, 'Do you know what happened there?'

'On that bridge?'

'Yes, that's where your grandfather went. In the olden days hearses were pulled by horses with black plumes on their heads. It used to take hours and hours to cross Liverpool by hearse so there would be stops at pubs along the way. Father – your grandfather – was burying your uncle, your father's brother who died young. Father had a drink at all the stops. And in those days, did they drink! Like open sewers they were. By the time they reached the graveside your grandfather was fully drunk. As they came out of the cemetery, he decided to climb up on to the pillion to join the coachman. Going over the hump-bridge the hearse jolted. It threw him off the top. He landed bang on his head. And that was that. That's how your grandfather died, burying his son.'

To Father's funeral I wore a dazzling canary-yellow suit. The Catholic service had recently been changed from Latin to the vernacular and the use of English revealed the priest's boredom with funerals. Soon after, Mother married Bernie.

Through a friend of Robin Maugham's I met a young man called Edward Madok. He was slim, extremely good-looking and wasting his time at Besançon University. Back in London I forgot about him completely and went to stay with an acquaintance in Cornwall Gardens.

There were many dinner parties there. Eric and Blanche Glass, Robin's agents and later mine, came, the most devoted couple in London. And Barbara Back, the only woman Somerset Maugham ever respected and his *confidante*. Her husband, Ivor Back, had been a celebrated surgeon with a house in Regent's Park where Barbara would entertain the rich and fashionable and the following day pass all the latest gossip on by letter to the Villa Mauresque. She was famous for having introduced the Charleston to England and taught the upper classes to dance it. But when Ivor died, there was no money to speak of and she was obliged to take up journalism.

Barbara was invited to a dinner with Gerald Hamilton and they loathed each other on sight. But Gerald fascinated me. His opening remark was, 'You know I'm Mr Norris from the Isherwood books, don't you?' I did. He had a hideous, heavy face with mottled skin which hung in drapes as if drained of a lifetime's excess, a lower lip drooping down towards his chin like a giblet, bloodshot bloodhound eyes, and bristling eyebrows which he trained upwards in order to lift a visage upon which gravity exerted too devastating an influence.

Like Cecilia he had been born in Shanghai, the son of a British merchant, and wherever the raffish were to be found so was he – Berlin before the war, Tangier after it, the King's Road in the 1960s, conning his way from one extravaganza to another. He threw names around like confetti. 'My *darling* friend, Nicholas of Romania, he never *touches* water – he brushes his teeth with a light hock.' Gerald exuded criminality, vice, corruption in high places, but this, like his snobbery, was so unbridled, so theatrical, that one never felt threatened by it, only enthralled. He seemed to be the repository of secret knowledge, like a jovial version of Aleister Crowley. But fact and fiction cross-fertilised so riotously in his imagination that one could be sure of nothing. I know at one time he carried two cyanide capsules under his wig in the event of finding himself in an impossibly tight corner. And during the Second World War he was arrested attempting to escape across the Irish Sea to Dublin disguised as a nun.

Winston Churchill interned Gerald twice for his supposedly pro-German sympathies. There was a feud between them. When Graham Sutherland was commissioned by the House of Commons to paint an official portrait of Churchill, Sir Winston could give the artist only a few sittings. Therefore Sutherland approached Hamilton to model the body because their measurements were similar. This was one of the reasons why Churchill so took against the picture. Another, said Gerald, was that Sutherland had caught the tragic emptiness of Churchill's eyes. (I like Churchill's verdict on the portrait to Somerset Maugham: 'I look as if I were having a difficult stool.') A year after the Sutherland sittings, Hamilton again modelled Churchill, this time for Oscar Nemon's enormous bronze. These modellings he called his 'revenge'.

I used to call on Gerald for conversation in his small, woebegone flat above the Good Earth Chinese Restaurant in the King's Road, where a willowy Oriental youth, who was devoted to him, supplied his various wants. 'You naughty baggage,' he'd say to me, 'I see you've been in the papers again. I can't offer you much, the whisky's gone I'm afraid.' From the way they lived one gathered he had no money at all.

Flushed out of Besançon, Edward Madok turned up penniless at the door. Neither of us had our own base in London so I suggested we share a place as brother and sister. We found an icebound slum room in Elm Park Gardens where we slept together for warmth because it was winter and the gas meter gobbled all we had. At one point there was so little cash we ate nothing but boiled potatoes for three weeks. I couldn't find work and refused to go on social security. We lived off my ring most of the time. Each morning I awoke with a numb head. I went to the doctor but it turned out to be a leaking gas pipe on my side of the bed.

It was such a relief when Juanita Kensington, a call-girl, said, 'Look, I'm away a lot. You can use my place at weekends.' Her flat was in a well-known block in Chelsea on the then notorious eighth floor. There were peculiar calls from her clients. I'd pick up the phone and say hullo and off they'd go into fantasy-land. Edward would put his head on my shoulder and listen in. He became so excited by one of the calls that he took me there and then on the floor. Which is how we became lovers.

Back in Elm Park Gardens, the linoleum, the greasy wallpaper, that bloody gas-meter – its appetite was so voracious that to take a bath involved rearranging the week's budget. 'If I take a bath, Edward, it means we can't go out until Thursday, but that's all right because Thursday is Margot's party where we can fill up on oysters and lobster claws, and there's Ziggy's thrash on Friday – remember, you've got to smuggle a chicken out of that one for Sunday lunch, and Janie tells me Ziggy keeps his champagne in the fish-pond if you want to make a mental note.' So I ran my bath. But when I went to take it, I saw floating on the green surface of the water a dead bumblebee. In the middle of winter. It horrified me. I don't know why but it seemed the most appalling thing. It was a piece of great fortune that Amanda Lear's departure for work on the Continent coincided with this traumatic event. She let her flat to us. This was in the same block of flats in Chelsea but on a lower, more genteel floor. It was tiny but it was warm and inviting, with a draped bedstead and endless hot water.

Harvey Sambrook, a friend from the Chelsea Potter, asked me to help out at the Gasworks, a penny-bun-cum-junk-shop at the wrong end of the King's Road. At night red-felt sheets were thrown across the stock and it turned into a cheap restaurant. My wages were thirty shillings a night plus tips. But since I served the customers in a black-crêpe evening dress and two ropes of pearls I never saw a tip.

Joan Shivarg did the cooking, Harvey waited upstairs, I did downstairs, and between us we'd fend off Joan's would-be lover who tended to burst in and hit her halfway through the evening. Joan was born a Wyndham and had she been born a boy she would have inherited Petworth House in Sussex. As it was, the house went to the National Trust and she went to the Gasworks. This restaurant was one of those improvised successes which flourished in the 1960s. When Harvey left, Edward came in to help and loathed every minute of it. He got a kick out of picking old salad out of the dustbin, wiping it with a dishcloth, and serving it to the customers. Then Joan left and the place began to fall apart.

By now it was Easter 1967 and I said to Edward, 'If I hock my engagement ring again, we'll be able to live in Ibiza until the autumn – that'll take care of summer at least.'

We went along to Sutton's in Victoria where all the dowagers take their tiaras when they've been betting too much on the horses. I had sworn to myself I'd never pawn the ring again and when I came out I said to him, 'I'm so upset, I'm going to be sick.'

'Quick, quick!' He steered me towards a litter bin halfway up a lamp-post. I shoved my head in, but there was no bottom to the bin and I was sick all over my shoes. I felt dreadful. Poverty gets to you in the end, especially when you've come to expect more.

It was the Summer of Love and the island was very druggy, so I don't remember very much about it. On our return Edward began studying law, and we calculated that if a school friend of his from Downside, Micky Mullen, joined us, then Robin Maugham's flat in Charing Cross Road would be cheaper to rent than Amanda's. Micky followed Edward everywhere.

I met Tony Singleton in the Strand, who said, 'What are you up to?'

'Nothing! It's abysmal. I'm just drifting with the tide. I need a job.'

'Come along and see my boss.' Tony's boss was Geoffrey Plumley. He ran a sales consultancy and employed out-of-work actors, models and such fluff. My job was map-reading, keeping track of salesmen for Cadbury's, the chocolate manufacturers, and Gallaher's, the tobacco company. A number had to be stuck on to a card to correspond with a number on a map. The office was above a porn shop near Charing Cross Station. With the starlets tripping in and out, the patrons of the shop presumed there was a brothel upstairs and were always making uninvited entrances. The space was cramped and its decorative order bad. I had to wear a headscarf because when the people overhead walked about, flakes of plaster snowed down from the ceiling. Whenever Geoffrey had a new client he'd never invite them up to the office but say, 'Right, I think the best thing is if we meet at the pub opposite for a friendly drink.'

'How shall I recognise you?'

'I've got two big dents in my forehead.' This was because he'd been a forceps baby.

At Shaldon Mansions I was the housewife with two men to cook for. Like me, Edward was a Northerner and loved meat pies and thick peasant soups made from bags of beans. There was often great silence and contentment between us. Of course we went to parties but not if we couldn't afford a taxi, which was quite often. It's no fun going to parties on a bus. At first Edward loved the fact that I was a celebrity, that we attracted all the attention. Robin Maugham said to him, 'Going out with April is worse than going out with Marlene Dietrich.' But Edward came to hate it when we were introduced as 'April Ashley and her boyfriend'.

Edward's parents strongly disapproved of our living together. His father was a self-made man from Preston in Lancashire. One night I was going to a hippy party given by the Shivargs – clothes in London were then at their barmiest – and wearing the crazy pink get-up which Roger Dawson-Denver had made from his curtains, plus bangles, beads, necklaces. I was in a pair of Richard Smith (of the Chelsea Cobbler)'s outrageous Roman sandals with straps and chains all the way up the legs (when he brought out a new line he would sometimes give me a pair by way of advertisement). Edward said, 'My parents are calling this evening. They're going to see *The Canterbury Tales*.'

'What time are they coming? Because I don't want them to see me in all this.'

I left before they were due. But at Cambridge Circus I realised I'd left my purse behind and would have to go back. There they were, he standing in tweeds, she sitting in pearls.

''Ow d'ye do,' said the father in a broad Lancashire accent.

'Very well, thank you. I should explain, I'm not always dressed like this. I'm off to a funny party, I mean . . .'

Edward didn't bat an eyelid. It was one of the nicest things about him. He giggled. Apparently, his father's only remark was to another member of the family: 'I've met April. She 'ad chains on 'er legs.'

At the invitation of Klaus, I did Bavaria. I'd longed to visit Munich ever since the onset of my Ludwig II period. Christopher Hunter, who was always such an angel when times were bad, said he'd treat me to a holiday. I decided to do Munich properly. It was winter – that was apt. I wanted to go by train, and arrive in the early hours of the morning. It was snowing. I stepped off the train in a big red-fox hat and a black velvet coat sweeping the floor. I'd only managed to get one foot on the platform when Klaus said, 'Don't move an inch. You are Anna Karenina. I want to remember you like this. *Immer.*'

'But Klaus, the train is about to disappear with my luggage.'

We drove to his parents' small apartment. His father had been a Nazi and Klaus introduced me as '*die Herzogin Ashley aus Groß-britannien*'. The father bowed slowly and deeply, righted himself and clicked his heels. Then he refused to sit down. The mother was the kindest Hausfrau you could imagine, with apple cheeks and a horror of not doing the right thing by her English guest. 'It's the war,' I thought. She kept appearing with schnapps and coffee and napkins. Every time I thanked her for one thing she would dash off and bring me another. While Papa clicked away in the shadows, Mutti kept saying, 'Vood you like . . .' After three days of it I said to Klaus, 'Are they always like this? I haven't relaxed for a second.'

'They think you're an English duchess.'

'What do you mean?'

'*Herzogin* is duchess.'

'Oh, Klaus, no. Disabuse them at once. I thought it was something idiomatic like Mrs.'

'It'll do them good to have an English title in the house. Papa's such a silly old Fascist, he'll have the puppies.' He teased his parents mercilessly. 'Look at the walls! No pictures, no books, no civilisation, no taste, no class! Typical Nazis!' At the same time they were very dear to him. The three of them had shared frightful experiences at the end of the war.

Munich was freezing. We kept going on Johnny Walker Red Label day and night. I wanted to go to Herrenchiemsee, the Wittelsbach palace modelled on Versailles. We didn't get there. Every time we approached the station Klaus would develop shaking fits of nerves. I'd noticed this on the Ibiza ferry, too: a terror of being transported with strangers on something he couldn't get off, presumably a throwback to his childhood. But we visited the Nymphenburg Palace by car so that I could view Jane Digby's portrait in the Galerie des Beautés. Ludwig II was born here. His sleighs like gilded plants were on show. So was his favourite horse – stuffed. In the grounds is the Amalienburg, whose principal chamber in the Wittelsbach colours (blue and silver) Chips Channon copied for his dining-room in Belgrave Square (I heard something interesting about Channon the other day – he used to fix his cocktails with benzedrine to make sure his guests shone).

I went half-a-dozen times to Bavaria, always in winter, and never did see Linderhof, Herrenchiemsee, Neuschwanstein. Klaus's nervous attacks conspired against it. I did meet the last Wittelsbach princess to be born at Nymphenburg, the Baroness von Hönning-O'Carroll. We spent the weekend with her and the Baron at Schloss Sünching and she gave me nothing but long stony looks, although he was a dear. While we were there some destitute Obolenskys arrived from Czechoslovakia, fleeing the Russian invasion. They had left everything behind and were sitting quietly in a *salon* patching old clothes. As usual when weekending with the nobility, I was fully rigged, in a rhinestone mini-dress with encrusted sling-backs and a ton of rocks around my neck. 'Baron, I can't go in there dressed like this. I mean, look at them. They look as if they've been attacked by dogs. It's too cruel.'

'April, you will be their very first sight of the modern West. They are on a voyage of discovery, they have many things to learn.'

'In that case, let's go in. I'm all for education.'

It was Shrovetide, the time of *Fasching*, and after tea we descended to the fair in Sünching. The village boys trailed us in their *Lederhosen* (always rather silly outside Germany, but madly sexy *in situ*), munching sausages and winking their blue eyes. They kept rolling on the ground in order to glimpse up my skirt. Not that they need have bothered. Skirts were so short then, they were little more than gestures. The Baron was shown much deference but said to me, 'Being a baron in Germany is finished. The castle's falling down, I don't know what my son will do.' I couldn't help feeling this was a pose. He owned a brewery among other things.

Viva and I were now very close. While staying in Florence she had slipped and broken her collar bone and had spent the rest of her holiday in stiff wadding from the waist to the neck. The moment I saw her I said, 'Viva, I don't care what the doctor says, I'm cutting you out of this rancid filth. We can get a doctor in the morning.' She stank like an Airedale, poor thing. I dug in with a big pair of scissors, eased it off, washed and powdered her with talc. As always Viva was embarrassed by her 'roly-polys' but the colour flooded back into her face. And then I sewed her into a sling. The doctor said I had done a good job because Viva's back was a mass of festering mosquito bites where the insects had crept in and been trapped. I had a touch of my recurrent bronchitis and Viva said, 'What we both need is a holiday. I'll treat you.'

For some reason we decided on Malta. On the plane a middle-class English couple started chatting to us. They were going out there to retire. The woman said to me, 'I'm sure I know your face. Do you mind my asking your name?'

'Ada Brown. I used to be quite a well-known model.'

The plane broke down in Rome and we had to spend the night at a hotel in Parioli. I wasn't at all sure I shouldn't be arrested on Italian soil. Going through passport control Viva was even jumpier than I was. She kept hanging back.

'What the hell are you doing, Viva?'

'I'm getting ready to grease his palm.'

'What with?'

'I've got a 1,000-lire note.'

'That's about ten bob. It won't get us anywhere. Now pull yourself together and stop attracting attention.'

At the Parioli Hotel the couple appeared again. 'Can we join you for dinner?' How could one say no? And as expected the woman didn't stop playing with her pearls (artificial) all through the meal. 'I know I'm going on a bit. But it's nagging me dreadfully. I can't help feeling that I know you. In fact it's driving me mad.'

'Don't let it do that. You've probably seen me on a lot of hoardings.'

Viva was twitching, playing with *her* pearls (plastic poppers), dying to tell. 'You dare, Viva,' I muttered, 'you know how I like to go unremarked when abroad.'

At long last we arrived in Malta. The hotel put us in an annexe, far from the main building. You gained it by climbing over the swimming pool on a bridge with only one railing. Viva, though moderate in all her habits (except sex, and that only late in life), was no stranger to the bottle and it was likely she'd fall in at some point.

The only other room was up three flights of stairs. We tried it but after the first flight Viva was already expectorating.

'Is this really the best you can do?' I asked the manager.

'I'm afraid it is.'

'Then would you be so good as to call us a taxi.'

'Why?'

'Because we can't stay here. And will you fetch our bags while you're about it.'

'But you've already booked in.'

'Then you'll have to unbook us. Mrs King is an old lady. She can't climb skyscrapers last thing at night.' Viva looked daggers at me. She detested being described as an old lady.

She tugged my elbow. 'What are you up to now, April?'

'Don't interrupt, Viva.' We'd been bickering since Rome. 'When it comes to hotels, I know what I'm doing.'

We bundled into the taxi and I said, 'To the Hilton, please.'

'To the Hilton!' Viva exclaimed. 'The Hilton, good Lord! It's me who's footing the bill! I can't afford the Hilton.'

'Yes you can. Five days at the Hilton will do us both far more good than a fortnight in that pit!'

Our first morning at the Hilton we went down to the Coffee Shop for breakfast. It was full except for one table which we grabbed. And who followed us in, with nowhere to sit except at our table – the retired, middle-class couple. During my Dover Sole the woman started up. 'I hate to be a bore but I can't get over the feeling that I know you.'

Viva said out loud, 'Can I tell them? I want to.'

'You say one word, madam, and you'll regret it. I told you in Rome, now I'm telling you in Malta – shut up.'

By now the couple's tongues were lolling out. 'Oh, do tell us, do!' The woman's pearls were all twisted up in her knuckles.

'I'm sorry. I'm on a private holiday with my' – I sniffed in the direction of Viva who was squaring up to a plate of bacon and eggs – 'friend, Mrs King here. Who keeps opening her big mouth.'

Then Viva looked up with the devil in her eye. 'She's the famous sex-change!'

Wicked creature! The couple died of embarrassment, simply *died.* The woman was choking herself, then the pearls snapped and shot all over the Coffee Shop. I stormed out. I'd checked in as the Hon. Mrs Corbett, as was my wont – it got one marginally better treatment. Now it was round the hotel in ten seconds.

Twenty-four hours later Viva and I made it up with tears and champagne in the discothèque and finally got round to 'doing' Malta. We met the Plugges, visited Rex Warren and Eric Crabtree, who have the only house on the island with a lift in it, saw the house where my friend Dippy de Piro was raised, and as a climax went to view Caravaggio's 'The Decapitation of St John the Baptist' in the cathedral and were immediately asked to leave. A men-only Mass was in progress. But the wait was worth it. A dark, dramatic picture. The flesh was breathing. Such intensity from that most hot-tempered of artists (who is said to have died from a fever brought on by an attack of rage).

Edward and I had decided to find a flat just for ourselves. Joan Foa was letting the top floor of her house in Clarendon Road, in Holland Park. But just before moving there Edward said, 'Darling, will you come for a walk?' I put down my maps and we ambled towards St Martin's Lane.

'I've got something awful to tell you,' he said.

'Awful for you or for me?'

'Awful for you, I think. What I want to say is – I'm not going to make love to you any more.'

'Why not?' A bus boomed by and wet my skirt.

'Because that part's over. I'm not going to pretend.'

If we had been in an American soap opera I should have said, 'Can't we talk about it?' Talk. Air. When Edward had made up his mind he was immovable. We were walking arm-in-arm past the Duke of York's Theatre. John Osborne's *Time Present* was on, starring Jill Bennett, and the audience was spilling out with excited faces.

'Can we go back now?' I said.

We walked back in tumultuous silence. Later I said, 'What do you want to do about Joan's flat?'

'That's O.K. I don't want to stop living with you.'

'Do you think I'm made of lead? I couldn't live with you like that.' This had been a terrible shock because by now something very deep had grown between us.

As I prepared to move out he became more unsettled, saying he would never get through Law School without me, that he would probably kill himself.

'It's all very well for you to tell me coldly in the middle of the street that you don't want to make love to me any more but that you'd like me to stick around to play nanny – what can you think of me, Edward? I'm not going because I decided it but because you did.'

'You don't care what becomes of me? Whether I try to kill myself?' He started to develop an asthmatic attack which he sometimes did when we argued.

'Yes, I do care.' How I cared! 'But it's a risk we'll have to take.'

Finishing with Edward had one magical consequence. I discovered Oxford. A schoolfriend of Edward's, Percy Curran, had invited me many times but Edward would never let me go. I think he realised too keenly that Besançon had been a mistake. Glancing back over the last few pages it seems that a certain gloom had seeped into my existence. Oxford dispelled it.

Percy asked me to be the Guest of Honour at a dinner he and Duncan Fallowell were giving at Duncan's college, Magdalen. My first inkling of the university spirit was walking from the railway station with Michael de Piro. He was sobbing into a spotted Turnbull & Asser neckscarf. 'You'll never understand,' he wailed, 'this is the first time I've been back since I left.'

After changing at the Randolph Hotel we continued along higgledy-piggledy streets, under gothic towers, down classical colonnades – to live amid such architecture as a teenager must surely give you delusions of grandeur for life – ancient gardens glimpsed through arches, the smell of an autumn bonfire, barking from the Deer Park, a row of fierce gargoyles against the moon, up steps, along a stone corridor, more steps (as Queen Mary said, 'I never mind steps when I'm interested') and into the Oscar Wilde Room. A dozen young men rose languorously to their feet. Roger Brockway, Benjy Buchan, Fluffy Dent-Godalming, Lord Charles Hay, Dicky Wallace, Count Adam Zamoyski, I forget who else. They were already tipsy in black silk, bottle-green velvet, frothing with lace, flashes of gold and diamonds at cuffs and necks in the wood-panelled candlelight. We ate game and afterwards some of them smoked drugs with their liqueurs. I couldn't believe teenagers could be so sophisticated. It was unnatural. And in fact as the inebriants took hold, the drawling mannerisms faded; youth, beauty, privilege started beating up the room. The butler, Bill, asked if he might sway quietly against the wall and watch. I shouted 'Ana de Pombo!', leapt on to the table, and danced a flamenco. Bill made a lunge for the silver candlesticks but I told him to leave them exactly where they were. Swirling in and out of flames is an important part of the effect.

My next impression of undergraduate life was when I went to Duncan's rooms to freshen up. We climbed a wooden staircase whose steps had been worn into curves. In his sitting-room I was taken aback by a giant pyramid of empty Gordon's Gin bottles built between the desk and the ceiling.

'It's Pop Art,' he said.

'Don't you do any work?'

'Yes, I'm writing a percussion ballet called *The Pink Swastika*. Do you like the Velvet Underground?'

I recall hectic dancing somewhere, smoked salmon and Krug in the early hours, and when at last I got back to the Randolph the young Count Zamoyski was lying on his back outside my bedroom door holding a large sunflower. My heart was full of Edward but I realised life must go on. I unlocked the door and we went in.

So on a succession of Friday nights I would arrive from a dirty office in a dirty train, change at the Randolph or one of the colleges, and at sunset join an enchanted world of viscounts, maharajahs and drug fiends crossing green lawns in silver boots, drawn by the hiss of champagne.

But the traffic between Oxford and London moved, like the telegrams, in both directions. I like to think that in return I managed to introduce them to some of the glamour of London and the wider world. They swelled Viva's parties and lowered still further the average age there (as did girls like Arabella Churchill, June's daughter, or Katie Pakenham, killed tragically in a car crash). At the time I didn't realise how important the support of the young people was to become.

10 Divorce

In 1965 I decided to try to enforce my claim on the Villa Antoinette. As I stated in my letter to him, I did not expect money *per se* from Arthur. But I was very broke and had understood that the house had been given to me; although I had no deeds in my possession I had also been led to believe that these existed in my name among the papers in Arthur's safe.

My manager's solicitor had been a small, slight, bespectacled man called Terry Walton. I had liked Terry from the beginning and asked him to handle my affairs. He had worked his way up the hard way, had plenty of drive, was open and unaffected, and I felt I could tell him anything. As events turned out his exertions on my behalf were extraordinary.

Terry wrote to Arthur in Spain but elicited no response. Difficulties arose over serving the necessary proceedings on Arthur while he resided out of the jurisdiction of an English court. After months of stonewalling, we decided in February 1966 to flush him out by initiating proceedings for maintenance as a substitute for a direct claim on the villa. In this the question of jurisdiction would not arise because of the assets held by Arthur in England.

Arthur went down with hepatitis and there were further delays, but as Terry and I pursued the claim Arthur was eventually advised that the best way for him to resolve the dispute was to seek an annulment. Therefore in May 1967 he filed a petition praying for a declaration that the marriage was 'null and void and of no effect because the respondent [i.e. me] at the time of the ceremony was a person of the male sex; or in the alternative for a decree of nullity on the ground that the marriage was never consummated owing to the incapacity or wilful refusal of the respondent to consummate it.'

I countered by seeking 'a decree of nullity on the ground of either the petitioner's [i.e. Arthur's] incapacity or his wilful refusal to consummate the marriage.' These and subsequent quotations are taken from the Law Report, except where credited otherwise.

At this time, before the reform of the divorce laws in 1973, all divorce proceedings demanded that guilt be affixed to one or other of the parties. A quiet dissolution was not possible. But our case, even if it had come to issue after 1973, could have taken a no less sensational course because of its contentious nature.

So Further and Better Particulars began to fly.

Arthur's contention was that since marriage is a biological relationship between a man and a woman and one's biological sex is fixed at birth at the latest, I could not be regarded as a woman for the purposes of marriage. My contention was that since the scientific definition of sex is not clear-cut in all cases and since marriage is also a legal and social relationship between a man and a woman, I should be regarded as a woman for the purposes of marriage because, as a result of my operation, I could function in no other way. That the judge confined deliberation to my original biological classification, disregarding the psychological factor and the functional developments to which it gave rise, was the central weakness of the case and the reason for its unsatisfactory outcome.

Alimony Pending Suit was granted to me at £6 per week because Arthur was working as a barman in Marbella at an estimated £18 per week (however, if his assets had been taken into account he would have been counted still a rich man, despite having been cut off from his inheritance).

Intimate details of my social and biological life would have to be brought before the court and therefore I was subjected to a series of physical and psychological examinations, firstly by the medical inspectors to the court, then by Professor Hayhoe, a chromosome specialist at Cambridge (he didn't see me – only my blood), then by the doctors for my defence. They were Dr C. N. Armstrong, consultant physician at the Royal Victoria Infirmary, Newcastle upon Tyne; Professor Ivor Mills, Professor of Medicine at Cambridge University; and Professor Martin Roth, Professor of Psychiatry in the University of Newcastle upon Tyne. Dr Armstrong reassured me enormously. Professor Roth was very hard on me but also reassuring in the end. Then to Addenbrooke's Hospital in Cambridge for a full physical examination. I almost ran out.

'Miss Ashley,' said Professor Mills, 'do you realise I'm on your side?'

'Then why all these dreadful questions about my body before the operation?'

'Because we have to be able to explain you and your body in court. Now lie down. I'll leave you and come back in about ten minutes. Think about it. I'm on your side but I have to know everything.'

I grew to like him very much. He was down-to-earth but not unkind. Later he attended the court every day, although he wasn't obliged to. But after these examinations I was in a frightful state. I'd just finished with Edward. There were so many consultations that I lost my grip on the map-reading at Plumley's and had to give it up. Everything seemed unreal. All attempts to communicate with Dr Burou failed. He answered none of the letters, not even those from august professors who signed themselves with all their qualifications.

A little way into the trial the court went into recess and I was examined all over again by the three doctors on Arthur's side. They were Professor John Dewhurst, Professor of Obstetrics and Gynaecology at Queen Charlotte's Hospital; Professor Dent, Professor of Human Metabolism at the University College Hospital; and Dr John Randell, consultant psychiatrist at Charing Cross Hospital. Dewhurst performed the three-finger test which is the standard method of determining whether the vagina can accommodate a normal-sized penis. I passed that one. The net effect of all these medical examinations was to bring me face to face with my almost forgotten pre-operative self and this was a most painful experience.

Terry asked me to visit Mother to see if she would be of any help to us in explaining to the court how odd a child I was. She and Bernie were now running a corner grocery shop at Denton on the outskirts of Manchester. They had achieved their ambition of moving into a bungalow. I rang her at the shop.

'Mother, I must come to see you.'

'Why?'

'It's complicated. I'm getting divorced from Arthur.'

'You always were silly. He's a lovely man.'

A few days later I rang the ding-dong doorbell in Frederick Street.

'Hullo,' she said. 'When are you leaving?'

'Tomorrow morning.'

'Are you hungry?'

'Not particularly. I've brought some wine.'

'I'm not mad about wine. Don't stand there, come in. I've cooked a pan of Scouse.'

The wine was rosé – I knew she liked the colour. Bernie joined us for the stew. He was quieter and floppier than ever and went to bed soon after we had finished eating.

'You won't get Bernie's name in the papers, will you?'

'Mother, they're not *interested* in Bernie.'

'Oh, that's good. Do you like the bungalow?'

'Yes, it's very nice.'

'It's lovely.'

We chatted and opened the second bottle of rosé. She relaxed more and more but I didn't. I tried to explain to her about the divorce, its implications, but she couldn't take it in and preferred to enlighten me about Theresa's awfulness, how Theresa wouldn't speak to her, how Marjorie came to see her only when she wanted something, and how the boys were much better only she didn't see much of them either. I ended up having a polite battle with a mother I didn't know and couldn't reach. But the more we talked the more I realised that she was much fonder of Arthur than she was of me. And that she was a scatterbrain and would be anybody's under cross-examination. I'd gone up to see if she could testify on my behalf, and came away terrified in case she did. Terry visited her himself and said she could be useful to us, but I said I didn't want her to be called if it were avoidable.

My leading counsel was J. P. Comyn Q.C., assisted by Leonard Lewis. They both had their work cut out in seeking to grasp abstruse and mostly hypothetical medical principles in a field where even the experts did not agree. Mr Comyn was one of the most persuasive and feared advocates at the Common Law Bar and was extremely fashionable. But I think he underestimated the complexity of the argument which would have to be mounted in my defence and the force with which it would have to be prosecuted if we were to succeed. He held too much faith in putting me in the witness box and letting appearances speak for themselves. By contrast Arthur was represented by Joseph Jackson Q.C., a thoroughly rude and unpleasant man and, probably for this reason, one of the best divorce lawyers in the kingdom.

The complexity arose because, as the judge wrote:

> Since marriage is essentially a relationship between man and woman, the validity of the marriage in this case depends, in my judgement, on whether the respondent is or is not a woman. I think with respect, that this is a more precise way of formulating the question than that adopted in paragraph 2 of the petition, in which it is alleged that the respondent is a male. The greater, of course, includes the less, but the distinction may not be without importance, at any rate in some cases. The question then becomes what is meant by the word 'woman' in the context of marriage, for I am not concerned to determine the 'legal sex' of the respondent at large . . . It appears to be the first occasion on which a court in England has been called on to decide the sex of an individual, and, consequently, there is no authority which is directly in point.

Joan Foa was superb. I must say it is amazing how people do rally round and, however much it may be due to their love of vicarious excitement, it is essential not to be alone during such ordeals. Joan said, 'If only we could get Roger Ormrod to be judge. I know him. He'd surely understand.' When the letter arrived saying that the case was indeed to be heard before Ormrod we hugged each other and danced round the kitchen. 'I know it's going to be all right now,' she said. Justice of course does not turn on such blatant considerations, but because it is so cold and impersonal a force, out of fear one catches at anything which will give it some human aspect. Ormrod had been a doctor before the war and I believe this was one of the reasons he was chosen.

The night before the trial opened I watched some television with Joan and her husband Giorgio, went up to my room and thought about what to wear. This in itself was a devilish decision. Too severe and I would be called butch. Too feminine and I would be accused of trying too hard. I shelved the problem and collected a Vindaloo curry from the Indian take-away opposite. This is a very hot curry which, after our first experience of it, we christened the Windy Loo. When eaten with a Mandrax it either shot you skywards in a fireball or knocked you out dead, depending on whether or not you were supine at the time. I took the liberty of two Mandrax but it was no good. There was too much adrenalin in me for sleep.

11 November 1969. I rose and had a cup of coffee. I dressed, deciding on a black-velvet maxi-coat and the fox hat I'd worn for the snows of Bavaria, and was ready when the car came to take me to the Law Courts in the Strand.

The car (which had been laid on by some people who were setting me up in a restaurant) dropped me at the back entrance to avoid the press. The reporters saw what was happening and swarmed across the courtyard. I was ushered across the famous Great Hall, a Victorian Gothic masterpiece designed to reduce to the size of a mouse anyone who sets foot in it. Terry and Mr Comyn were outside No. 2 Court.

Arthur was there with his lot. He was in a dark suit and tie and looked much older than I had expected. 'How silly,' I thought, 'that I can't go over and greet him.' More than all the probing questions and the probing fingers, more than the endless consultations, this simple fact made me realise that I was now in the grip of something inhuman. I had surrendered my soul to the lawyers and would have to watch while they not very skilfully kicked it about among themselves.

Abnormalities of sexual identity are divided into two broad categories, the psychological and the physical. Of the psychological two main abnormalities are recognised – the transvestite and the transsexual, although transsexualism may possibly have some physical origin too. A transvestite is someone with a strong desire to wear the clothes of the opposite sex. This is usually intermittent and not accompanied by the corresponding desire to live and pass as a member of the opposite sex. Transvestite males are frequently heterosexual. The transsexual on the other hand desires to become to the fullest possible extent a member of the opposite sex. Transvestism and transsexualism are both far more common among males than among females.

While disagreeing strongly on where the emphasis should lie, the medical witnesses on both sides agreed that there are four fundamental criteria for assessing the sexual identity of an individual. These are:

Chromosomal sex. Normally a person has twenty-three pairs of chromosomes in his ordinary body cells. All ova carry the X. There are two varieties of spermatozoa, one X, the other Y. Fusion of the ovum with an X spermatozoon produces an embryo of XX chromosomes and eventually a normal female. Fusion of the ovum with a Y spermatozoon produces an XY embryo and eventually a normal male.

Gonadal sex. This refers to the presence of either testes or ovaries, and the hormonal ratios which they regulate.

External body form or genital sex. The presence of a penis and scrotum or a vagina, plus secondary sexual characteristics.

Psychological sex. The standard tool here is the Terman-Miles Test, an extensive questionnaire which the patient is asked to complete.

In the great majority of individuals there is no problem. All four will be congruent. But naturally there are exceptions. There can be errors at the stage of chromosomal fusion resulting, for example, in an XXY chromosome pattern or an XO (i.e. single X). The XXY is Klinefelter's syndrome, an undermasculinised male with atrophied testes and some breast enlargement. At puberty the secondary sexual characteristics fail to develop in the proper way. The XO is Turner's syndrome. An X goes missing, producing an individual with the external appearance of a female but no ovaries and again failure of the normal changes at puberty.

The development of a normal male or female is not governed exclusively by the chromosomes. The correct chemical balance in the embryo is also critical. For example, the adrenogenital syndrome. Here the chromosomes are XX but the external genitalia may appear to be male. What has happened is that abnormal enlargement of the clitoris produces the appearance of a penis and fusion of the labia the appearance of a scrotum. But there are no testicles and further examination reveals the deception. In most cases hormone treatment and surgical intervention enables the woman to live as a normal fertile female. Alternatively a subject has XY chromosomes and testes but the external genital appearance of a woman, with well-formed breasts (testicular feminisation syndrome) due to the tissues being insensitive to male hormones. Testes are usually found in the abdomen. Surgical resolution of this problem is far more difficult, since it is always easier to remove an excess than it is to supply a want (it is not yet possible to build a convincing penis; for the same reason transsexual surgery on males is more feasible than that on females).

All the doctors agreed that the above examples, which are not very uncommon, would be classified as intersex. The physical criteria fail to agree. Many doctors, including Dr Armstrong, define intersex as the state in which any of the criteria, including the psychological, fails to agree. But because our society demands that we be either male or female, the medical profession has to assign the subject to one sex or the other. As Professor Dewhurst put it: 'We do not determine sex – in medicine we determine the sex in which it is best for the individual to live.'

So what about me? Could I be classified as intersex and therefore be reassigned to the female sex as being that in which it was best for me to live? That was the medical consideration.

And were I not to be classified as intersex, would my post-operative transsexual status none the less entitle me to be classified as a woman for the purposes of marriage? That was the legal consideration.

Of my chromosomal sex there was no doubt. Professor Hayhoe found it to be XY, male.

Of my gonadal sex there was no evidence, although presumed male at birth. Professor Mills and Dr Armstrong thought that I was a probable case of Klinefelter's syndrome. This occurs in the case of XXY chromosomes but occasionally in XY too. They accepted my statement of spontaneous breast development and small testes and generally feminised figure prior to the taking of oestrogen, underlined by the report from the Walton Hospital (poor on detail though it was). Professor Mills attached much importance to the reference to 'little bodily or facial hair'. His examination of my body found no evidence of male hair-growth whatsoever, either on my face or elsewhere, and once such hair develops evidence of it can never be entirely eliminated.

Professor Mills, an endocrinologist, felt that subjects with a decidedly abnormal ratio between male and female hormones might also be candidates for intersex. He referred to a chemical test carried out on my urine which indicated that my hormonal balance was strongly female in character. Another test carried out during the trial produced a more ambiguous result. Neither test was allowed in evidence because they were not carried out under legal supervision.

Of my genital sex, it was now female due to vagino-plasty, though male at birth.

With regard to psychological sex, I took the Terman-Miles Test. The average male scores 65+, the average female −31. My score was −15, the conclusion being that my psyche was emphatically female in orientation. Unfortunately this test was likewise inadmissable because it wasn't carried out under legal supervision. Dr Armstrong and Professor Roth felt that transsexuals could not be classified as properly male or female and could only be usefully described as intersex. All their attempts to broaden the discussion along these lines were cut short by Ormrod, who agreed with Professor Dewhurst and Dr Randell that in questions of sex-determination little regard should be given to psychological factors when chromosomal, gonadal and genital sexes are all the same.

This, crudely, was the medical picture. But let's go back and into court where we were all sitting with solemn, even perplexed, faces.

I would have liked to do a Perry Mason on the trial but no transcription was made and to attempt, therefore, a dramatic reconstruction of the procedure would be hazardous. The risk of misrepresentation in a matter such as this, in which the reasonableness, or the futility, of an argument may rest upon the correct placing of a comma, would be very great – even as it is, it's like writing on eggshells. So what follows is, I'm afraid, only an impressionistic account which is, however, in keeping with my numbed, incredulous state of mind.

The court was deep, pit-like. We sat on the front bench with our solicitors and the Q.C.s one bench up behind us. Everyone stood for the entrance of Mr Justice Ormrod, who wore a little wig and spectacles (not half-moons). At first the public gallery was thinly populated but this changed as the trial got under way (seventeen days spreading from 11 November to 9 December).

The first matter to be discussed was what to call me. I was happy with 'April Ashley' but they settled on 'Mrs Corbett'. I felt that Ormrod didn't like me, a gut reaction. I mentioned this to Terry and Professor Mills over lunch in the basement of the courts and they laughed it off. But I knew Ormrod was disconcerted by me. He never once looked me straight in the eye but glanced furtively in my direction and mumbled his references to me as if they were distasteful to him. His behaviour towards me was contemptuous. Judges are the absolute rulers of their domain, and can play at being God, a temptation they do not always resist. Solicitors and counsel alike are obsequious to the point of grovelling, each side desperately keen to get into better books than the other by adopting ever more extravagant genuflections. And the sycophantic laughter when the Judge attempts humour – well, the atmosphere is terribly unnatural, stiff with formalism against which common sense has to fight for breath.

Arthur's case was opened first. When questioned he was very frank about his personal life. In this he had been cleverly advised. He explained that he had had sexual relations with many women before, during and after his marriage to Eleanor. He also described his deviations, the male brothels, what happened there, his need to dress as a woman, which he did about four or five times a year. About being so dressed he remarked, 'I didn't like what I saw. You want the fantasy to appear right. It utterly failed to appear right in my eyes.' From the first meeting he said he had been mesmerised by me. 'This was so much more than I could ever hope to be. The reality was far greater than any fantasy.' And later: 'It far outstripped any fantasy for myself. I could never have contemplated it for myself.'

Suddenly I realised what he was doing. So did my medical and legal advisers. Arthur was emphatically presenting himself as a deviate, in vivid detail, some of which was new even to me. For example, I had not realised the extent of his homosexual experiences. By adopting this confessional approach, by posing as the pervert since struck by contrition, by casting a pall of sulphurous depravity and transgression over our entire relationship, he was able to convey the impression that our marriage was no more than a squalid prank, some deliberate mockery of moral society perpetrated by a couple of queers for their own twisted amusement. By implication, I too was a deviate, and no more than a deviate. He appeared to be apologising in court and sympathy was forthcoming. I was not apologising for being myself and sympathy wasn't forthcoming.

This tactic involved an urgent reconsideration of my defence. It was the first turning-point of a case which was now revealed as something quite different from an objective consideration of my status for marriage purposes. I now had to defend myself against an all-purpose stigma of indecency, against the prevailing opinion, led by Arthur's testimony, that our marriage was a shameful joke because I myself was a shameful joke.

A few days into the case Ormrod suddenly asked if it were necessary to continue wasting the tax-payers' money. Both Arthur's representative and mine protested that it was important to hear the evidence in full and Ormrod grumpily agreed to go on. In the face of his alarming lack of interest in the debate, my counsel began to look very worried indeed.

Professor Mills said, 'There is a great deal of snobbery in this case, April.' By this I assumed he meant not only the obvious prejudices against transsexuals and the usual gestures of male chauvinism but also a more subtle association between Arthur, Arthur's counsel and the bench, the subconscious intransigence and *hauteur* of educated gentlemen who had no intention of being made to revise, or even examine, their notions of what a man, a woman, a marriage might be, especially not at the behest of a parvenue such as myself who, having been born into a Liverpool slum, not only refused to stay there but had the damn nerve to change her sex into the bargain, and not only that, but more, much more, cheek of all cheek, had the impertinence to marry into the peerage as well! I was in all respects an *arriviste* and so in their eyes not worthy of serious consideration. I have little doubt that my position and my arguments would have been accorded far greater respect had I been born into a family of distinction (on the other hand, perhaps not, perhaps I should have been pilloried for letting the side down. One thing you have to admire about these castes – they sure know how to protect themselves, from without and from within.)

Dr Randell's psychiatric examination was, to say the least, curt. At one point I had my head X-rayed because Professor Dent said it would show male characteristics – but he turned out to be wrong. Dent, by far the friendliest of the opposition, seemed to regret having been caught up in the affair, as later did Professor Dewhurst, whom Jackson on several occasions had to prompt with words which suggested he was thinking 'Whose bloody side are you on?' The provisional nature of Dewhurst's conclusions became obvious under cross-examination.

They say that if your shoulders are wider than your hips it is a sign of masculinity. My shoulders were half an inch wider than my hips. When the discussion turned to the question of my beard, the subject was raised of the races of the world who do not have hairy faces, Orientals, Mongolians, Red Indians. I longed to cry out, 'But I'm not a Red Indian!' Both men and women have hair on all parts of their bodies except the palms of the hands and the soles of the feet. This varies in amount and character according to sex. My face is in fact quite downy but of female type and my pubic hair is in the classic female pattern. I used to worry about my legs and would have them waxed. I remember my beautician saying to me, 'Miss Ashley, if you think you've got hairy legs, you should see Elizabeth Taylor's shoulders.'

Dr Vaillant was subpoenaed by the opposition. He was still head of the psychiatric department at Walton. But I was shocked when they brought him in because he was in a desperate condition, a terrified man. 'What have they done to him?' crossed my mind, suddenly imagining myself in Russia or Fascist Germany. He was dragged in, hunched up and trembling, eyes darting everywhere. The ushers had to shove him physically into the witness box because at the bottom of the steps he began moaning, 'I can't go up, I can't, I suffer from vertigo.' He was wrenching his shoulders, pulling in his arms, pulling bits of himself away from the ushers, the picture of a man trying to avoid being strapped into a strait-jacket. The judge said, 'Mrs Corbett, will you please stand up.'

I stood rigidly to attention.

'What do you think of the respondent now, Dr Vaillant?'

He screwed up his face and his eyes started out on stalks. He hissed one word: 'Mincing!' After extracts from the Walton Report were read out they let him go, to his very great relief. Vertigo? A few feet up in the witness box? It was cruel to bring him in. He had no useful testimony for either side.

Jackson tried to imply that I was a gold-digger and had conned Arthur into marriage. Both these insinuations were discounted. Arthur said he knew all of my history at the time of our marriage and that he felt for me the love which a man feels for a woman. The judge said his impressions in this area were inclined to be fantasies and were not important (although elsewhere the judge commended him for the straightforward honesty of his testimony).

'But,' said Jackson, 'you received and accepted many presents from Mr Corbett.'

'Yes, every single one chosen by my husband and never asked for by me.'

When cross-examined about the anatomy of my body before the operation I broke down and cried a little. For any transsexual this is the most distressing memory of all – we bury it, we try to forget it, we push it further and further into the recesses of the mind, and therefore it remains at the root of our insecurity. In my case this is especially ironical and annoying because in all other respects I'm a great one for getting things out in the open.

I have already described my male genitals as 'meagre' and that is exactly what they were. I have already stated that to my eyes my appearance was otherwise more female than male. My inability to be more clinically specific counted against me and the absence of proper detail in the Walton Report made it difficult for my doctors' belief in an XY case of Klinefelter's syndrome to be taken into account. Let me put it to you like this. How would you like the most personal details of your sexual mind and body, with all its doubts and vagaries and imperfections, to be paraded for public scrutiny in a court of law? Not very nice. And you are one who (setting aside the intersex readers for a moment) has the basic security of knowing yourself to be either male or female. Multiply therefore your sensitivity to such exposure a hundredfold and you might be able to grasp something of how horrible it was for me.

Having said that, it is wise to add that all unpleasant truths have finally to be faced if one is to free oneself from them. So having been *forced* to take stock of my previous self in public, unambiguous terms, in the long run – in the very long run because it took years to get over it and this is still the most difficult chapter to get out of my system, a kind of catharsis – I did emerge a stronger individual, having been obliged to acknowledge aspects of my past which in my weakness I should have preferred to regard as simply not being there.

An analogy would be the working-class boy who works his way into the middle-class – his biggest problem is coming to terms with his origins. My working-class origins never bothered me in the slightest, as it happens. They were completely upstaged by my more fundamental and harrowing transference from male to female. For post-operative transsexuals the greatest test is accepting *in full* what it actually means: that they were never natural males and can never be natural females either. On these grounds alone, it seems to me, we are the most obvious of all intersex types.

Towards the end of the trial, in early December, I was coming out of the courtroom with Terry and Professor Mills when there she was, standing in the corridor in boots and a full-length black mink and heavy dark glasses. Rita.

By this time I was so spaced out that all I could say was, 'Hullo, Gigi. I'll be right with you.' The feeling for 'time' had gone in me and with it an important aspect of normal perception (the other being a feeling for 'space'). We went across the road for tea.

'How's your son? David?'

'I've got four,' she said, 'three boys and a girl.'

'You must have done an awful lot of trembling.'

She laughed and said, 'But I'm divorced from Marcel now. Let me drive you home.'

At Clarendon Road we brewed endless pots of tea and talked and talked. Only then did it dawn that I hadn't seen or heard anything of her for twelve years. Apart from a broader American accent and a generalised aura of uptown Hollywood, she hadn't changed at all, the same beautiful round face with shining green eyes and not a line to be found, the same extraordinary sense of fun which disconcerts so many people and which I find impossible to convey. But in its very different way her divorce had been almost as traumatic as mine was being because, underneath the jocularity, it had clearly taken a similar toll on her self-assurance and sense of identity. She had returned from the U.S.A. only a few months previously and had moved to Aylesbury to be near her favourite sister and bring up her four kids single-handed, which I thought was really gutsy. When we'd last met I had been Toni April. But she had recognised me from the newspaper photographs. Joey she'd been unable to trace. I told her that he'd gone to Canada, bought a boat which he'd christened the *Cockney Panther*, and was at that very moment probably floating past an atoll in the Pacific. I hoped so. It sounded so much more attractive than the pickle I'd got myself into.

The trial ended on 9 December. The reserved judgment was not to be read until the following February and the interim would be an endurance of nerves. Arthur flew back to Spain, but not before Terry Walton had chased him down the Strand and slapped a writ on him, seeking a court declaration that Arthur held the Villa Antoinette in trust for me. This was a precaution in case the judgment went in my favour. I went up to Oxford to a dancing party at Lady Margaret Hall with Duncan and Richard Doyle, and Rita came with me. She took to the place directly and her high spirits awed them. She could party all night, have one hour's sleep, and be as fresh as milk for more excesses the following day. The only person who could keep up with her was Duncan and even he had to retire with conjunctivitis after two consecutive nights without sleep. His parents were arriving to take him out to dinner and he greeted them with a blue complexion, sinister dark glasses, and two eyes full of pus. 'I don't know what you're on,' his father said, 'but it's costing me several thousand a year.'

I looked like a skeleton, having dropped from nine stones to seven, but the undergraduates were fine therapy for the simple reason that they were less interested in the trial than in their own exotic affairs. Richard Doyle, also painfully thin, great-nephew of Sir Arthur Conan Doyle and now a novelist himself, paid me all manner of exquisite attentions at a time when my self-esteem was at its most vulnerable. Having left Oxford, he kept me going with a stream of letters from his family home in Essex. They were never more than a couple of pages, and his writing was such that he could never manage more than one sentence per page, but they were amusing and companionable.

> Dear Ashes, Our new drive is being constructed today so we have a bulldozer working away. This rather spoilt lunch since this machine was working just outside the dining-room windows while we were eating. It is a trifle upsetting to have a huge sweaty machine and driver of similar description thrusting away some ten feet from the table.
>
> . . . Many thanks for the lovely note and also the cutting about the Daimler. As you say, a lovely car and dirt cheap at 5½ grand. The trouble is I think if I got one of those just now, people would think I was embezzling . . . a huge lorry has now got stuck in the mud of our new drive.
>
> . . . My mother has just bought a new grand piano in my absence. This, after I had spent much time and effort persuading her to get rid of the old one . . . I have your photograph prominently displayed on my dressing table; however as yet no one has been in to look at it.

The ordinariness and the simplicity of these communications meant a great deal to me during that nerve-racking winter.

By 2 February, the Day of Judgment, I had lost another half-stone and was down to six and a half. At 9 a.m. that morning Arthur was found in a coma at the Villa Antoinette, which further fattened the headlines. He was discovered face-down on the sitting-room floor by the maid, who had come in to take Mr Blue for a walk. His friend

Guy Sitwell said, 'Arthur must have been unconscious for at least sixteen hours – he was supposed to catch a plane from Málaga to London last night to be in court. The doctor says he has a head injury and may have fallen.'

Towards the end of the judgment, long after my last hope had slid into obscurity, one of my restaurant partners who'd come along said, 'Come on, we're going.' The press were outside and he told them, 'If you want to speak to Miss Ashley, there will be a press conference in half an hour at the restaurant premises, 8 Egerton Gardens Mews.'

The judgment had been: ' . . . I hold that it has been established that the respondent is not, and was not, a woman at the date of the ceremony of marriage, but was, at all times, a male. The marriage is, accordingly, void . . .' In this any consideration of intersex was discounted by the judge, who in some instances did not believe the testimony relating to it and in others held it to be irrelevant. The psychological sex, he said, would have importance only when the biological criteria were not congruent. Transsexuals therefore lost all marriageable rights. As for my villa – I could whistle for it.

I remember very little of the press conference, I was in robot gear. They asked me what I felt about Arthur's coma.

'I'm sorry about it. But I shan't be flying out to see him. That part of my life has ended.'

'Yes, I'm still to be regarded as a woman for social purposes – woman's passport, woman's prison, woman's national insurance, woman's hospital, etc. I shall get my pension at sixty.' (Although there was a case recently of a transsexual who applied for her pension at sixty and was told she'd have to wait.)

'What are you going to do now?'

'Carry on. What else can one do? It just means I can't get married for the moment but I have no plans to anyway.'

Joan didn't know what to say to me. She was stunned by the judgment. All I wanted to do was go up to my room and hide. I lay on the bed, shut off my mind, and eventually went to sleep. Nothing had yet sunk in.

The Simon Dee Show on television was the first Sunday after the judgment. I said I couldn't go on unless they gave me a large glass of whisky to have on the set. Eventually they relented. John Lennon and Yoko Ono were on with me, talking about their bags. They would climb into them and stay there. Bag for Peace. Bag for Love. Bag for Whatever. They kept climbing into these bags. We were all clowns together.

But I was in a state of shock. As I came out of it, I went into a deep depression. The judge's words went round and round in my head like an unstoppable tape loop, provoking ugly nightmares and the physical sensations associated with fear. I felt guilty. Hideously so. My pride had taken a beating from which it never fully recovered. I had been proud of escaping from the Liverpool slums, I had been proud of finding by myself the solution to my problems of sexual identity, and now it was just thrown back in my face as worse than nothing. Physically I was completely run down. I had to check into a health farm; Forest Mere in Hampshire.

At Forest Mere I spent most of the time alone. I had to face people but I couldn't. I didn't know what to say to them and they didn't know what to say to me. Ava Gardner was there, trimming up for a film. I longed to introduce myself but all my confidence had been wiped out overnight. Meals were served in my room. I didn't visit the public dining-room once. They started me off on health food – nuts, raisins, salads, beans – because I'd virtually stopped eating and could take nothing more substantial.

My mental state was horrific. It was like being on a helter-skelter, going down very fast in an agony of despair and panic with no one to help me apply the brakes. Why was I alone? Why had I no family to help me? There was nothing solid inside me. All my certainties had turned into meringues. I would rush away from the lip of one abyss to find myself at the edge of another. When your confidence in yourself as a person is knocked completely away – and I do not mean dented or bruised but knocked completely – it produces a rapid and uncontrollable oscillation of intensely unpleasant feelings which amounts to suffering from acute claustrophobia and acute agoraphobia simultaneously. Your reason tells you that it is vital to cling on to people and fills you with the dread of being left alone. But your emotion fills you with a dread of all encounters. In this way reason and emotion wreck each other and the battle between the two produces rushes of panic, confused perception and patternless palpitations and muscular spasms. It is the patternlessness which is so frightening. Everything is out of control. Which being the case, I was frightened of hurting myself. Since the operation I have never done this in a deliberate way but my aloneness increased the apprehension that I might do something silly, by mistake as it were, not because I sought death but because I sought a respite from these tortures. Was there nothing which could

> . . . minister to a mind diseas'd,
> Pluck from the memory a rooted sorrow,
> Raze out the written troubles of the brain,
> And with some sweet oblivious antidote
> Cleanse the stuff'd bosom of that perilous stuff
> Which weighs upon the heart?

I had brought a bottle of Remy Martin to help me sleep. Each night I stared at it, longing to crack it open and swallow the lot but knowing that if I did it would destroy whatever drive remained in me. It was one of the modest challenges I set myself, which kept me sane by giving my willpower something specific to bite on. When one is in this sort of state, one has to begin with the small accomplishments. I love reading but couldn't manage it. My focus shifted wildly about. Either the page was an impenetrable mess of print or the phrases would eat into me with a queasy intensity. So I decided to put the television on and leave it on all the time, even with just the test card, just for the noise. I often slept through it. I kept nodding off or cutting out. The awful thing about depression is losing one's powers of discrimination. This is compounded by the fact that one's grip on oneself is so weak that sleep is continually interrupted by outbursts of lurid dreams and unwanted flows of adrenalin, and therefore wakefulness suffers from the constant drag of exhaustion. In consequence the distinction between the waking hours and the sleeping hours begins to be lost and one comes to occupy a twilit interzone of drifting anxiety and sudden vertigos. But it was essential for me to have episodes of complete rest at whatever cost, so I continued to swallow Mandrax at night.

Forest Mere has excellent stables and I wished to go riding but was found to be too debilitated and had to be content with long walks. I was staying in a row of chalets, the walls between which were very thin. In the adjacent chalet a man was on the telephone and I heard him say, 'You'll never guess who's in the cabin next to mine – that monster April Ashley.' I have had great experience of loneliness but at that moment the feeling was never more complete. More than an anguish of friendlessness, it was a bleak and limitless conviction that

I was outside humanity altogether and therefore that humanity was meaningless and had no existence. This lasted for, oh I don't know, some timeless moments during which I lost all sense of perceptual identity in a universe of indifferent chaos. Then something happened. I became angry. Or rather I became aware of a tiny strand of anger somewhere within me, the merest filament, but it existed, and it was ME. I was angry with the man next door. I had gone way beyond the confines of self-pity, towards the foothills of insanity, and anger was leading me back into the flock.

I tried the sauna bath. It was crowded with obese women. I looked like something out of a concentration camp and was embarrassed by my body which, after the court case, was the object of their uneasy curiosity. They were embarrassed too. I told Big Blonde Betty, my masseuse, 'I'm not going in there again. I don't like saunas anyway. Are there any steam baths here?'

'Oh yes, they'll be much nicer for you because they're individual, private.'

Betty was fantastic, my contact with a nourishing reality, because I was in genuine need of some mummying. 'April, you're *so* thin – we'll have to take good care of you. Forget all about the court – we've got more important things to do now.'

She gave me a massage every morning. I asked for as much oil and cream as possible because my skin was out of condition and flaking off. Followed by a steam bath, more oil, beauty treatments, my daily walk, rabbit food, TV, dozing, fitful sleep.

But I didn't want to stay at Forest Mere for more than a week because I became very frightened that if I didn't plunge back into the world immediately the depression would settle on me and I should go into an absolute decline. This understanding in itself marked progress. But the prospect of leaving filled me with foreboding. How would my friends and acquaintances react? The judgment quickly sorted them out. In some cases I was upset to discover how bad a judge of character I'd been. But these were more than compensated for by the reverse surprises, those people secure enough in themselves not only to accept me, in all my vivid headline sinfulness, but also to champion me. Close friends like Viva weren't bothered in the least, except for my welfare.

Strangers reacted in all sorts of ways. There was the usual screwed-up minority who made a point of referring to me as 'him', especially if I were within earshot. Some poked me in the breasts to see if they were real, or pulled my hair to see if it were false. What amazes me is that in other respects these are usually normal people. Sex cases seem to bring out their weird secret obsessions. They acted as if they had a perfect right to humiliate me in this way, as if my past meant that I had surrendered all rights to the basic courtesies.

But on the whole, people – from the London taxi-driver upwards, or downwards, whichever way you want to go – were unexpectedly kind and went out of their way to boost me. One woman who had attended the trial every day ran across me in the street. In Sloane Square I felt a tug on my sleeve and turned round. I recognised her at once. About sixty years old, very slim and smart. 'Miss Ashley, do you remember me? I hope you won't take any notice of that idiotic judgment. You would be foolish to do so. Live your life, be wonderful. I watched you. You are very brave.'

I mumbled something and ran off. It was terrible, running away from her like that, but I felt the tears coming. Right up until that moment I'd kept it all in. I'd read the letters alone with the odd little tear. But now this woman in Sloane Square had simply reached across and touched my heart and had almost triggered the flood. I wanted to sob it all away. I should have done. But I held it back – just. It was a long time before I recovered the courage to let myself go in this respect. Crying is not given to us for nothing. It is a release for distressed emotions. It has been discovered that emotional distress builds up certain chemicals in the body. They ran an analysis of real tears and these chemicals were found in them. But in tears induced by onions these chemicals were not present. It would be interesting to know what would be found in tears of laughter.

There were many letters of course, mostly from women, mostly kind and encouraging. Only two were truly abusive. 'You're a bloody man, get back into trousers, who do you think you're kidding?'

As part of my brazen-it-out therapy I again went to Oxford. Those qualities in myself which I like least – my stubbornness, my bluntness, my egotism – were now the very ones I had to draw on to pull myself up. Not only did I intend to stick around, I intended to make noises too. But going to Oxford was a nail-biting business because the undergraduates didn't belong to my generation, my world, my set. They were independent and they were young and therefore their reaction was especially important. I made myself as glamorous as possible and went up to a party given by Baron Paul de

Gaiffier d'Hestroy at New College. And had a sensational time. Their behaviour towards me hadn't altered in the slightest degree – except that they were rather excited by the publicity – and this helped me to feel that perhaps nothing very crucial had happened to me after all. There was only one piece of bother. We had all gone on to another party on the first floor of a large private house in the Banbury Road. A Rugby Blue the size of a bus roared, 'You're a bloke, you'll always be a bloke, and I fancy you!' As he advanced I side-stepped, he overbalanced, and like a pelican diving for food, went plummeting down a grand staircase to the bottom where he was left to sleep it off.

There was the question of an appeal. Terry was very keen on this. 'Everything is moving in our direction.' He even offered to help financially. Money was of course the problem. I had received legal aid for the case but this is not granted for appeals. The *Sunday Mirror* had paid me £5,000 for my side of the story. My partners suggested I sign this immediately over to the restaurant, on an investment understanding, otherwise I should forfeit it all in legal costs (Legal Aid has to be paid back if one comes into money within seven years). The cost of the appeal was assessed at £7,000 and a substantial part of it had to be placed with the court by 24 August 1970. Joseph Jackson said that I had deliberately disposed of my assets so as to be unable to pay the cost of the appeal. This is untrue. My assets would have been swallowed up by the previous costs. At one point an American foundation dealing with transsexuals was willing to underwrite the appeal but this had to be dropped when it was discovered that Professor Dewhurst sat on their English committee. I must admit that I had little energy for fund-raising at this stage but I do regret not trying harder while the opportunity remained. The drift of subsequent debate was towards my side, as were certain legal developments in Europe and America. But it couldn't be managed in time. And because there was no appeal, there was no transcription. This alone would have cost £872.10*s* for the top copy, plus £72.12*s*.6*d*. for each duplicate copy required by the court.

Let's get the sour grapes out of the way right now. I was bitter.

A month after the decision went against me in London, a court in Grasse in the south of France ruled in the case of Hélène Hauterive, a 35-year-old transsexual who underwent in Casablanca an operation identical to mine, that she is a female for legal purposes and can marry if she wishes because 'she possesses external genitalia of a feminine type and because her psychological behaviour is without doubt that of a woman.'

In New York Dr Harry Benjamin commented on my case: 'The judge's ruling is terribly illogical. It is a very inhuman decision . . . While we should be very careful and very conservative in advising the operation, once it has been done we should do all in our power to make life easier for them . . . Chromosomal tests are a purely technical thing and of no practical value, but could nobody see this?'

Dr Howard Jones Jnr, of Baltimore's Johns Hopkins Medical School, America's leading institute for transsexual research, commented: 'Sex can be identified in a number of ways – by chromosomes, by identification of the gonads, by examining the genitalia, external and internal, and by looking at the hormones. The sex an individual considers himself to be is an equally important factor . . . It isn't the operation that changes the sex. The operation merely reinforces a decision that has already been made. One who is familiar with this particular problem soon comes to the conclusion that you can't disregard the fact that someone believes he is a female.'

Christine Jorgensen said: 'The judge's decision is a cop out.'

What it effectively did was create a third sex for whom marriage was not possible, this third sex comprising not only all transsexuals but also certain intersex categories. The *Lancet* posed this recondite but still important question:

> . . . operations might be carried out which subsequently make it impossible for the person to fit either sex for marriage purposes. What, for instance, is to happen in the case of a female child with the adrenogenital syndrome who has a complete penile urethra and labia fused to form an empty scrotum, if a surgeon when exploring for undescended testes finds a uterus and ovaries and removes them (such a case is recorded)? On the decision of Mr Justice Ormrod the patient is female and one must 'ignore any operative intervention'. This would be a heartless decision . . . There is no doubt that these two decisions about assignment of sex and what is an acceptable artificial vagina raise problems of great importance to the medical profession. The work of paediatricians, endocrinologists, and gynaecologists in dealing with problems of intersex will now be immeasurably more difficult and surrounded by a frightening air of uncertainty. Although the marriage of such

> a person might possibly not be annulled during the lifetime of the partners, the challenge could still come after the death of one of them, from a third party who was interested in the inheritance.

One does wonder why the question of whether or not I was an intersex was not properly investigated. Professor Mills wrote to the *Lancet*:

> . . . there was abundant evidence that this individual did not go through anything remotely like male puberty, and since I believe her statement that the breasts developed spontaneously, I consider that she was endocrinologically an intersex. Thus I believe that an artificial vagina was constructed in an intersex patient, which is something we frequently invite such experts as Professor Dewhurst to do.

Why didn't Ormrod order the hormone tests and the Terman-Miles Test to be properly carried out? I wish he had done so, because if I had been proven to be an intersex I should no doubt have received a far more sympathetic hearing. But whether or not I am an intersex is a question marginal to my feelings on this subject, which are that just because Arthur and I made a farcical mess of things it is unfortunate that a general principle had to be extrapolated, denying transsexuals marriageable status altogether. To deny a small but distinct social group such a right is a very serious matter and yet Ormrod did not seem to take it seriously. He came to his conclusions irritably, as if it were only what we deserved, that we somehow had to be penalised rather than accounted for. To my mind the medical arguments should have been only a preamble to the central issue – how can the law respond intelligently and usefully to the predicament of all transsexuals? I'm not asking for sympathy, you can get sick up to the back teeth with professional sympathy, but I am asking for a sense of what is practical in life. Had he not taken such a narrow view, we might have made some progress here because however you look at it, it is simply not very bright to say that one must ignore the consequences of operative intervention. If we were always and only to refer back to first causes, then civilisation could never happen at all. These operations don't take place for the hell of it, they are not a branch of light entertainment – and yet Ormrod persisted in viewing the operation as a kind of wantonness on my part.

Is it the function of the law to create non-people? And if we had as our inalienable rights 'Life, Liberty, and the Pursuit of Happiness', what then? Tension between the male and female principles (or the positive and negative) is the mechanism through which the universe propagates itself. It is understandable that the court should pay some attention to this mechanism as it applies to humans. And having done so, conclude that I am not a natural female. However, the greater does *not* include the less. From this it in no way follows that I am or was a natural male. But this is slightly beside the point. Because marriage is not a biological relationship. The biological relationship is called coitus. Marriage is the cultural institution developed from this and when a relationship develops it changes its character. I do not see that it makes sense to treat marriage as something entirely separate from the currents of social life of which in fact it is one of the key components. Procreation is an important factor in marriage – the most important in most marriages – but from this one must not assume that marriage and the procreative relationship are the same thing. The overlap may be immense but the distinction is obvious.

Dr Armstrong and Professor Roth were especially upset at the dismissive way in which all their attempts to broaden that argument were treated. In *The British Encyclopaedia of Medical Practice* Dr Armstrong with Professor Hall concludes thus:

> In spite of the fact that the assigned sex of a patient with intersex may be challenged as not meeting the criteria of a man or of a woman for the purposes of marriage, the authors would not advise against marriage in the sex assigned provided the other partner was fully aware of the situation and agreed. It seems unlikely that society and the medical profession would in general wish to deny the comradeship and social benefits of marriage to those unfortunate patients who fall into the category of intersex.

Since Dr Armstrong regards transsexuals as a species of intersex, this advice would also extend to them. I too would say – Go ahead! But tell your partners all. Be Mr and Mrs Bloggs if you can. Or more to the point, if you want to. A lot of transsexuals living in obscurity were unmarried by my judgment and remain helpless before the law should a conflict enter the relationship. But the situation is bound to be resolved before long. It will take another court case – more time and money – and a more far-sighted judge than the one I was blessed with. As Christine Jorgensen's lawyer, Robert Sherman, said: 'The legal entity of changing sex is only now evolving. It will take twenty years before it is established.'

But of course the right of a transsexual to marry by no means solves all his or her problems. Arguments still rage about the wisdom of the operation itself. The Johns Hopkins Medical School suspended its transsexual operations after a report by Dr Jon Myer suggested that transsexuals were no happier after surgery. This is often true, alas. There are many suicides. Their dream is to become a normal man or woman. This is not possible, can never be possible through surgery. Transsexuals should not delude themselves on this score. If they do they are setting themselves up for a big, possibly lethal, disappointment. It is important that they learn to understand themselves *as transsexuals*, and if they find this difficult, various groups and associations are there to help them. It's all very civilised and chatty these days.

Research into the problem continues. More clues are revealed. In 1979 at the Fourth World Congress of Sexology in Mexico City, Dr Wolf Eicher of Munich announced that his team had discovered that the H-Y antigen present in all normal skin tissue was significantly absent in an experimental group of male-to-female transsexuals. This could be a crucial discovery. In the last ten years psychiatry had tended to feel more and more that examination of the DNA and RNA, rather than chromosomes and hormones, is a more profitable line of investigation. Dr Armstrong believes that recent work on the sexual differentiation of the brain might provide an answer to the origin of such a clear-cut and deep-rooted condition as transsexualism. The amount of androgen required for masculinising the brain is greater than that required to masculinise the genitals, so that sufficient androgen might be present in the foetus to produce an anatomical male but still leave the brain improperly differentiated. This also provides some argument against the feminist proposition that the differences between male and female outlook are essentially due to cultural environment and conditioning. Another argument against this proposition is provided by the tragic case in America of a normal baby boy whose penis was accidentally cut off by the doctor during circumcision at his birth. After discussion, it was decided that the best thing to do was perform a sex conversion on the infant and have him raised as a girl. But now at puberty the 'girl' is revolting against the female role, the masculine gender is strongly asserting itself. The medical profession is severely agitated by this case.

The matter is immensely complex. While we were preparing this book, Sir John Dewhurst wrote to Duncan: 'I believe the judgement to be correct for the reasons which Mr Justice Ormrod set out in it and do not think I can helpfully amplify this without going into considerable detail which you ask me not to do. Certainly no reconsideration of the matter has changed my view.' But he added: 'I find the whole field of transsexualism one of the most difficult that I have ever encountered in my medical lifetime, so difficult in fact that I felt obliged to give up my work in it and concentrate on other things, since for one reason I felt I was making no progress.'

I admire Sir John's frankness but I hope not too many other doctors follow his example, because I can't help feeling that a simpler, less agonising method must be found for solving this problem so that in the far future sufferers from it will not be obliged to go through what I went through in Casablanca – and in the courtroom.

11 AD8

I now gave myself to my subterranean *boîte de joie*, AD8. A for April, D for Desmond Morgan (Dizzy), 8 for 8 Egerton Gardens Mews. My partners founded a company, Freshrise Ltd, to run the restaurant and I entered into a five-year contract with this company which took all my earnings, including the £5,000 from the *Sunday Mirror*, in return for which I should officially receive £60 per month and free accommodation in the studio above the restaurant. This was the only arrangement, I was persuaded, whereby my income would not be forfeited in legal costs, although when reviewing my position Lord Justice Winn observed, 'Slavery has been set aside, but this agreement comes very near it.' The principal backer was Eagle Star Insurance. Kit Lambert, manager of the Who pop group and son of the composer Constant Lambert, put up £2,000. Alan Kaplan, an American doctor, put something in too. He was an addict who prescribed his own drugs. Not very long after we opened, I was having dinner with him in the restaurant. As usual he was in an abject state, rambling on about why he wouldn't be around for much longer, why he'd be doing himself in. I listened to his morbid talk for an hour or more, I thought it part of the job, then he staggered to his feet and had to be helped upstairs to a taxi. A few hours later I heard he was dead. Alan had swallowed a bottle of pills in the restaurant but no one had seen him do it.

The restaurant opened on Monday, 2 March 1970, with one hell of a party. Between five and six hundred people passed through what was in fact a rather small underground room. Several weeks later Shirley Bassey was opening at the Talk of the Town, and Chris Hunter had got together a group for our first night off. We were about to leave the restaurant when a wheelchair appeared at the top of the stairs. This was the trademark of London's most influential restaurant critic, the paraplegic Quentin Crewe who wrote for *Vogue*. The cars were waiting for us and I thought it would be too toadyish to cancel the evening, so I gave him a drink and left.

Quentin's review was savage. The basis of our salmon pâté was soap, and so forth. All the same, he gave AD8 the longest write-up of the month. Actually the food improved enormously when in due course Pepe joined us as cook from La Popote.

It wasn't until later that I could get back at Quentin, when Henry Pembroke and Christopher Thynne bet me a bottle of champagne that I dare not accompany them to the Crewe wedding reception at the Barracuda. In fact, I felt quite confident going along between two lords. When Quentin said, 'April, I do hope you've forgiven me for the write-up', I was ready.

'I never read my publicity, darling. I just measure it.'

It was at this reception that I first met Princess Margaret. I was standing by one of the bars, flushed with introductions, and a young boy approached me.

'Is it true you're April Ashley? I'm Jeremy Sykes. You know my brother Tatton Sykes. Can I get you a drink?'

'But I've already got this big glass of champagne.'

'No, something stronger.' He plonked a tumbler of whisky into my other hand.

'Isn't that Princess Margaret behind you?' I asked.

'Yes it is. Have you met her?'

'No.'

'Hang about then.' Cockney turns of phrase were still popular among the *jeunesse dorée*. Jeremy turned round and said, ''Ere, Maggie.' He poked her with his finger and it sank into the flesh of her shoulder. 'Maggie, come and meet April.'

With a glass in each hand I bobbed and said, 'How do you do, Your Royal Highness.' I was so nervous I got mouthrush and jabbered. She was skilful at sustaining a conversation with 'Yes' and 'Really' and 'I'm sure it was'. I finished up by saying, 'Will you do me the great honour of dining at my restaurant? We'll take good care of you. There are private booths at one end where you can see everything that's going on without anyone seeing you.'

'I'll send someone along to look at it,' she said.

'Do you mean you'll have someone case the joint first?' I couldn't help myself. My big mouth again. The words came tumbling out. She moved away. And never came.

Thoughts on Princess Margaret: a highly emotional woman. I was reminded of a Frenchman's description of Jane Digby: 'Her passions could be seen agitating in their imprisonment.' I was fascinated by how sexy she was. Soft perfect skin, Prussian-blue eyes, thick sensual lips, an overweight voluptuous body very well held – she seemed more confident in her body than in anything else. One felt she would bruise easily like a ripe fruit. In the course of being used a great deal she seems to have become a little lost along the way, so that one thought all the time what a shame it was that fate had called her to a station in which she is prevented from fulfilling her passionate nature.

I don't think she liked being called 'Maggie' in front of me. It must be a great trial for her to be handed round at parties. But of course she lays herself open to this by her desire to mix as freely as possible in the real world. Her roles were a source of confusion to her, being familiar one minute, pulling rank the next, torn between 'Maggie' and 'Your Royal Highness'. Of course, had she been blessed with greater wit and lightness of touch, the incongruity might have given her more amusement and therefore more power. Instead, this incongruity had become a predicament and there was about it a breath of tragedy. Obviously she is a woman capable of great love. In another age she would have inspired poets and adventurers. In ours she has increasingly found ease only among those younger and of considerably less distinction than herself. None the less it is lovely to see her looking so beautiful and slender these days.

The restaurant was hard work seven nights a week and I had to be groomed for it. Nearly every penny I made, the paltry £60 a month and any cash bonuses, went back into the business via make-up, hair-dos, clothes and shoes. My work began with a cup of tea and 'Crossroads' on television. Then to the cosmetics, nearly always Max Factor and Revlon Ultima II. First, on with the moisturiser, followed by the foundation and a little powder to fix it. It was always a long night, and one during which I was being kissed every five minutes, so I could never get away with sticky make-up. Then eye-shadow, mascara and false eyelashes. Masses of blusher on the cheeks to give colour and bring out the cheekbones and some more on the forehead because my complexion is quite colourless (but very heavy shading on the face went out with the 1960s). Indeed, without make-up my whole face is blank. It is a plain canvas on which I can paint almost anything. I'm sure that's why I gave up painting, because my face became my canvas. Making-up is also my meditation in the concentration of which I compose my inner self.

Eyes: masses of blusher under the eyes to take away any bags or dark circles. My top eyelashes grow straight downwards and without make-up the eyes look quite small. So I apply plenty of mascara, rolling the lashes again and again to make them curl upwards. And this opens up the eyes enormously. Everyone thinks I have huge eyes but I haven't, it's an optical illusion. My eyes are deep set, so I favour a dark eye-shadow to bring them out. This also makes the irises appear much darker than they really are, almost black in fact. To separate the eyes, I thicken all the lines slightly towards the temples. Eye-shadow carried above the eyelids raises the eyebrows. My eyebrows are very high up anyway and excellently shaped with the minimum of plucking.

Nose: I have a slightly *retroussé* nose and since I detest such noses I put a little white on the tip of it to make it look straight.

Mouth: the best thing in the world for making a mouth look young is to have a very precise one. My mouth was never very precise at the best of times, so I outline it in dark pencil, then fill it in with lipstick. Then I cover it with gloss to make it last all night. The best ever was California Gloss by Max Factor. Can't we get it back? I can't imagine why they discontinued it.

Skin: only two commandments. Clean it and feed it. That's all. Once a day before bed, with cold cream and moisturiser. Diet is not crucial. A bad diet won't necessarily kill a good skin, but it pays to be reasonable. If you drink, a lot of moisturising is essential. Alcohol, champagne most of all, is very dehydrating. Hard-drinking men would look far less haggard if they fed their skin.

Hair: I had a lot of white in my hair which I wasn't inclined to hide. But with the place fogged with cigarette smoke, it would turn a vile yellow. So regularly I'd blue rinse it which brought up the white a pale blue and made the black very black.

Clothes: always long because the patrons expected glamour. I was the main attraction and so of course went overboard. Once I wore jeans to work and some Americans who'd brought friends in to see me in all my finery were frightfully disappointed. They said they felt cheated, as if the understudy were on for the night, so I didn't do it again.

Shoes: the staff reckoned I walked five miles a night up and down the tables. With all that walking, you must provide the foot with a norm. Chopping and changing of height and weight and shape would soon ruin the feet. So virtually all my shoes were the same high-heeled evening sandals from the Chelsea Cobbler, in a variety of colours to match various outfits. They were very light and made from kid.

Now I'm getting older I don't try to keep up with the latest fashions. I think it best to stick with the style one feels most at home in. In my case this is rather early 1960s with futuristic touches (I've always wildly mixed things up). My face especially looks early '60s and this makes people think me grand. Any middle-aged or older woman who wishes to give off that indefinable air of grandeur would do well to avoid being too up with the latest fashions, which is usually viewed by others as trying too hard to stay young – and nothing is more ageing than that. For the older woman the secret of looking impressive is to be dressed up to the nines in the style of one or preferably two generations previous to the present.

Unless I had parties, I would go into the restaurant at 8 o'clock to check the tables and flowers. But there were always parties, sometimes four or five a night. It was good advertising. The opera likewise. So long as I appeared in public my partners did not object. But it was always on to the restaurant afterwards.

AD8 was a long warm pinkish cave, small enough to be intimate, large enough to be profitable. The staff were given the choice of dressing casually or formally, but either way they all had to wear the same. They chose to dress casually. Black trousers and red shirts. Some of them, especially when they returned from holiday full of zest, would try to flog themselves as well as the food and hope to get away with shirts open to the waist. But often people don't like warm hairy navels being pressed gently to their cheeks while they're eating, and I had to insist that only the top two buttons were undone.

Jean-Pierre, our French barman, was a true find. Customers tried to outsmart him by ordering some obscure hideous cocktail they'd picked up in Montevideo or the Phoenix Islands and he'd always plonk it down in front of them. I'm convinced he studied these things at night under the bedclothes with a torch.

Our first manager was Roberto, and Dizzy did the cooking. Dizzy looked very young for his age and was eager to preserve his youth, to which end he'd have himself injected with vitamin compounds and miracle custards from Switzerland. But unfortunately meat and vegetables would jerk up and rush for cover the moment he appeared. He's now doing very well on Fire Island, but at the time everyone agreed that he was better out front as the manager. Still, if a big star came in, Dizzy would rush round clucking, 'Wadda we do? Wadda we say?' Then I began to grow suspicious because he wasn't a great drinker but was getting tipsy.

'Jean-Pierre, are you fixing Dizzy's drinks?'

'Oh no, Madame!'

'Jean-Pierre, you *are* fixing Dizzy's drinks. I know him. He's only had three and he's got to sit down.'

'Yes, all right, I admit it, but we all decided it was best so that we can get on with the work.'

'O.K., thanks for telling me, carry on, because it keeps him out of my hair too. But nothing poisonous please.'

Our new cook, Pepe, was a classically handsome Italian usually with a moustache. And he could cook too. He was tremendously honest and hard-working but if he didn't have a woman in his life his temper was dangerously short. He would chase the waiters out of the kitchen with a meat cleaver. They'd be too terrified to go back in and come running to me because at such times only I could pacify him.

'Now listen, Pepe, the boys have got to come into the kitchen because they've got to collect the food because the customers are getting hungry.'

'Those bastards! I'll chop their heads off! O.K., let them in . . .'

Then we had the screaming lulus who came in to do the washing-up. They were always fighting too. Blood everywhere. Our most gracious washer-up was Dizzy's friend, Eleanor Clutton-Brock. She was big and tactile, the heiress to Chastleton House, one of the most beautiful Jacobean houses in the country. It has hardly been touched since the eighteenth century, mildew everywhere, and was used in the filming of *Joseph Andrews*.

Micky Mullen or his enchanting sister Allison often worked on the till and our porter, who cleared out the rubbish during the day, was David, an angelic Irishman. When I lived in the studio he would bring up my coffee and toast each day at lunchtime. David lived in a bed-and-breakfast place. Because of his untidiness and his drunkenness he could never keep rooms. I thought he was well into middle-age but discovered that he was only in his thirties with a wife back in Ireland. Often I'd find him wandering about drunk in the street.

After he'd done his work, I'd say, 'Right, David, one drink with me in the bar before the customers start to arrive.' When he'd had his whiskey he'd obediently shuffle off, never pressing for more. One day in a stupor he walked in front of a bus and was killed outright. I really missed his sweetness when he went.

The first couple of years were full of variety and gaiety. My dream was that we should become an established restaurant and go on for years. The divorce trial had given us a headstart, we were booked weeks ahead, but I had a battle on my hands to overcome our original reputation for bad food. Such reputations are the hardest of all to lose because, although people often give the impression of knowing the difference between good and bad food, in practice they rarely do. The reason for this is that they don't pay attention to it. As with wine, their reaction is governed by hearsay or the remarks of someone who appears to be in the know rather than by their own immediate experience, which they are inclined to distrust for fear of making a *faux pas*. One of our most successful dishes was Champagne and Camembert Soup.

We were flooded several times when the drains became blocked in the Brompton Road and the water would pour down the stairs. The customers started yelling, 'We'll be electrocuted, we'll be fried to a crisp!' And I'd have to do my bit. 'Ladies and Gentlemen, fear not, the wiring is all in the ceiling.' We'd throw dozens of aprons and tea-towels on to the floor and carry on as usual.

Gradually I was recovering confidence, learning never to forget a name – as the Queen will tell you, this is a priceless asset in dealing with the public. Most people expect to pass through life entirely unnoticed by the world. The joy which overcomes them at being remembered can often make for a successful evening all by itself.

The restaurant had genuine glamour and genuine characters and was the stopping-off point for many hardcore Knightsbridge and Chelsea socialites. One of my main obstacles was that a new member of staff would cotton on fairly quickly that when it came to the nitty-gritty I had little say in the running of the place. Occasionally I'd throw a tremendous tantrum to remind them that I wasn't to be disregarded. The only improvement in my position was that the studio proved to be too small and the company therefore took a lease on a flat in Eaton Square of which I had the use. It was on the first floor and so I had the original drawing-room. This room was vast and beautiful but unfortunately had no furniture whatsoever, so I would dance around barefoot in it to my Puccini and Rodgers and Hammerstein records.

Everyone came to the restaurant, from John Osborne to the Chinese Ambassador. Elaine Kennedy brought Ingrid Bergman, Denny Daviss brought Placido Domingo, who sang Neapolitan love songs until 1 a.m., accompanying himself on the baby grand. Ava Gardner taught me how to drink tequila. Stretch out thumb and forefinger and place salt in the hollow between the two. Cut a lime in half. Lick the salt, slug the tequila, suck the lime in quick succession. It's as if someone had thrown a match into the Brock's Fireworks factory. Ava was living in semi-retirement in Knightsbridge with her little dog. She loved London because she had discovered that it was a very personal, very private city and she loved her privacy. She came to us about once a month, always very simply dressed, and sometimes she drank a great deal, sometimes nothing at all. She visited her old flame Howard Hughes when he was staying at the Inn on the Park. I pressed her about him but she refused to divulge anything. She had caught the secrecy bug which he spread, the high drama of being one of the exclusive club that knew him, membership of which was conditional upon saying nothing. She did say that he infuriated her so much that once she hit him with a frying-pan.

Kit Lambert said he would eat his investment and he came almost every night. Usually he was alone but pop people sometimes came in behind him, especially Keith Moon. (Keith had the wildest reputation, he'd drive his Rolls-Royce into his swimming pool, that sort of thing, but really he was the softest of men with a passion for schoolgirls – he reminded me of Robert Newton, who also drank himself into the ground.) Francis Bacon came, bringing the young artists, always falling over and having to be helped up the stairs afterwards.

Barbara Back always had to be helped in as well as out. Barbara was the world's worst driver. She would stop at Belisha beacons and wait for them to turn green. She took me to the première of Robin Maugham's play *Enemy*. There was a big party afterwards at the Ivy Restaurant. It was torture driving there with her. Even though she went at only 15 m.p.h. one always felt in the utmost peril, and because of the slow speed this apprehension seemed endless. As we went into the restaurant she said, 'Darling, I've got my high heels on, please take my hand, I'm getting vertigo.' I looked down at her shoes. The heels were scarcely an inch high. She was always tall and skinny but by now her legs were mere bones.

I decided to give dinner to my three oldest lady friends – Barbara, Gladys Calthrop and Viva. They already knew each other very well and decided not to compete but the glad rags came out none the less. Gladys wore hunks of primitive jewellery à la Nancy Cunard. Barbara, who had a daring colour sense, wore a yellow-silk pencil dress with emeralds. And Viva wore a white blouse and the inevitable black-velvet skirt which was her 'going out' skirt and covered with the stains of two dozen dinners past. Viva suffered from the Crowning Glory syndrome and only really bothered with her hair, which was always spun into ice-blue candyfloss.

'We're the three oldest fag hags in London,' said Barbara. She was Somerset Maugham's, Gladys was Noël Coward's and Viva was Norman Douglas's.

'Do you realise,' said Viva, 'that there are well over two hundred years between the three of us?'

'Jewels burn brighter on a fading skin,' said Gladys.

'And how many men?' said Barbara.

'Not enough. The waste, the waste!' said Viva, warming to her favourite subject. It turned into an extremely bawdy dinner. At the end of it Barbara offered them both lifts home but Gladys 'longed' for a taxi and Viva insisted on walking.

Pat Dolin brought Evelyn Laye and Rudolf Nureyev, Bobby Moore brought the footballers, Johnny Dankworth and Cleo Laine brought each other. Danny La Rue came and invited me to dinner with Liberace at his house. Very *luxe de Harrods*. Even Danny's toilet paper hung out of a dolphin's mouth. Liberace I couldn't believe. He wasn't at all amusing but extravagantly sentimental instead, lachrymose even. When he spoke it was like molasses dripping out of the Virgin Mary. Incidentally, for kitschiness Danny La Rue's house couldn't compete with Lionel Bart's. Lionel had a musical staircase which played selections from *Oliver* when you walked up it. He also had a musical lavatory. It played 'Food, Glorious Food' when you flushed it by depressing a large gold crown.

One who never came to AD8 was Amanda Lear, which hurt me. She still telephoned to say how low she was. 'You know you have a standing invitation to dine with me.' But she wouldn't. After finishing with her German and Brian Jones, she moved further into the pop world via David Bowie and Bryan Ferry, and I heard from her less and less until I heard from her no more. I think the root of her unhappiness was her unease about her sex identity. She had the bone structure but lacked the nerve. Even when she became the Disco Queen of Europe you could hear it in her voice – a moose at bay.

I was always giving free meals to worthy causes, much to my partners' fury. One such case was Sir Francis Rose, Lord Berners's friend. Vikki de Lambrey started to bring him in. He was small, grubby and poor, and sometimes slept at Viva's house. He had succeeded to his father's title while still a child and had been vaunted as a prodigy in the Parisian art world of the 1920s. Gertrude Stein thought he was as good as Picasso and apparently as a teenager he was terribly promising, if his seventeenth-birthday party is anything to go by. It took place in Villefranche at the Hotel Welcome where his mother lived. Lady Rose imagined herself in touch with the spirits of the dead and wore sailcloth dresses painted with roses by her son. The party was organised by Jean Cocteau and the guest of honour was Isadora Duncan. It ended in a fight – Lady Rose was attacked by a lobster – between the French and American sailors who'd been urged to attend. Despite this rapid start, or more likely because of it, Sir Francis failed to develop and ended up designing wallpaper in a disgruntled frame of mind.

What a frightful shame it was, so I gave him free food with half a carafe of wine thrown in. One night Sir Francis arrived and we were chock-a-block. Roberto asked me what we should do and I told him to set a place in the corner of the bar. I always had my own meal there if I were eating alone. On this night I was sitting at the other end of the restaurant with Polly Drysdale and Lord Antrim. After he had eaten his fill and wiped his mouth, Sir Francis approached our table screaming abuse.

'How dare you put me in the bar. Don't you realise I'm the 4th Baronet! My mother was the daughter of a French count!'

I was so upset and so angry that I whacked him one across the chops, told Roberto to throw him out and never to allow him in again. His vanity, unappeased in consequence of the world's disregard, had eaten up all his self-respect.

'Who was that?' asked Lord Antrim.

'Francis Rose.'

'Not *Sir* Francis Rose?'

'Yes.'

'You've just done what I've been longing to do ever since I was at school with him.'

Vikki de Lambrey was another case but at least he was well-meaning – I say 'he', but Vikki was indecipherably androgynous in appearance, with long rats' tails of various tints, plucked eyebrows, and a high thin voice like Japanese water torture. He was always sending me letters by recorded delivery marked 'urgent' or 'confidential' or 'strictly private' and I would open them gingerly to find enumerated therein his reasons for not living. He once sent me an eleven-page telegram, beginning *I just had to send you this short message* . . . Vikki's favourite pastime was to hire a white Rolls-Royce from Harrods, put big stickers in the front and back windows with his name on them, and tell the driver simply to drive round and round London all day. Vikki's desire for status was like a plant's desire for light. It was constitutional. It was also doomed. When he started to call himself a Rothschild, the banking family had to threaten him with the law. The last I heard, Vikki was out of prison (I don't know why he went in), had decided to put unreality behind him, and to this end had started up an organisation called the Marianne Faithfull Rehabilitation Society.

Rita was at the restaurant almost as often as I was; her children came down on their birthdays. And Terry MacNamara turned up one night. He looked so sweet with his suitcase, just seventeen years old.

'I've run away from home,' he said.

'Right, Terry, hold on a moment.' The place was packed but I called up Roberto and told him I'd be gone for half an hour. I took Terry to Eaton Square where I had camp beds for emergencies. He couldn't stop trembling.

'Why have you run away from home?'

'Because I can't take my parents any more.'

'Well, darling, I can't talk to you now. I'll give you something to help you sleep and we'll have a proper talk tomorrow.'

I tucked him up in bed, gave him a couple of Valiums, left the lights on and the number of the restaurant, and told him where I'd be. At AD8 I sent his parents a cable. *Terry with me and O.K.* When I returned from work he was fast asleep.

The next day I took Terry out to lunch, filled up his wine glass, got him drinking a bit, and said, 'So what's the problem?' It all came flooding out. It was nothing to do with his parents. Although he had all the feelings of a young man of seventeen, he was short for his age and looked scarcely twelve years old. He would make passes at the girls and they would turn round, pat him on the head and say, 'Dear little Terry.' I'd also called him this and I bit my tongue. But the temptation was considerable because he was small, cuddly, and so beautiful.

'Don't despair. I have an idea. One good thing about my divorce case was that I learnt a bit about endocrinology. We'll get you a doctor and see what can be done.'

I explained everything to his mother Pat and took him off to see his G.P. in a grim surgery in Hammersmith.

'It's rather difficult, doctor, but Terry isn't growing at all well and I know of an endocrinologist called Professor Dent, he's a professor of human metabolism at – '

'Yes, I know of Professor Dent.'

'I think Terry should see him because – '

There is nothing the medical community hates more than being made to feel that curative knowledge is not exclusively its own . . . The doctor went red in the face and said, 'What on earth do you know about endocrinology?'

'Not very much but I've picked up a bit along the way.'

'Maybe they could help him, maybe they couldn't. It wouldn't do to raise the boy's hopes, Mrs MacNamara, because these things are by no means straightforward.'

'Doctor, I'm not Mrs MacNamara.'

'Who are you?'

'I'm Miss Ashley.'

'You're not the boy's mother?'

'No.'

'Then I'm afraid this conversation is at an end.'

I returned to Pat and said, 'It's no good, you'll have to do it, but at least the doctor knows the problem now.'

As it turned out, Terry did start to see Professor Dent, who put him on a course of something and Terry grew up without any more difficulties.

There were three Americans I always loved to see in the restaurant. First Johnny Gallier, voted several times Best Dressed Man in the World. The second was Billy McCarty, exquisite manners, way over six feet tall, who gets younger by the year. The third was

Tommy Kyle. He was the most outrageous of the three by far and he was the richest.

Tommy I'd first met ten years before at a dinner party given by Mrs Ting-a-Ling, Joan Thring, Rudolf Nureyev's manager. I liked him, he was so mischievous, so outspoken. Tommy loves to stir it up and he can be very brutal. Then he walks out of the room to leave the rest scratching each other's eyes out.

Tommy was the personal assistant, manager and chief designer to Gustav Leven, Mr Perrier Water, and when in the south of France lived either at Gustav's dreamy Château Croix des Gardes on a hill overlooking Cannes or at his own smaller but scarcely less sumptuous house, La Bastide, adjacent to the main property. Gustav worked most of the time in Paris but he would fly down in his aeroplane for quick weekends with his girlfriend, Jacqueline Citroën.

Christopher Hunter took us to a first night at the Hampstead Theatre Club. During the interval Tommy said, 'When are you coming to the south of France?'

'When you send me the ticket.'

The following day the ticket arrived at the restaurant by special messenger. I flew to Nice Airport. The housekeeper of Croix des Gardes, Madame Lolo, was there to meet me and the chauffeur, Sonny, who wore a bright fluffy orange wig with a cap stuck way up on top of it. He was standing beside an open Rolls-Royce in *café au lait*, the same colour as his uniform.

We climbed the hill and stopped outside iron gates. Sonny pressed a remote-control button inside the car and we passed up a long drive planted with leafy English trees filled with white doves. Everywhere one caught glimpses of gardeners clipping and hoeing and wheeling barrows. Eventually, after what seemed time enough to traverse a county, a cream house in the Palladian style floated across the windscreen. It used to be a redbrick Victorian mansion but Tommy changed it.

The Great Hall goes the full height of the house, three floors, a crystal chandelier hanging forty feet down from the roof and a lift in one corner. Straight ahead is the *salon* with a circular sofa in the middle. The floor is patterned with a circular design concentric with it, so that when sitting there you are on a golden carousel. The *salon* looks out to the sea beyond the swimming-pool, which is designed to give the impression that it has only three sides with a fourth flowing over the cliff. In the centre is a single jet fountain which rises to a hundred feet.

The house is filled with valuable furniture, some of it made for Versailles, but Tommy has the American gift for updating the antiques of Europe with uninhibited adaptations, daring upholstery and outrageous bravura effects, quite the opposite of the English custom of wearing history on the sleeve, letting everything acquire a certain decrepitude.

My bedroom was the Lavender Room with a view across the Mediterranean. Even the soap in the bathroom was lavender. Tommy's own bedroom was in pinks and greens, with a collection of Dufys to match. His bathroom was completely mirrored. The bath was in the middle of the room and appeared to float in mid-air. Every interior was so over the top that it worked.

Like many Americans who come to live in Europe, Tommy was a stickler for doing things right. We always dressed for dinner, except on Sunday when there were no maids on duty and we'd play about in the kitchen. In the evenings Tommy would come up to my room for a whisky and Perrier while I was finishing off my hair. And then I'd go into his bathroom and chat while he bathed. About 8 o'clock we'd go down to the library to meet the guests and have Dry Martinis prepared by the butler, Rudi. Dinner was usually simple. Then we'd drop the formality, tumble into the Rolls and charge down town for fun at Les Trois Cloches which was open until 6 a.m. We did all the bars but usually ended up here. It was sleazy but fashionable. You'd meet everyone from the local fisherboys to David Hicks.

One night we were dining out in St Tropez (I had swordfish, my favourite fish after sea bass). Paying attention to us from a nearby table was a large flushed woman in middle years, accompanied by a pretty young man dressed in white. She turned out to be Madame de Juste, from Haiti. And the boy in white turned out to be a girl, one of France's top tennis stars. When the tennis star learned of my identity she said in that pugnacious French way, 'I don't believe you're April Ashley.'

'And I don't believe you're a woman – show me your tits.'

'Only if you show me yours.'

We unwrapped our respective bosoms in the best restaurant in town and satisfied each other's curiosity – such behaviour is very St Trop. The upshot was that they were invited up to Croix des Gardes for dinner the following day. 'I've heard so much about that house. Can I bring my husband? And my dog?' said Madame de Juste.

The next evening, corseted in beige satin, Madam de Juste arrived like a galleon being tugged into harbour, with her husband, her poodle and a young male lover. As far as one could tell they were all from Haiti, except perhaps the poodle. There was a handful of other guests, including Lil, Marquise de Valois (a regular visitor), and after dinner we went tipsily into the *salon* for music.

Tommy had arranged for a group of gypsy musicians to come up from the town to entertain us during digestion. They went into their routine. We sat sipping brandy, half-smiles on our faces. They wailed about various lost homelands, fiery stuff, melancholy stuff, more fiery stuff. Just as one felt the end was in sight, the violinists would rev up again, another lament, another blitzer. I've as good an ear as the next for a Romany jig but we were drowning ourselves in brandy. When they started to fly round the room, I saw Tommy wince. I said, 'Are you going on for very much longer?'

'We go on until you seize up,' said the ringleader.

'I guess, Tommy, that means they're prepared to be paid off.'

When they'd shuffled out, the brandy hit us and everything grew much friendlier. Madame de Juste said to me, 'This is an extraordinary house. I'd luff to see your bedroom.' I took her up there. We'd hardly crossed the threshold when she ripped my zip down. It was one of those strapless black crêpe shifts – once the zip is down the weight of the brooches carries it to the floor at once. I was standing there in my bra and panties and pearls. She jumped on me and threw me across the bed (she was a fine figure of a woman, no wimp in a scrap):

'Madame de Juste,' I said, struggling for breath, 'you have your husband downstairs and your boyfriend too and now you want to make love to me.'

'Yes, yes, that's right,' she panted.

'Obviously you're gifted with sensuality, but where will it end?'

'I giff anyfing to make luff wiff you.'

'All right then, I'll have that on your left hand,' pointing to a conker of a diamond set in claws of platinum.

Her manner changed completely. She buttoned up her bodice, smoothed down her hair, and marched out of the bedroom slamming the door behind her. We hadn't realised it but her poodle had followed her upstairs and was now trapped inside with me.

'Hullo, darling,' I said, 'how are you?'

It came trotting up in its encrusted collar, wagging its tail, and it smiled at me. I was astounded. It grinned and in its mouth there were no teeth. When I returned downstairs I said to Tommy out of the side of my mouth, 'Not only has she got a husband, a lover, a tennis star, and wants to jump around with me, but she's also got a toothless dog – now what do you think that's for?'

'You've got to be joking. I knew she was after you – but no, surely not the dog.'

'Watch . . . Come along, my boy.' And the little oddity came wagging up, grinning from ear to ear, showing a fine set of pink gums. Tommy and I collapsed. Madame de Juste started crying again and called me a bitch and a number of other names. I asked her if the poodle were a lap-dog. At this she hurled herself at the french windows. Luckily these gave way and she blew out on to the terrace and disappeared. When Tommy realised where she'd gone he went white, because after dark they let out the hounds. He managed to retrieve her before she was torn to pieces. The husband was no less strange. He didn't say a word all evening. Just smiled throughout. With a shudder I suddenly realised that he was the dog in human form.

It must be something in the air down there because Lil, Marquise de Valois, had her turns too. She was Norwegian and wore black-silk trouser suits, with her hair pulled severely back. She used to sit on the edge of sofas with her knees apart. On this occasion I was sitting next to her in the *salon* after a dinner.

'Phew, the weather's been so hot lately, hasn't it, Madame de Valois?'

'Do call me Lil.'

'All right, that's nice. Lil. I do like you.'

'And I like *you*.' With a tremendous lunge, she went for me. When Tommy came back into the room, Lil was chasing me round and round the circular sofa, trying to lassoo me with her arms. My heels were much higher than hers, so I was jolly glad to see him.

I think it was Dame Edna Everage who said, 'Lesbianism leaves a nasty taste in my mouth.' I've nothing against it myself. Who am I – who are you, come to that – to tell people they mustn't love each other? Many lesbians have fallen for me. But I suppose the reason I've never been able to fall back is that I'm always so smitten with men.

From 1971 on Tommy gave me some exceptional holidays from reality but the big trip that year was to Tokyo, as the guest of Fuji Television's programme 'The Secret of the World'. Tokyo was just like Manchester, grey, cold and wet. They put me up at the New Otani Hotel and the next morning I was woken up by the twittering of birds. Since I was a dozen floors up I couldn't work out where it could be coming from. Then I realised it was the radio – if you don't switch it off, they rouse you in the morning with bird-song. From that moment I was in love with the place.

'The Secret of the World' is a panel game. A group of Japanese television personalities have to guess one's special secret. Funnily enough Sarah Churchill had been on the week before. The chairman more or less had to tell them my secret in the end. We all chuckled and that was that. The Japanese seem to take transsexualism far more casually than Westerners do. I might almost have been a bus conductress.

We travelled to a house in the hills for the tea ceremony. I was wearing a gold kaftan with a burgundy-velvet opera cloak on top and I towered over everything (the Japanese men were rather nervous of my height). The mistress of the house asked me how many outfits I owned of the sort I was wearing.

'About thirty or forty,' I replied, which I thought quite a few. 'And how many kimonos do you have?'

'Over three thousand.' She had sample fabrics from each bound into a large book which was divided by occasions: weddings, birthdays, New Year, etc. They were numbered and she would make her choice, give the numbers to the maid, and the clothes would be brought to her.

Though the lady was demonstrably an aristocrat, her house was not large by European standards. On the return journey to Tokyo, I put it to Koko. 'All the houses are small and all the walls are so thin and all the families are so large and yet the Japanese are very keen on privacy – how do they make love?'

'That's one of the great secrets of Japan. We are the world's most silent lovers.'

A few months before my visit, the writer Yukio Mishima and some romantic friends of his had committed ritual disembowelment followed by decapitation. Man A disembowels himself; A is decapitated by B; B then disembowels himself; B is decapitated by C; and so on. The last man has no one to decapitate him and so has to be content with disembowelment. I was flicking through the pages of a magazine in the Otani lobby, waiting for the car to the airport, and screeched to a halt at a macabre double-page spread. My last image of Japan: all their heads on a table like a collection of crazy flowerpots.

My business relationship with the partners was terrible. I should have sorted it out – but I didn't, and this was soon to cause me great pain. Meanwhile, Edward had done brilliantly at Law School and was about to enter the Webber-Douglas Academy of Dramatic Art. He had 'glittering future' stamped all over him.

A flat was now taken for me on the corner of Elm Park Road. I was happy here and felt safe. My landlady, Mrs Denehy, was thoughtful and uncurious. My daily, Mrs Anne, an Irishwoman who'd come from service with Princess Margaret at Kensington Palace, made it feel like home.

Robin Maugham organised a dinner party in honour of Gerald Hamilton's eighty-something birthday at the flat which the Hon. Lady Joan Assheton-Smith shared with Hermione Baddeley. Joan was a tremendous cook and hostess. She hailed from Australia and affected eccentric corsages. A plastic rhododendron might be affixed to her generous bosom, or a stuffed cockatoo. Gerald sat in an armchair like an old potentate in his best baggy suit. As a special concession to us, he agreed to stay up late, explaining that usually he retired at 9 p.m. in order to be up at 5 a.m. to begin writing. He was very emphatic about this writing without ever giving the smallest clue as to what it was. We toasted him and all said how wonderfully fit he looked. A few weeks later he was dead.

Two other legends I met at this time were Cecil Beaton and Noël Coward. Beaton was giving a party at his home in Pelham Crescent. Numerous celebrities and assorted American women dripping in jewels were gossiping in a drawing-room with black velvet walls. Cecil Beaton was snooty. I think he felt I wasn't out of the right drawer. Beaton didn't have the gift of mixing. His range was narrow and he could be unpleasantly precious, with that high thin voice running like string out of a mean tight face. In fact all his being seemed to be concentrated up in his head. Very homosexual by nature but in practice the least sensual of men, his blood was cold with self-consciousness. His involvement with Greta Garbo, I always thought, had the pathetic quality of a joke from which only Beaton was left out.

Noël Coward was also at this party and much more of a man, one of those magicians who fills a room with champagne bubbles by his presence alone. Coward's charm was irresistible, not at all brittle, but warm, astringent and puckish all at the same time.

I didn't meet Cecil Beaton again but I did Noël Coward, once, at Johnny Gallier's house. He'd come over to pick up his knighthood. In the few intervening years he'd aged markedly. Despite obvious discomfort, he insisted on climbing to his feet, saying, 'I always stand for a lady.' His face was covered with black spots.

Julia Lockwood came to the restaurant with her husband. She was in a curious mood and we didn't connect very well. Sarah Churchill came – she was slightly easier but the old intimacy had gone. To my delight, because Sarah is a magical person, it improved again when together we went to Arabella Churchill's wedding to a young schoolteacher called James Barton. June had rung me and said 'Arabella's got so many hippies coming to this thing, we thought we'd smooth it over by asking everyone to come dressed that way, so do come hippified.' The reception at Mary Soames's house in Cheyne Walk was full of vegetarians and squatters.

There were many visitations from the past, not all of them a treat. One of the happiest surprises was from Goebbels's sister-in-law, Ariane. She wrote from America, addressing the letter 'April Ashley, c/o April in Paris, London, Chelsey'. To my amazement the G.P.O. delivered it to me at the restaurant – professionally speaking, it was one of the most flattering things ever to happen to me.

Ariane had a story to tell. While still living in Germany, she had opened a magazine and read in it a story concerning a man called Sam Shepherd who was being charged with the murder of his wife in America. Beside the story was a photograph of him, and Ariane fell in love with it. By this time she was already disenchanted with Germany. Years before, when she telephoned me, there were tell-tale clicks on the line which she said was phone-tapping (the authorities were worried in case she became a rallying point for old Nazis). She was always escaping from Düsseldorf to Paris and the south of France and had kept up her friendships with Les Lee and Everest.

So in 1963 she sold up in Germany, moved to the U.S.A., and made contact with Shepherd. The photograph had not lied, her love for him was confirmed, and she went to work on proving his innocence. Over a quarter of a million dollars later, having spent the best part of her fortune, she was successful. In 1964 they were married and moved into Sam's all-American house in Cleveland, Ohio, with yellow awnings over the window, where the now unsolved murder had taken place. But bliss did not await her. Shepherd became a motorbike and leather fiend and degenerated into a hopeless alcoholic and drug addict. Several times he tried to kill her. It became obvious that he was guilty of his first wife's murder and when, she wrote, he pulled *a gun on me, I ran away and filed for a divorce so I could get police protection. I was hiding in a motel for three months until I had the court order to protect me. The divorce was final in 1968.* Shepherd then married a foolhardy teenager, but died soon afterwards. *The autopsy showed that two thirds of his brain were gone. The whole thing was a nightmare. I'm slowly recovering from it all and have started dating . . .*

A film was made of her story, starring Nina van Pallandt as Ariane.

Now, in the autumn of 1972, I also had to face a tragedy. One evening in the restaurant two uniformed policemen came down the stairs. They said, 'Miss Ashley, would you like to sit down?'

'No. What is it!'

'We've some bad news, I'm afraid.'

I went very cold.

'Do you know Edward Madok? There's been a car accident north of Paris.'

'How serious is it?'

'He's dead.'

'Why have you come to me?'

'Yours was the only address they found on him.'

Edward had been driving back from St Tropez to begin his second term at the Webber-Douglas Academy. It was a wet night, a head-on collision. The driver of the oncoming car had been killed too.

Dizzy telephoned Edward's parents. Although Jack and Julia Madok didn't approve of me they did invite me to the funeral. I booked into the local hotel and was summoned up to the house. Jack had been crying I think. He put his arms round me and said, 'April, I didn't understand.' Julia took me up to Edward's bedroom where I saw many things that I'd given him. But the room was empty. The spirit had gone out of it.

Eight months almost to the day after Edward's death, Micky came down to the restaurant to take over on the cash-till from Allison, who had a date. 'I'd love a drink,' he said, 'I haven't even had a pill today.' About 1 a.m. I said to him, 'I'm off now, Micky. I've got to be up early tomorrow, I'm going into the country to stay with John and Wendy North. Don't be too long after the last table.'

'No, it's O.K., I'm going to Kit's house afterwards.'

The next thing I heard about Micky was that he was dead. Apparently he'd got up in the middle of the night at Kit's, feeling unwell, and had taken a shower. At 9 a.m. he was found dead in his bed. He had had some kind of apoplectic or asthmatic seizure and had choked to death. He had no history of seizures. Micky's death disturbed me far more than Edward's because there was something spooky about it. Edward's death was grief. But Micky's wasn't quite explicable and so one's sorrow was agitated by the sharp odour of something malign.

Not long after, Kit's house was gutted by fire. And then he lost the Who. With Chris Stamp he had managed them from the beginning and success preyed on all his weaknesses. I was very fond of Kit and it would be incorrect to leave you with the impression that there was deliberate evil in him. He was an intelligent and witty man, blessed with great generosity of heart and pocket. It was his lack of ruthlessness and guile which made it impossible for him to remain on top of the exploding Who empire. Sadly he died recently after falling down a staircase.

During AD8 I again took up my flirtation with show business. It began when Frank Dunlop asked me to play Eva Perón at the Young Vic. Copi, a well-known Argentinian cartoonist, well-known in Argentina anyway, had written a black comedy about her. Vegetables had been thrown at it in Paris. So Frank Dunlop, ever interested in the Theatre of Abrasion, wanted to bring it to London. He dined frequently at the restaurant and out of the blue asked me to take the lead. Copi thought it a good idea too. When I turned round, the project was off.

But my taste buds had been aroused, so I tried again with the film *Human*. This was a Mexican enterprise, produced by George Schwarz, and directed by an assistant of Buñuel's. It amounted to little more than the filming of a London party of which I was to be hostess, *cinéma vérité*-style, the last decadent gasp of Swinging London. They must have been watching the films of Andy Warhol. When we discussed it at lunches beforehand, it sounded decidedly intellectual. Nanette Newman and Joan Collins were also present. I was impressed. The party was to be held in a beautiful rented house in Neville Terrace.

When I turned up there on the night I couldn't believe my eyes. They'd trawled for every freak in London and pulled most of them in. It was packed solid, a madhouse, full of drink and drugs. Everybody had been paid £1 as they went in and told to go wild. Leather queens, transvestites, trendies and weirdoes, debutantes, Bertie Woosters, the Oxford lot. Obviously, incongruity and surprise were what they were after. I never quite understood what I was supposed to do – they'd bought me an expensive frock, loaded me with make-up, and then turned me loose among the crazies while cameras, booms and lights elbowed about.

A man in chains took a girl so violently on a green marble table that it cracked down the centre. It required seven men to carry the two pieces out of the house which should give you an indication of the violence of their congress. I glimpsed Duncan and Rita having a conversation in a wardrobe among a pile of shoes, then I was jostled on. I entered a bathroom for a pee. Ju-Ju, who used to live with Charles Hay, was in there. She was outrageously fat. That was her gimmick. She was in there naked. In the bath. Bubbles all over the floor.

'Ju-Ju, what are all those teethmarks down your breasts?'

'That's my role. Having my tits bitten. D'ya want a bite?'

'No!'; and I fled. What on earth had happened to Nanette Newman and Joan Collins?

A reporter asked me, 'What do you think of it all? There are two men over there kissing.'

'Good luck to them – I'm glad someone's getting something out of this.'

I'd given Rita a bunch of cash to stay sober, lest I got drunk and needed help. But I couldn't get high to save my life. There was one moment when I thought I was getting off the ground, when I found myself with a black nun on a sideboard doing a tango to David Bowie music, then somebody hit me with a chain and I sobered right up again. I was crawling up the stairs to the top of the house for a rest when I saw two studded leather legs planted in my path. In a rapid double movement he unzipped his fly and pulled out a monstrous floppy pink piece and wagged it around in my face. He was so drunk. And so ugly. That did it for me. I was off.

I saw the final cut at Shepperton. There wasn't much of me left.

The plot had changed. It was not particularly complex: two young people go to a party, then go to bed. It was released only in Mexico, where I'm now considered quite avant-garde. But they ought to show it in England, if only at a late-night art cinema, because it was certainly a unique record of something or other.

Mrs Denehy sold the house in Elm Park Road and I moved yet again to 235 King's Road, above another restaurant, but the polishing of Mrs Anne who came with me provided a welcome feeling of continuity. A journalist friend, F., rang me, desperate for accommodation, so I invited her to stay until she'd fixed herself up. After ten days or so of being the model house-guest, she said, 'I've got a boyfriend – would it be all right if he spent the weekend here?'

It didn't make much difference to me because I had the small bedroom so that the large double bedroom would be free for guests. I went to work on the Saturday evening and didn't see who he was. I returned at about 3 a.m., read a little (a biography of the Emperor of Mexico, my current pash), swallowed a Tuinal with lemonade (bottles of each always beside my bed), and switched off the lamp. By and by I was roused from my light preliminary slumbers by a sound similar to that of a dripping tap.

My first thought was: 'Damn these Tuinal.' The capsules have a most ravishing colour scheme, tomato red and turquoise, but sleep was so much easier to come by in the Mandrax era. However, the widespread prescription of Mandrax had given rise to such outrageous behaviour among the young, and not a few inadvertent deaths, and the drug was so little used for strictly soporific purposes, that the medical profession had discontinued it. My second thought was: 'But we don't have any dripping taps.' I lifted both ears off the pillow in order to gauge the sound's direction. It was coming from the bedroom, down the hall. On and on and on it went. Tak tak tak, regular and prim. What could it be? Rats, mice, the plumbing? Then the penny dropped. It was a slapping sound. Finally it lulled me to sleep as a grandfather clock might. But in a slightly different mood it could have gone the other way and driven me insane.

Next morning I was woken up by the aroma of fried bacon curling under the door, so decided to get up and investigate. F. and her boyfriend, looking very *Private Lives* in their silk dressing-gowns, were at the breakfast table tucking into plates of eggs, bacon, mushrooms, tomatoes and fried bread.

'Good morning, April,' said F. 'You know Kenneth Tynan.'

'Good morning, Mr Tynan. You should always grill tomatoes with oregano, you know. It's the only way.'

'I must try that,' he said.

When he'd gone I said, 'Who slaps whom?'

'Well, mostly I slap him.'

'In future give him half a dozen from me. You might have warned me, darling. I can hear everything that goes on and it's not everybody's cup of tea.'

These weekends went on for months. Likewise that restrained and obsessive slapping. There was something so fretful, so middle-class about it. I longed to shout through the walls, 'For God's sake, let yourself go for once, forget the neighbours for once, show some passion for once!' He wouldn't have survived five minutes with Sheherazade. The sound of that slapping symbolised for me the whole predicament of Kenneth Tynan's life, the failure of nerve or imagination or whatever it was which prevented him from fulfilling his promise, from achieving anything robust, anything truly genuine or independent. The more loudly he revolted against the bourgeois temperament the more he revealed his entrapment within it. Such a dainty and colourless bondage, the sound of dandruff striking the shoulders.

Sometimes I had to dash into the vacated bedroom before Mrs Anne arrived, to put away the photographs which had been mistakenly left on show. They decorated their love-nest with Victorian photographs in silver frames of girls being spanked. Or there might be garters and various convolutions of thongs hanging from the bedpost.

One day, like a complete fool, I said to F., 'Why are you wearing a gym slip? Every time you bend over I can see everything you've got.' She had it all on; black stockings, suspenders, black peek-a-boo panties trimmed with blood-red satin, a school tie. It seemed eccentric for tea-time.

'Ken likes it,' she said. 'He's coming round later.'

And then parcels started to be delivered in plain brown wrappings. They were love-aids of a sado-masochistic character. Whips, leather bras, marble eggs covered with leather, etc. What shocked me particularly was that they were all posted from Somerset. F. soon had a bottom drawer full of tricks. She showed it to me.

Finally I decided to bring down the curtain. The ostensible reason was that my niece, Tess's daughter, had rung up wanting to meet me.

I invited her for a weekend (she was a dark and vivacious teenager and reminded me of myself) and was averse to her finding me living in a bondage parlour. It would have confirmed all the family P.R.

As I'd not asked for any rent during this period, I didn't think it unfair to ask them to pay half the bills. I didn't mind having F. stay for nothing but didn't see why I should do the same for Kenneth Tynan, especially as he had a habit of sitting on the telephone and his weekends often lingered into the middle of the week. F. was pretty penniless but Kenneth said he would cover her cheques. But they bounced and bounced. Next the police showed up. There had been a robbery. A red Audi had been used. At that time there were only a few in the country and one of them was Kenneth's. The police had noticed it parked outside. He wasn't connected of course but having to explain to the police made me even more annoyed with him. Then I went to a party given by the feminist pundit Dee Wells. Kenneth was at the party too. He cut me dead, and this on top of all the bouncing cheques. I thought, 'To hell with you, Mr Tynan – this is where I go for the jugular.' I sent a telegram to his house in Thurloe Square, demanding he pay his bill. He wrote back: *What a charmless thing to do.* I cabled back: *Where money's concerned, charm doesn't enter into it.* He paid. The plain fact was that the mood was so uncertain at AD8 that I simply couldn't afford to let him off the hook even if I had wanted to (which I didn't).

The restaurant finally struck its iceberg. Friends had urged me to make my position secure but I hadn't bothered, imagining the future would somehow be wonderful. It wouldn't, apparently. Things were bad, but every night I'd still have to be there on show, smiling, kissing, trying never to express a negative emotion. I was expected to be wise, giving and dramatic. Sometimes the mask slipped and I had my outbursts too. On several occasions I vented my spleen by throwing plates of food the length of the restaurant, provoked by some ineptitude from the staff. Towards the end, there was a new member of staff virtually every month. Some of them couldn't even wait properly. I know many of the customers came in the hope of witnessing a scene. My nerves and resentment were being held in check by Valium and booze. One night one of the waiters came up to tell me that the kitchen was closing and would I give my order. I asked for Pacific Prawns and said to Jean-Pierre, 'I'll have another Dry Martini while I'm waiting.'

'Madame, do you know how many Dry Martinis you've had tonight?'

'Do you mean you've been counting my drinks?'

'The staff asked me to count because they couldn't believe it. If you have this one it will make thirty-two.'

'Then let's make it thirty-two.'

Walking about and chatting so much, one hardly noticed it. But I should have taken note. My liver had started to play up. And Ina Barton had recently died from a combination of booze and pills. I believe an open verdict was recorded but that's splitting hairs – in effect she killed herself. Already I'd had one nasty accident at Elm Park Road.

One night I had passed out in bed with a leaky hot-water bottle. Next morning I awoke with a balloon blister on my ankle. I stuck a pair of scissors into it and the water shot out. Then I bound it up and went to the doctor. 'You've given yourself a severe burn,' he said, 'I'm afraid you'll be scarred for life. You'll have to rest that leg.'

But I had become a workaholic and with all the walking up and down the restaurant the leg wouldn't heal. Some weeks later, after work, I went off to Tramp nightclub where I was always made welcome, regardless of my condition. As I was going down the stairs Ju-Ju's boyfriend John shouted, 'April!' The greeting was so abrupt that I swung round in my long skirt, tripped and fell. I was wearing a blouse with leg-of-mutton sleeves and could hear the poppers unpopping as I bounced down the stairs. At the bottom the waiters rushed to help but I said, 'No, don't touch a thing, leave me for a second, I want to count my bijoux. Well, they all seem to be here. Right, I'll have a large whisky.'

My right wrist swelled up. They wrapped it in a napkin. At dawn I found myself at St Stephen's Hospital in the Fulham Road. The wrist was broken. It was set in plaster but a few days later the hand started turning black. 'This plaster's got to come off,' I thought, because I knew enough medicine to understand that black fingers are the road to gangrene. I squatted dejectedly in the bath for two hours to soften the plaster, keeping myself going with wine-gums, then cut it off. When I returned to the hospital, I was told that the wrist had been set incorrectly. They tried to repair the damage but to this day the joint is misshapen and is turning into a claw. But breaking my wrist had one fortunate result: I had to take a week off work and this healed my leg.

The arm was in plaster for a couple of months. At the restaurant I wore plenty of white so that the sling would glare less. Being right-handed I was unable to prepare myself for work. But luckily my friend Oscar da Costa, the Uruguayan cartoonist and make-up artist, agreed to attend me every afternoon. The South Americans have such baroque fantasies, the baroque of swamps and crocodiles and skeletons of the Saints; I would arrive at AD8 looking like something untoward seen in a mescalin vision. My protests were useless. One day it would be Cleopatra from Mars, the next Dolores del Rio *à la Grècque*, the Duchess of Hong Kong, or Madame Bovary in Zululand.

At the end of the day all I could do was peel off my eyelashes, smear off the paint with a little cold cream, and flop on to the bed. Mrs Denehy would come up when she rose at 7 a.m., to help me out of my clothes and off with my hairpiece, so that I could have a few hours' sleep before Oscar arrived to start all over again. 'Today I see you as the Virgin Mary – divorced!'

Mrs Denehy was a most uncomplaining woman. She made you understand how London survived the Blitz. 'Daddy' Pat Dolin came to take me to see *Charlie Girl* and as we were about to leave he said to her, 'Ah, my good woman, will you find me a taxi please.' She went rushing down the street before I could recover from my embarrassment. I apologised the next day and she said, 'Was it really him? I've been a fan ever since I was a little girl. I'd run to the end of the earth for him.'

Eventually the plaster came off. They bandaged the wrist and put it into a fresh sling. That same night I was unsteadily making my bed when I tripped. Extending my left hand to break the fall, I jarred against the skirting board and smashed the other wrist. Now I came into AD8 with both arms in slings. I looked outrageous. Now I was swallowing Valium like Smarties. I'd go from uptightness to down-tightness in one skid. Of the two, I think I prefer uptightness. At least you know where you are. But I hardly knew where I was from one moment to the next. For three weeks I sat in the bar nodding like something in the rear window of a car as the customers filed past. The two slings gave the impression that I was wearing a strait-jacket.

Just before I had to quit Elm Park Road, something happened which made it possible for me to endure many things. Rita came down to the restaurant one night, her hair a shock of curls like Shirley Temple on a thousand volts (Oscar had been getting at her too), and said, 'You'll never guess – Joey's back in England.'

'Where?'

'In Greenwich.'

He wouldn't come to the restaurant, so we met at Elm Park Road. Although he'd disowned England, he had sold his boat and returned to see if his back could be sorted out once and for all.

'I've rented a house overlooking Blackheath,' he said rather coyly. 'I've a new wife, Nina, and two kids – you haven't changed at all.'

'Neither have you.'

It was true. He was still very athletic. It was like stepping back into a pair of comfortable old slippers, as though he had never been away, as though we were teenagers again.

We'd do the pubs at lunchtime, spend the afternoon in bed (I'd regained the use of my arms), then he would go, and I would get ready for work. I feel as if I should be making more of a song and dance about this. But it wasn't like that. It was so easy.

He'd married the daughter of a rich Canadian merchant who'd taken Joey into the business as the son and heir he'd never had. Joey had hit his groove and was now a successful man.

Then he appeared with his four-year-old son. The boy was prone to sudden bouts of seriousness like his father. We'd take him into the park and sit on the grass while he romped all over us, and I'd pretend that he was our child. I know it was silly, I tried not to, because it only sharpened the painful truth, but all the same I did. Joey was so happy with his son. I'd never seen him so relaxed and yet so filled with delight.

Then he said he wanted me to meet Nina. 'No, Joey, I don't want that. I don't want to be able to visualise her, because I'll start getting guilty.' But he insisted, so we met one Sunday afternoon at the Natural History Museum. She was a tall, elegant woman, very capable, very beautiful. I liked her. Right away the guilt started.

By the beginning of 1974 I was swallowing over a dozen Valium a day. Eventually Dizzy said; 'Dr Atkinson tells me you've got to have a holiday.'

Old friends Beverley and Larry lived on Barbados and invited me over. I met Oliver Messel who was small, wiry, very tanned and extremely mannered, like a monkey who had been raised at the Court of the Sun King. Although on his last legs, he sang and danced famous numbers from *Gigi* for us on his terrace. And I visited Verna Hull who often came to AD8 when she was in London. She lived next door to Claudette Colbert with whom she'd shared a house for many years. But they'd fallen out and despite living only feet apart they didn't speak at all.

Upon my return the battles with my partners started up immediately. The crunch came when they threatened to pension me off to Greece for the six months which remained of my contract.

'I'm not going.'

'Then we'll sack you.'

'There's nothing wrong with me!'

But there was. Having to be charming to customers with the rage burning inside – it eats you up so fast. Finally they geared themselves up and said they wanted me out of the restaurant, and I agreed.

'We'll give you £3,000 as a pay-off.'

'But I put in five! And four and a half years of my life.'

'You can either go for £3,000 or find yourself in court fighting us and ending up without a penny. You'd better take the money or you'll have nothing – and who wants to employ a middle-aged sex-change?'

I didn't have the energy to fight. What was there left? A few nights playing Countess Dracula at the Collegiate Theatre. I fled 235, span round town like a wheel without a pin, and then I fled London.

12 A Woman of Property

I hit forty years of age at a hundred miles per hour and, darling, it hurt. Where was I this time? Oh – in another agony of the soul. Technically speaking, I was at Viva's house, the last party she gave for me, wearing an expression of frantic insouciance and beneath it a bosom of heaving cockfeathers, the smile a silent scream flashing at intervals like the warning light on top of that dam in *Earthquake*, brave, so brave. I looked magnificent but it was all cardboard and paste, every moment on the verge of exploding, smithereening, leaving me starkers, the slightest chip of gravel might do it. And when they'd all gone I slumped, the last dregs of a Knickerbocker Glory. I was past it. And I'd missed it.

The reason I looked magnificent, setting aside the ennobling effect of tragedy, was that I'd just returned from seven weeks in California. I had been hiding away for months at Rita's house, then she'd gone east to India to look for Duncan, who was said to be strawberry-picking in the Nilgiri Hills, and I went west to San Francisco to help a friend sob his way through a nervous breakdown. The west coast was full of distractions. I met Lenny Plugge, who had moved to Los Angeles; Roddy McDowell gave a dinner party for me in Hollywood; we visited the San Andreas Fault, unnaturally green, no sound of birds or animals. I threw a rock to break the ominous silence and said, 'Let's get out of here', and then we drove down to Mexico to watch the whales making love in slow-motion off the coast of Ensenada.

Unfortunately it was nothing but distractions. I had to return to London, the city I love so much and where I have never found any real happiness. This latest collapse had happened so abruptly. I was the toast of the town, on everyone's invitation list, the telephone always ringing, my days a constant parade of novelty, and the next moment . . . When you place your sense of identity in the reflections you see in other people's eyes, what happens when the people go away? When the lights are switched off?

I was profoundly disenchanted. The sudden loss of exterior stimulus left me lethargic and empty. Thrown back on myself, I didn't know what to do. I ventured into Chelsea on a bicycle and was arrested and convicted for drunken driving. It was the night of some I.R.A. bombings in that part of London, so the police were hypersensitive. I rowed with the people with whom I was staying and moved on to Michael Crossley's house in Wimbledon. Every day I walked on Wimbledon Common, talking to myself, screaming at the world, trying to find a route out of the cold and acrid smog which seemed to smother me. By the age of forty, one presumes certain basic expectations will have been fulfilled. Even if one hasn't achieved anything, one expects at the very least to have acquired something. But I had nothing.

After a few weeks' further cogitation, in Ibiza as it turned out, I decided to get right away from it, to move to Hay-on-Wye on the border of England and Wales. Richard Booth had suggested the possibility of opening a restaurant in his castle there, but this wasn't an important factor. What was important was for me to escape the hard (and expensive) glare of city lights, carry off to a quiet place the little knotted scarf containing the fragments of my life and buckle down to the serious business of sorting them out. Those I chose to keep would be pieced together into a simpler and smaller but more sturdy structure.

I had first visited Hay with Viva in the early 1960s. Sited on a dramatic bend in the leafy Wye Valley and overlooked by the Black Mountains, it was Arcadia. The town is exquisitely self-contained, gathered mossily about the castle in precipitous streets built at odd angles to defeat the squalls, and encircled by operatic landscapes – the Brecon Beacons and the snow-tipped Welsh wilderness to the west, the softer undulations of the Golden Valley towards Hereford in the east, to the south the Black Mountains whose baleful if often unseen presence makes the logs in old fireplaces burn more blissfully, and to the north Hergest Ridge and the Radnor Forest. Curving through these set-pieces, like a fertile voluptuary beset by her lovers, is the salmon-laden Wye, most beautiful of rivers. And through all of it move the seasons, four film directors each of distinct personality.

Hay resembles a settlement in a story by Mervyn Peake and is as aloof from outside influences. There are no industrial centres in any direction short of a day's expedition. Therefore no pylons invade its eloquent horizons. The countryside is substantially unchanged from that of the eighteenth century. Not being on the road to anywhere else, it is a destination in itself. The air is abundant and rich in oxygen. The blue sky is alive with green or purple clouds. At night it alters to a dome of stars fixed with a moon unnaturally large and bright. Owls hoot from turrets, bats swerve from steep gables, storms roll out of the mountains and disperse in a pastel sunrise.

It lies exactly on the border, a theoretical line which the inhabitants have widened to make a small domain all their own, owing allegiance neither to the Dragon nor to the Lion. Food and beer are excellent. On festal days the town ripples with coloured pennons. They are tough people with a vigorous sense of humour, sometimes melancholy, occasionally violent, and inclined towards eccentricity. They are accustomed to the passage of outsiders and neither impressed by nor hostile to them. One of the town mottoes is 'Stuff Tourists', which explains much. One cannot hide behind London sophistication because they have their own variety which penetrates it. Hay appreciates the individual, not the type, and it is the visitor who is bewitched by Hay rather than the reverse. He will find himself drinking more than he usually does and prancing more than he might wish. Since the ceilings are low, he should be careful.

Distributed through the town in a number of buildings is Richard Booth's book business amounting to the largest second-hand bookshop in the world. 'When I started,' he said, 'the most prosperous feature of the Hay economy was probably the fruit machine at the British Legion Club – it was making £400 profit per week.' Without altering Hay's fundamental nature, the book business has none the less given it something of an international atmosphere. It wasn't always like that. Richard's first driver, Terry Parton, had never been more than twenty-five miles from the town in his life. When they made their first buying trip to Cardiff, Terry said, 'Cor, isn't London big.'

Richard's maxims for buying stock are 'Never offer a high price – it arouses the seller's suspicions' and 'There's never any good gear in a house with an illuminated doorbell'. But his basic philosophy is 'Buy everything and sort it out afterwards', and so by the time I moved to Hay in September 1975, the town was congested with millions of books – in the castle, in the old cinema, in the converted workhouse. In Richard's wake other booksellers opened up. When they gather together the collective noun is 'a conger' of booksellers – to see them tottering along the streets with armfuls of heavy old volumes gives credibility to this term.

Richard's reputation for eccentricity increased when in 1977 he declared Hay-on-Wye an independent kingdom and crowned himself King, with much roasting, quaffing and jigging. He conferred on me the title of First Lady, Duchess of Hay and Offa's Dyke, and there is no denying that he is a man of some dottiness, given to falling off horses and inadvertently backing his car into other people's sitting-rooms. When his castle burnt down a few years ago, he said that what woke him was the sound of applause. He got out of bed to see why his subjects should be demanding his presence at the ceremonial window in the early hours of the morning. Only then did he realise that it wasn't applause at all but the sound of crackling beams. Typically it was during the firemen's strike. But such lunacy is not without underlying purpose and his flair for Hay promotion is envied by the advertising executives of Mayfair. As the book trade prospered the town drew more and more eccentrics into its sphere, specialising for some reason in unfrocked priests.

With the help of Rita and her battered brown Cortina – a remarkable machine which keeps going despite many inducements to stop, it is just a lump of rust with big holes in it, and over the years has become familiar outside every public house between Aylesbury and Lord Hereford's Knob – I moved into a flat above one of Richard's shops. My new address was terrific: No. 1, The Pavement. And I loved its pitched ceilings and small gable windows which looked out to the Radnor Hills. In the immediate foreground was the town clocktower whose chimes with their lyrical ignorance of Greenwich reminded me of Oxford (that city is full of clocktowers, all telling a different time; they begin to chime midnight at ten-to and go on until ten-past, twenty minutes of brazen uproar).

But my transference to the hills was accompanied by vomiting. I hadn't been well since returning from Ibiza and put it down to something I'd eaten or my squiffy liver. After Rita departed for the Home Counties, I took to my bed and stayed there with a bucket beside it. The following month, October, a friend called Val was coming for the weekend, so I pulled myself together and got out of bed for her visit. On the Saturday evening we went to the Baskerville Arms for dinner. This is in Clyro, a village on the other side of the Wye. The inn takes its name from the hound-loving Baskerville family who built Clyro Court in the early-nineteenth century. It is a strange house. Hallucinogenic mushrooms grow on its lawns. After staying there Sir Arthur Conan Doyle was inspired to write his macabre story *The Hound of the Baskervilles*, although in consideration of his hosts he changed the location to Devon. *Kilvert's Diary* mentions both the house and its occupants. An entry for 1870 tells of a great storm which destroyed the gable in which the housekeeper slept. She and her bed passed through two floors before coming to rest in the shambles of a morning room. On examination she was found to be still asleep, smelling strongly of brandy.

With the decline of Baskerville wealth, Clyro Court sought other keepers, none of them normal. It became a health hydro and a swimming pool was added, fed by mineral springs from the hillside. At one point nobody was sure *what* was going on there, except that Arabs kept landing on the lawns in little helicopters and never stayed above a moment. Then Colin Stone, who had made a fortune selling garden gnomes to the Americans and was even more eccentric than Richard, bought it and tried to turn it into the ultimate pleasure dome for jaded pop stars and dispossessed peers. It really was extraordinarily opulent inside, Liberace Louis Quinze, Walt Disney Scottish Baronial, Tommy Kyle Rainbow Chic. But the house retained its curious ether. Colin always said, 'The house is far more powerful than the people who live in it.' He was right. It was a disaster for him. The last I heard he was languishing in Shrewsbury Gaol.

At dinner with Val I felt better than I had in ages. It must have shown because people I hardly yet knew came up to tell me that I was glowing. But on the way home I began to feel breathless and decided to walk in the air. I had a black-out and came to, feeling terribly shaky, in the doorway of Golesworthy's Outfitters opposite my flat. Val helped me up to my bedroom and as I was recovering on the bed a sharp pain shot under my ribs. Val held my hand for a moment or two, then I said, 'It's O.K. now, go to bed, I'll see you in the morning.' Just as she was about to switch out my light, a much more severe pain hit me in the centre of the chest. It was like being kicked by a horse. My neck was thrown back and my shoulders forward. Dr Harvey arrived at midnight and said, 'I think you've had a heart attack.'

'But, Dr Harvey, I don't smoke, I'm underweight.'

'You do drink and you've been under a lot of stress lately. I'm almost sure that's what it is.'

I was taken to the Nuffield Clinic in Hereford. When they traced a cardiograph they found my heartbeat all over the place. The first twenty-four hours is the critical time. If you survive that, you're likely to survive the heart attack. Every hour or so they woke me up to trace another cardiograph. I'd lost much of the feeling in my arms. Between the shoulder and the elbow they were dark and puffy.

The following weekend Rita visited me with the kids, Denny Daviss rang, and Joey too.

'Do you want me to come down?'

'No, please don't. I don't want you to see me like this.'

'Well, in that case I shan't see you at all. We're going back to Canada next week.'

I was inside for just over two weeks. They wanted me there for a month because Dr Wood said my heart was still very scratchy, but I was terrified of having another attack worrying about the bills. I didn't know how much I was insured for. As it turned out it was up to £10,000. They instructed me to avoid cholesterol, dark meat, chocolate, sweets, salt, white sugar, not to overdo the stairs and to acquire a potty, no sex for the time being – I behaved myself for ten minutes then thought, 'What the hell, if I'm going I might as well go with the few comforts I can muster.' Out came the bowls of sugar, the boxes of sea salt – and there are worse things in life than dying in the arms of a big Welshman.

After a few more weeks I felt fit and went to London to see Viva. She was on good form, lining herself up for imminent celebrity, because her memoirs were due out. I was sitting on a sofa in the drawing-room when suddenly I felt most peculiar. It was as if the floor had given way. My face drained of blood and expression and no longer felt part of me. 'Viva, something's happened.' But I didn't know what.

The doctor suspected that I'd had another heart attack, a minor one, a hiccup as they say, which is really quite common even for healthy people, but coming after the major one it frightened me very much. I returned to Hay at once and took to my bed for five months' solitary confinement. By now I had only a few pounds left. I did a careful budget and calculated that if I cut out all alcohol and most food I could afford to rent a television set, which, with sea salt, was my only luxury but it did prevent me from going gaga. I lived on cabbage and baked beans, my own private recession, madly Jarrow, with occasionally a wine-gum for pud. I would sleep all through the morning if possible, to make the days shorter. And I hardly went out – you don't when you can't afford to buy someone a drink. I stayed in bed to avoid losing weight. My only contact with outside reality was provided by the visits of Pat Wigington, and Gerry and Vera Taylor's sumptuous dinner parties at Winforton Court. Reality? Going to Winforton Court was like going to Samarkand.

For want of anyone else, I struck up conversations with Edward. I'd shake my fist at the ceiling and say, 'Hey, Edward, what's going on up there? You're supposed to be looking after me so put that angel down and pull your finger out.' There was plenty of time to think and I began to make notes for my book.

Eventually I'd had all the cabbage I could take. It is in fact a fine vegetable but day after day, week after week, even with sea salt on, you begin to turn pale green and start dreaming of Holland, definitely a danger sign, so I went up to London for a few days to stay with Colin Stone. While there I thought, 'I'll give Tommy's London number a ring.' It was August, I expected him to be frolicking in Cannes, but he picked up the phone and said, 'What a wonderful birthday present. Today is my fiftieth birthday. I've been trying to get hold of you but everyone tells me you've vanished into thin air. Come to my party tonight.' Afterwards we went to eat at La Popote.

'So what are you doing these days?' he asked.

'Recuperating in the country.'

'Poor lamb, how gruesome. What are you doing for the next couple of weeks?'

'Nothing, always nothing.'

'You are now. You're coming to France.'

'No, I'm not. And for one reason.'

'What's that?'

'I don't even have the money to tip your staff.'

'Don't worry about that.'

'I'm serious, Tommy. My purse is a howling void.'

'I know, I heard – I'll take care of everything.'

The next minute I was sitting on the golden carousel up to my chin in chauffeurs and chambermaids. At one point Gustav said, 'I know a lovely place for lunch – in Geneva', and we flew off in one of his private planes. Aren't wings wonderful? We were back at Croix des Gardes in time for cocktails. Tommy took his yacht out, the *Casa Nina*, and we bumped along the coast for a few days with Mrs Ting-a-Ling and the singer Lulu, who had married one of the Bee Gees. In St Tropez we tied up opposite a coffee bar. I was on deck taking the southern air in my curlers and spotted Amanda Lear among the coffee drinkers. I said to Tommy's friend, Brian, 'Do go and ask her on board for a drink. I can't cross the road like this.' I saw Brian talking to her, I threw her a tiny wave, and she hopped on to her bicycle and pedalled off as if pursued by devils. It was the last time I saw her. Harold and Grace Robbins were tied up nearby and invited us across for dinner. Linda Christian was with them and I thought, 'How can some people stay in this *milieu* without ever suffering?' Linda floated through the *beau monde* as effortlessly as a cork. Nothing sank her. At the end of the holiday, Tommy quietly handed me envelopes to give to the staff.

Back in Hay I decided it was time to improve my own earthly circumstances. I went to the Social Services offices in Brecon. I hated doing it because I come from the generation which considers such things shameful. The official said, 'Why haven't you worked?' I said, 'Because I've had a heart attack.' She gave me £14.50 on the spot and I went bright red. Their doctors decided I was to be registered as a disabled person because I wasn't supposed to stand for more than four hours a day nor stretch my arms above my head. Mr Evans of Wrexham made contact with me, a charming careers officer who suggested I go on a rehabilitation course learning to put tops on bottles.

'Mr Evans, it's very kind of you but I haven't come all this way to start putting tops on bottles.'

'Veronica Lake worked in a factory in her time of troubles.'

'Did she? How heartbreaking. It's probably what killed her. What else have you got?'

'There's a short cookery course . . .'

I was famished and jumped at it, three months at Radbrook College in Shrewsbury, a very beautiful and very boring town. Richard let me keep on the flat in Hay and I went to Shrewsbury to look for temporary digs, tramping round boarding houses all day, one Edwardian door after another, with no luck. Finally I came to the last on my list, Mrs Williams of Park House. She opened the door and said, 'I only take men.' My face hit the doorstep and she must have softened at this because she said, 'You do look tired. Come in for a cup of tea and we'll talk about it.' She went on, 'All the girls I've had have been so dreadful, so untidy and noisy. I find men much more considerate, which isn't what you'd expect, is it?' I was about to go down on my knees and slobber in the style of a spaniel by Landseer, but she forestalled it by saying, 'I'll take you on for a week's trial.'

For the first two days at Radbrook I was anonymous. On the third day it was out. I went into the dining-hall and two hundred pairs of eyes turned and stared. There was an unhealthy murmur like marsh gas escaping from a bog. Any course connected with food demands that you hide your hair for hygiene purposes and so I was wearing a hairnet, one of those faintly wartime ones which make you look as though you were carrying a load of rolled veal on your head. Before, I had always relied on my glamorous shell to protect me in moments such as this. Now I had to face them as Mrs Mop. I was groping wildly for a champagne cocktail to quell the mutinies in my thorax but none was at hand, only canteen coffee and some fatigued sandwiches. 'Valour, dear, valour,' I said to myself, 'remember Ekaterinberg.' I sailed towards a table on sheer willpower and felt much better after I'd occupied a plastic chair and joined a discussion on student power and the Fight For Peace movement.

One of the women in my class said I was a rich bitch who was exploiting the tax-payers' money for a lark, but Mrs Williams saw through it. At the end of the week there was a little tap on my bedroom door. I put down *Daisy Princess of Pless* by Herself – at the point where a shorthand-typist, Mrs Leeds, was about to marry well and turn into Her Royal Highness Princess Nancy of Greece – and said, 'Come in.'

'It's only me,' said Mrs Williams. 'My, you have made it cosy in here. I hope you will stay, April. You never go out, you never eat. I don't want to speak out of turn but I suspect you're going through a rough time. So I'm dropping the rent a bit and I've got a television for your room.'

The class was of all ages, some young kids of seventeen, the majority in the middle years, and a widower of sixty-five who decided it was time he learned to boil his own eggs. Much of it wasn't new to me and although I wasn't the best in the class, I was the fastest, especially with the boning knife. One of our tutors, Mrs Bracegirdle, who for a cookery teacher had a remarkably hungry look, Kafka cheekbones with straight black hair chopped off at the neck, gave me any extra filleting which had to be done. One morning Mrs Bracegirdle came up to me with an extra chicken and plonked it down. 'Do that as well,' she said. Suddenly, feeling like something at the bottom of a pit in a film about oppression under Stalin, I rounded on her.

'Mrs Bracegirdle, you're a bloody bitch. Take that carcass off my bench. There are words in the English langauage such as please and thank you.'

'I'm sorry. Of course I mean please. Now, will you fillet the chicken?'

'No, I won't. It's too late. There are youngsters in this class. You should be setting an example.'

When we were taken round the Wem Brewery or the Shrewsbury Abattoir, we were supposed to ask questions. Whether stinking of beer or dripping with blood, I always asked dozens – every time I opened my mouth Mrs Bracegirdle's face took on the expression of someone who's just found a slug in the lettuce.

I was the only short-course student to be invited to the end-of-term College Ball. I was in my cockfeathers and a low-cut black dress and the Principal asked me to join his table for a drink. I downed a massive vodka and set off. Half-way across the hall my heel snapped, I lurched, and my breasts tumbled out. The whole place went up in a storm of laughter and I decided it was my bedtime. The next day Mrs Bracegirdle gave me the look of death.

'Good morning, Mrs Bracegirdle.'

'I heard all about you last night. 90 per cent fall-out.'

She wasn't being funny. At least she didn't look as if she was. Perhaps her sense of humour was very dry. Some people don't smile when they're amused.

On my last day I was packing up to leave when Mrs Williams came up to say there were eight women and one man to see me. I didn't know who they could be, because I'd kept entirely to myself and made no friends. They were from the class, including the woman who had called me a rich bitch. They didn't want to leave without telling me how much fun it had been having me in their class. It was a sweet thing to do but I couldn't see the back of Shrewsbury fast enough. My best friend had been Terry Wogan on the radio.

The main purpose of the course, from my point of view, was to push me back into life rather than provide a marketable skill. So I decided I'd like to do a proper three-year course in *cuisine* and contacted Mr Evans again. I wanted it to be in a different place because everyone in the border counties knew who I was and would never allow me to take study sriously. He tried Exeter University but it fell through. Then Bangor and that fell through. Finally he said, 'There's a place going on a one-year business course at the Coleg Howell Harris in Brecon.' Elementary mathematics, typing, book-keeping, etc. It was like going back to junior school but made tolerable by my tutor, Mr Jones, a dear.

But all my worst fears were realised. One day they were reading about the elegant Miss Ashley in the local papers, the next seeing me run for the 7.55 a.m. bus to Brecon. I was just as confused as they were and the Hay kids were a real pest.

Usually you can quip your way out of taunts. But when tired you either ignore totally or fight back totally. 75 per cent of my life has been a silent battle against rising to the bait. And some of the things they come out with. When you've been the object of public attention, you realise that most people don't know what they're talking about most of the time. You can't keep putting them straight. It's so exhausting. I've never wanted to go round justifying myself, as if I were ashamed of what I've done, as if the right to lead my life needed a special dispensation. Even in this book I'm not trying to justify – only to explain a little and not even too much of that.

It wasn't easy being accepted in Hay. I don't mean accepted like the locals who were born and raised there – one shouldn't expect that – but simply to be taken for granted in the local landscape without always causing nudges and loaded comments. I was accepted in this way eventually but it takes time and I'd forgotten that. Time moves more slowly in the country or rather each moment, because of fewer distractions, is subjected to a more detailed examination than in the city. Knowledge is narrower but goes deeper, everyone knows everything about everyone, and acceptance means acceptance in the round.

The kids were the worst, the eight to twelve year olds. Sometimes they were comic. 'She's a lesbian, you know,' I overheard one puppy say to his friend. Goodness knows how some of the more squeamish parents explained me to their offspring. The thought of simply explaining the facts of life causes most of them to blanch and gibber, they usually just take the kids along to a farm, so how they managed with sex-changes . . . and I'm sure their children would have asked at all the wrong moments, in front of Aunt Maud, during 'Match of the Day', when the whisky bottle was empty.

Yes, before long the kids were all-knowing, which is right, but sometimes they were horrid. 'Look at her. Are your tits real?' Usually I strode by on the other side, but once I was hung-over, Christopher Fry (the young landlord of my local, the Blue Boar) had had one of his Dionysian parties the night before, ale and Glen Morangie and great hams. I was running for the Brecon bus and I was late. They were young teenagers. One was being especially loutish. I wheeled round and charged at him.

'So who are you to jeer at people? Men don't jeer. How do you want to grow up? To be a nothing? To be a little creep sniggering in the corner all your life? If you want to know something, behave like a man and ask me to my face. Men are open and honest and courageous. They don't hang around in streets jeering at decent people. Do you want to be a man? Or do you want to be a coward and a baby?'

I walked away, smoke pouring from my head, the bus probably way past Aberllynfi by now, but terrified too in case they jeered again, because then I should know I'd lost, that the truth hadn't impressed them, that my attack had failed. But they didn't jeer. Perhaps the boy learned something important that day. Perhaps he didn't. Perhaps he's still shivering with the sheep.

However, I'm not so fanciful as to imagine that my history should arouse no comment. And I readily admit that what may have been tough for me nevertheless has many comic aspects. In fact laughter is usually my own first reaction when I think about my past, because a sex-change has one thing in common with every other man and woman – the comedy of being human in a superhuman universe, the incongruity between what we are and what we frequently imagine ourselves to be. Suicide is the complete failure of the sense of humour. I promised to thin out the suicides and I've done so. Caroline Stocker's. Duncan Melvin's. Duncan's surprised me. He always seemed so amused. But it must have been a front. Something must finally have called his bluff and he fell for it. June Churchill's was different. She was in the throes of terminal cancer and a member of the Voluntary Euthanasia Society. Even with all the modern drugs they could not control the pain and so when no one was looking she swallowed a handful of heroin pills and stuck a polythene bag over her head.

One of the problems of my newspaper exposure was that I became always a sex-change first and anything else second. I don't blame the *People*. It had to happen and the furtive life was always what I wanted to escape. But it also meant that to survive I had to be brazen and that can coarsen a temperament. Until the story broke I was learning, learning, learning. Afterwards I was notorious and it was left to me only to exploit my personality. I was forced to become an 'artist of life', which is close to the art of the actor in that in many respects one is the product of one's own imagination, but differs from it in one important respect. That is, one *is* what one appears to be. One has only one role. Or to be exact, one is allowed to have only one role. Most people play a variety of roles, whether they realise it or not. To have only one is a great privation and prevents one from doing many things which almost everyone else takes for granted, such as working in a shop if one has to, because one lacks the chameleon adaptability necessary for casual living. The image tends to require reality to bend to it, instead of simply colluding with reality in an informal way, and so of course one ends up an institution. This is not true of all celebrities, only of those whose celebrity is due to some singularity in their personal life as opposed to the singularity of their professional accomplishments. But there is one compensation here if one has the perspicacity to see it and the strength to grasp it. Most people all their life are the dupe of their self-image. Those of us whose self-image is made a widely public thing, either through scandal or a quirk of nature, are forcibly detached from that self-image, which is terribly painful, yes, but can be the beginning of many profound freedoms.

I need my solitude but I also need company. The manner of the break-up of AD8 severely damaged my natural liking for people but like everyone else I want to be used and be useful. So in Hay I found my good cause, a man in his eighties called Charles Simpson. He'd been a nervous wreck since the age of forty when he retired into leisure from the garage business, but being a hypochondriac, the attention which he lavished on his health meant that for his years he was as fit as an ox. Charlie had buried two wives and lived alone in a substantial house which had belonged to the second of them, the highest house in Hay after the Castle. I cooked for him, gave him the town gossip, to which he affected indifference, steered him away from the bottle, and tried to make sure he didn't muddle up his boxes of pills. I cheered him up by refusing to treat him like a two-year-old – the secret of getting on with old people is not to behave as if they've just strayed from the pram – and in general played the loving but exasperated daughter. In return he made me feel like Ingrid Bergman, full of good deeds.

Happiness. The Big H. The question they always ask. Are you happy? It is the inevitable question because it is what everybody wants to be and hardly anybody is. I have to reply – happy with what? With the operation, yes, of course I am. It gave me my chance for happiness and one cannot expect more. Although it did give me a problem as well, different in character from the social difficulties already mentioned. I had realised my dream, my goal, and that is rare. At the age of twenty-five it's rarer still. The purpose of a dream or an aim is to focus individual effort. Without it a life cannot develop, will simply pass from day to day in a haphazard fashion like a dog's; and if you live like a dog, you die like a dog. But such aims should always be placed just beyond the fingertips. I lost my central purpose by achieving it and the problem was what to do afterwards.

If you want to talk about life in general, then happiness is no less elusive for me than it is for everyone else. Nietzsche, my dear, said, 'One remains young only on condition the soul does not relax.' Youthfulness and happiness are at odds with each other. In middle age one can incline to defeatism or complacency but while recognising and accepting one's limitations, it is important not to abandon the dream, the self-criticism, the possibility for exultation, the inner exertion. I know my limitations but I often ignore them. There is a Chinese proverb which says, 'Nature takes the line of least resistance.' That is the distinction between Man and Nature, Man's fearlessness in pursuit of the impossible. Relaxation, acceptance, happiness belong to old age, one's very last moments. The greater the exertion, the greater the relaxation. Because I have nowhere near reached the time for relaxation, I am still insecure in many ways. For example, I tend to grab at people if I like them. This is due not to my transsexualism but to my upbringing. My childhood was the worst time but it geared me up for the rest of my life. After a recent television interview in which I mentioned this, I received a letter from one of the boys who used to bash me in Norris Green. *I felt so upset I was tempted to write but got cold feet. Then I saw the programme repeat and decided to, thinking they can't shoot you for it, so here goes*. He sounds like a real man to me.

Of that which has passed – what is the correct way to view it? As far as possible I have checked my facts because I know the memory can be a conjurer and, as Justice Ormrod remarked, transsexuals have a tendency to be selective historians, although the failing is by no means confined to them. All romantics – which includes all lawyers and all historians – view events through the spectacles of their adoption. But I don't think I have been gratuitously cruel or taken obnoxious liberties. I did want to be brisk and astringent and this is bound to make some people uncomfortable, especially when I have not underwritten their *amour-propre*. A phenomenon observed by two minds has a tendency to display divergent characteristics. Besides, people are famous for not seeing themselves as others see them. This is a very personal memoir and perhaps some of those in it never grasped the effect they had on me. Let them remember that I have by no means presented myself in a blameless light and that my partial view is not the end of the story or the whole story, but it is me.

I was attending Coleg Howell Harris when in November 1978 I was told of Viva's death. It wasn't unexpected and the loss took time to make itself felt.

During the last few years I had tried to visit her as often as possible, and always on New Year's Eve. After such a life it was awful to see her all alone in her bed, reading the *Evening Standard* on the last night of the year.

'Come on, there's a party down the road.'

'No, I can't, I couldn't, I mean I shouldn't, no,' but she'd already be climbing out of bed and making for the black-velvet skirt.

Her autobiography had not been received as she'd hoped. It lacked sweep. In fact it lacked everything. Stuffy, emotionless, decidedly ungay, it was so unlike her. She had left out so many important things. She hardly touched on the vital black market of life which seethes beneath the membrane of official transactions. At the same time she had nothing very nice to say about anyone, at least not about anyone who was alive, including me. I accused her of betraying fourteen years of friendship and – which was the criminal thing – doing so without wit. She said, 'Don't be so touchy – look at these', and held up a fistful of umbrageous letters. The book was her final gesture to life and after it flopped she took to her bed.

Viva's last time out was when I took her to lunch round the corner at the George and Dragon. I bullied her into it – she liked to be bullied, it excited her masochistic streak. The second we arrived I set her up with a large gin and tonic. She loved freshwater fish and had trout, whereas I love seawater fish and had sole. Afterwards she walked back to the house content and erect, having forgotten all about her stick. Back in bed she said, 'Do you think your friend Oscar would come round and do my hair?'

'No, I don't think he would, because you sneered at hairdressers in your book.'

A suggestion of the naughty old smile passed across her lips. She didn't go out again. She went into a rapid decline, started losing her teeth, developed bedsores which had to be covered with pads, and with her white hair sticking out on either side looked exactly like Michael Foot when he's rabble-rousing. Although terribly lonely she refused to see anyone except me. The maid and nurses kept everyone away. Viola Hall paid a visit but was turned away and had to leave her flowers behind in the hall. There must have been others. I smuggled Rita in one evening, to Viva's fury and Rita's consternation. Although Rita had become a visitor at the Stoke Mandeville Hospital for the Disabled and saw many unfortunate things every day, she wasn't prepared for the change in Viva.

But the mind was still wonderfully complete, wonderfully unclouded by false sentiment. Towards the end she wrote to me in Hay: *I am like Oscar Wilde, dying beyond my means, the china has all gone, but if it doesn't keep the night nurse I shall have to start on the pictures – I detest doing it, but I am too frightened a coward to end it all which would be the best way.*

In her will she left me all her pictures. On my last visit she said, 'Take Santiago de Compostella with you.' It was a carving which she knew I loved. 'Go on, take him. It doesn't matter to me, I'll never see my drawing-room again. Take him, the pictures are going so fast, you'll have nothing.'

But I couldn't take him. When she died there were still a few pictures left, though none very valuable. She left me a little capital too and so finally I was able to come off social security. I asked Richard if he were going to his aunt's funeral and if so to give me a lift. But he said he wasn't mad about death and wouldn't be going, so I didn't go either. She wouldn't have minded. Like me, Viva didn't believe in an after-life. I still miss her very much, more now than at the time of her death, and looking back I wish I had attended the funeral, because a funeral has nothing to do with the dead or with creating the right impression with the other mourners – it is to fix something in oneself.

Death, death, death! My goodness, and we still can't pack away the bombasine because there is one other I must record – Charles Simpson's – dear old Charlie's – and I mention it because the solicitor said to me, 'In his will Mr Simpson left you his house.'

'Well, I never. Thank you, Charlie,' I said sweetly like Irene Dunne in *The White Cliffs of Dover*.

Thus, for the first time, I became a woman of property.

As a householder I am now entitled to apply for a gun licence – I must get round to that soon. The Hay boys who play Devil's Leap by rushing unexpectedly and at top speed across my garden will provide excellent target practice. A few hefty blasts at them and I'll be in shape for a safari through East Africa or a trek across Australia.

I have been considering whether to go to the Court of Human Rights at Strasbourg to sue the British Government for marriageable status. But somehow there are so many more important things to do. Like having the house painted inside and out. When I suggested it to Charlie he said, 'But it's only just been done.'

'When was that? 1965?'

'No. 1952.'

All that dark House of Horror woodwork – fine – I like a little intimidation to back me up – but Dracula walls as well? Ian (my decorator), start stripping! Let there be light! He says he needs a blowtorch . . . 'Try the outhouse,' I shout as I rush to the door to take delivery of my new curtains.

'Can you pay now?' says the man from Hereford with a pencil in his ear.

'Of course I can – just give me a moment,' I reply from somewhere near his feet because the curtains are surprisingly heavy.

Then there's the garden wall, a noble edifice built of stones from the medieval town rampart, solid as a rock for centuries. As soon as I move in, it collapses, taking several embanked trees with it.

'Can you sort of pile it back up?' But apparently it is a major engineering exercise to be compared with the raising of the *Mary Rose*, so I'll have to stock up on tea-bags. While they're about it they can take out some of those gnarled dead apple trees which at night look as if they want to crawl in through the window and strangle me. I've been out there in my housecoat and wellies and hit them with an axe, but it's a man's job. And the Elephant Ears clogging the front – tea roses, I think. And some slates have slipped off the roof.

And the bills. You pay them and in return they send you some more. It's sick. Surely we could devise a civilisation which wasn't modelled on an Oriental torture? I'll be glad when my yacht arrives and I can sail off round the world for a year or two. Clockwise or anti-clockwise? The eternal dilemma . . .

And there's the dog to feed, a golden whippet, dear Flora, but she will break wind so. She is easily excited and has to control herself, I insist, and I think this is the way she expresses her tension. I've tried everything, all the diets. I've cut out her pasta, her French beans, anything containing cream and garlic, and absolutely no choccy drops, at most a Terry's Spartan, but it's no good. It doesn't much matter when we're alone together, one acclimatises, but if we have guests they flick each other rodent looks and the conversation falters and the Dry Martinis start to bubble.

And the central heating. Charlie died before he could initiate me into the mysteries of this esoteric system. There's the most frightful rumpus going on up in the attic, and down here the walls are shaking, the pipes racked with screams. I've turned every knob I can find but the steam is still spurting from the joints, filling the room with a scalding fog. One hears stories of violent explosions, appalling devastation. I try turning it off but it's got a will of its own and ignores me. And here I am, off to a hunt ball, dressed as Artemis of Ephesus with —— honking furiously from the car, the telephone's ringing, the dog's howling, lightning in the sky, and the wind is on the rise – let me tell you, something's going to blow, baby, and it won't be the champagne cork. Boom! Boom! Boom!!!

Index

Aberconway, Christobel, Lady, 191
Abraham, F. Z., 73
acting, 102–4, 145, 146, 252–4, 260
AD8 restaurant, 226, 236–44, 249–52, 256–60, 273
Ad Lib, nightclub, 110, 176–7
adolescence, 10, 21
adrenogenital syndrome, 212, 227
Alaria Ballet, 66, 93
Alba, Doña Maria, Duchess of, 131, 146
Alice, Princess, Duchess of Gloucester, 105
ambiguity, sexual, 73–6; *see also* transsexualism
America, S.S., 25
androgen, 230
Annabel's, nightclub, 176, 180
Anne, Mrs, 249, 254, 255
Antoinette, Villa, 126, 127, 131, 134, 144, 149, 206, 219, 220
Antrim, Lord, 241–2
Arena Club, Weston-super-Mare, 139–40
Aretusa Club, 176
Armstrong, Dr C. N., 74, 207–8, 213, 214, 229, 230
Armstrong-Jones, Carol (later Lopez), 108, 155
Arteaga y Martin, Inigo, 129–31, 135
Ashcroft, Lyn, 158
Ashcroft Theatre, Croydon, 157–8
Assheton-Smith, Lady Joan, 249
Astor, Nancy, Viscountess, 143
Astor Club, cabaret, 137–8
Audley, Lady, *see* Churchill, Sarah
Audley, Henry, Lord, 128, 138, 146, 165
Audrey, 46, 57, 65–6, 69, 70, 78, 93

Back, Barbara, 121, 146, 194–5, 239–40
Back, Ivor, 194
Back, Patrick, 146
Bacon, Francis, 158–9, 239
Baddeley, Hermione, 112, 249
Bagley, Richard, 163
Bailey, David, 175
Bailey, James, 192–3
Baird, Maxine, 148
Baker, Josephine, 68–9
Balmain, 89, 192
Bambi, 50, 53, 57, 62, 78, 80
Barbados, 259–60
Bart, Lionel, 108, 145, 240
Barton, Ina, 46, 104, 139, 140, 156, 257
Barton, James, 250
Bashford, Patrick, 108
Baskerville Arms, Clyro, 265
Bassey, Shirley, 72, 108, 232
Bavaria, 199–201
Beatles, the, 176–7
Beaton, Sir Cecil, 249
beauty, 153
Beauvoir, Simone de, 51
Bedford, Duke of, 104, 176
Beirut, 181–3

Belcher, Muriel, 108, 158–9
Benjamin, Dr Harry, 73, 227
Bennett, Jill, 115
Benson, Gale, 163
Benzedrine Inhalers, 33, 35, 36
Bergman, Ingrid, 239
Betty, masseuse, 224
Big Gloria, 29, 33, 36
Bismarck, Princess, 1, 132–3
Blair, Lionel, 145
Blond, Anthony, 191
Bluebell Girls, 66, 93
Blueharnis, Lady Georgia, 76
Bodin, Robert, 76–7, 92–3
Bologna, 72
Bonham-Carter, Lady Charlotte, 191
Booth, Richard, 191, 262–4, 276
Bowie, David, 241
Bracegirdle, Mrs, 270
Brahms, Penny, 185
Brecon, 271
Brenan, Gerald, 126
Bridgewater, Bentley, 191
British Encyclopaedia of Medical Practice, 229
Brockway, Roger, 204
Brown, Ada (later Jamieson), 2–3
Brown, Georgia, 108
Browne, Hon. Nicky, 175
Browne, Hon. Tara, 175
Brussels, 76
Buchan, Benjy, 204
Buchanan-Michaelson, Bob, 184
Buchanan-Michaelson, Jane, 184
Buckle, Richard, 191
buffet parties, 107–8
Burou, Dr, 79, 82–92, 104, 153, 208
Burou, Mme, 85
business course, 271

cabaret tour, 137–40, 142
Cadillac, Rita, 66
Caine, Michael, 158
calcium, deficiency of, 4, 83
California, 18–19, 22–3, 24–5, 261
Callas, Maria, 68
Callingham, Lance, 106
Calthrop, Gladys, 191, 240
Campbell-Becker, Ginny, 161
Campbell-Walter, Fiona, 100
Canada, 19–20
Cannes, 49, 62, 63, 244
Capparoni, Mimi, 170
Capri, 166–7
Caprice, 115, 118, 154, 181
Capucine, 67–8
Le Carrousel, nightclub, 49, 52–72, 79–80, 91, 92–6, 99, 120
Cartmel, Ada, *see* Jamieson, Ada
Cartmel, Bernie, 3, 7, 31, 183, 184, 194, 208–9
Casablanca, 79, 80–92, 153
Catholicism, 3, 5, 6, 34–5
Cauldwell, D. O., 73
Channon, Chips, 200
charity balls, 105–6
Château Impney Hotel, Kidderminster, 183, 184
Chelsea, 175–6, 177–8, 196
Chelsea Potter pub, 155, 175, 177, 185, 196
Cherkassky, Shura, 187
Cherry Marshall modelling agency, 98–9
Chester, 32
childhood, 2–11
Christian, Linda, 177, 268
chromosomal sex, 211–12, 213, 227
Churchill, Arabella, 205, 250
Churchill, June, 176, 205, 250, 272–3
Churchill, Sarah, 90–1, 94–5, 97, 113, 114, 122, 128, 138, 146–7, 149, 153, 157, 158, 164, 165, 171, 176, 248, 250
Churchill, Sir Winston, 158, 195
Clark, Ozzie, 175, 180
Clinique du Parc, Casablanca, 79, 82–92
clothes, 235–6
Clutton-Brock, Eleanor, 237
Clyro, 265
Coccinelle, 50, 53, 54, 55, 57, 58, 70–1, 75, 77–80, 95
Cocteau, Jean, 124, 241
Coddington, Grace, 99
Cogan, Ronnie, 33, 35, 40, 136
Colbert, Claudette, 58, 260
Coleg Howell Harris, Brecon, 271, 275
Collegiate Theatre, 260
Collins, Joan, 103, 252
Colony Room Club, 159
commercials, 101–2
Comyn, Sir J. P., 209, 211
Constantinople, King of, 171
Cooch Behar, Maharani of, 108

cookery course, 268–70
Coombe, Carol (later Lopez), 108, 155, 162–3, 166, 174
Cooper, Lady Diana, 191
Copi, cartoonist, 252
Corbett, Hon. Arthur Cameron, 116–18, 120–1, 122, 123–9, 131, 132, 137, 138–9, 146–50, 153, 154, 206–11, 215–16, 219, 220–1
Corbett, Hon. Bobby, 147
Corbett, Hon. Eleanor, 116, 117–18, 120
Cork, Clare, 37, 41
cosmetics, 234–5
Côte d'Azur, 49, 62–5, 93, 120, 244–7, 268
Coward, Sir Noël, 104, 240, 249, 250
Cowell, Roberta, 74
Crabtree, Eric, 203
Craven, Mrs, 48
Crewe, Quentin, 233
Cristóbal, 18
Croix des Gardes, Château, 244–5, 268
Crosby, Bing, 103–4
Crosby, Caresse, 186–7
Crosby, Harry, 186–7
Cross, Sir Ronald, 132
Crossley, Michael, 262
Crowder, Harry, 190
Cunard, Nancy, 190, 240
Curran, Dr Peter, 204
Cynthia, washerwoman, 17, 18, 22, 30

da Costa, Oscar, 258, 276
Dali, Salvador, 69
Damascus, 182–3
Dankworth, Johnny, 240
Danny, seaman, 13, 14, 18–19
David, porter at AD8, 237–8
Daviss, Denny, 155, 166, 239, 266
Dawson, Bumble, 191
Dawson-Denver, Roger, 177–8, 198
Dean Paul, Brenda, 44
de Lambrey, Vikki, 241, 242
Denehy, Mrs, 249, 254, 258
Dent, Professor Charles, 208, 216, 243
Dent, Marilyn, 112–13, 114
Dent-Godalming, Fluffy, 204
de Piro, Michael, 203, 204
de Pombo, Ana, 124, 138, 205
De Sica, Vittorio, 107
Dewhurst, Sir John, 208, 213, 214, 216, 226, 231
Dietrich, Marlene, 58
Digby, Hon. Jane, 182–3, 200, 234
divorce, 206–21, 238
Dixon, Edwina, 158
Dixon, Piers, 158
Dizzy, *see* Morgan, Desmond
Docker, Norah, Lady, 177
Dolin, Sir Anton ('Daddy Pat'), 67, 189, 240, 258
Dolphin Square, 96, 97
Domingo, Placido, 239
Donaldson-Hudson, Dorothy, 108
Donovan, Terence, 101
Dors, Diana, 177
Douglas, Norman, 240
Doyle, Richard, 219, 220
Dragadzi, Peter, 171
Drysdale, Polly, 186–7, 241
Drysdale, Stephen, 186
Dudley Hippodrome, 139
Duff, Lady Juliet, 190
Duff, Sir Michael, 189, 190
Duncan, Isadora, 241
Dunlop, Frank, 252

Eagle Star Insurance, 232
Earl's Court, 41–7
East, Roy, 121
Eaton Square, 238–9
Edge, David, 142
Egerton Gardens Mews, 232
Eicher, Dr Wolf, 230
Einstein, A., 34
Elbe, Lili, 73
Elm Park Road, 249, 254, 257, 258–9
Emperor's Gate, 107, 120
Endicott, Reggie, 3, 28–9
Ernestine, 43, 48
Establishment Club, 155, 158
Eunice (1st wife of Joey), 98, 100, 156–7
Evans, Mr, careers officer, 268, 271
Everage, Dame Edna, 247
Everest, of Le Carrousel, 53–4, 91, 250
examinations, medical, 207–8, 213–14, 216

Faith, Adam, 138
Faithfull, Marianne, 176

Fallowell, Duncan, 204, 205, 219–20, 231, 253, 261
Fallowell, T. E., 220
fan mail, 24
Farrell, Rita (later Wallace), 36
fashion, 236
Fashion Models agency, 99
Fata Morgana, 157–8
Fath, Geneviève, 66
Fazakerly: bomb factory, 4; hospital and cemetery, 193–4
Fedorovitch, Sophie, 190
Fellini, Federico, 166, 167, 173
Fernandez, Enrique, 100
Ferry, Bryan, 241
Fielding, Fenella, 108
Fielding, Rollo, Viscount, 176
Filben, Miss, 6
films, 102–4, 252–4
Finch, Peter, 106–7, 135
Fish, Michael, 175
Fitzrovia, 34
Fleet, Simon, 189–90
Florence, 72
Foa, Giorgio, 210
Foa, Joan, 203, 210, 221
Forbes, Sir Ewan, 74
Forbes-Sempill, Elizabeth, 74
Forest Mere, Hants., 222–4
Four, Dr, 53
'Frank', *see* Corbett, Hon. Arthur
Freshrise Ltd, 232
Freud, Lucien, 108, 114
Fry, Christopher, 272
Furness Withy Ltd, 24–5
Fürstenburg, Princess Ira von, 125, 144

Gaiffier d'Hestroy, Baron Paul de, 225–6
Gallier, Johnny, 243, 250
Garbo, Greta, 249
Gardner, Ava, 34, 222, 239
Garland, Judy, 67
Gasworks, restaurant, 197
gender, definition of, 207, 210, 211–14, 226–31
genital sex, 212, 213
Giancarlo, 95
Gibraltar, marriage in, 148
Gingold, Hermione, 112, 114, 176
Glass, Blanche, 194
Glass, Eric, 194
Godwin, Bill, 126, 148
Godwin, Doreen, 126, 148
Golan, Barbara, 99
gonadal sex, 212, 213
gossip columns, 121–2, 157
Gough, Simon, 63
Granger, Jamie, 184
Grey, Dr Geoffrey, 178
Grimsthorpe, Lincs., 112
Gulbenkian, Nubar, 115
Guppy, Mrs, 154, 170, 175, 178, 185

Haden-Guest, Anthony, 154, 176
hair, and gender, 216–17
Hall, Viola, 191, 276
Hamburg, Dodo, 66
Hamburger, Christian, 73
Hamilton, Gerald, 195–6, 249
happiness, 274
Harrington Gardens, 99, 106–7
Harrison, Rex, 58
Hauterive, Hélène, 226–7
Hay, Lord Charles, 204, 253
Hayhoe, Professor, 207, 213
Hay-on-Wye, Powys, 262–8, 271–8
heart attack, 265–6
Hemingway, Ernest, 51–2, 147
Hemmings, David, 157–8
hepatitis, 60–1, 83
Herbert, Hon. David, 142
Heseltine, Philip, 190
Heywood, Ship's Cook, 15, 17
Hicks, David, 245
Hildegard, model, 104–5, 119
Hill, Heywood, 191
Hohenlohe-Langenburg, Prince Alfonse von, 125, 132, 144
Hohenlohe-Langenburg, Prince Max von, 1–2, 125
Holroyd, Michael, 191
Hönning-O'Carroll, Baron von, 200–1
Hope, Bob, 63, 103–4
hormone implants, 64
hormone injections, 53, 64
Hory, Elmyr de, 187, 188
hotel work, 32–3, 37–9, 47–9
Hoyer, Niels, 73
Hudson, Rock, 34
Hughes, Howard, 188, 239
Hull, Verna, 259–60
Human, 252–4
Hunter, Christopher, 199, 232, 244

Hurst, Brian Desmond, 114
Hutch, 190
Hutton, Barbara, 142

Ibiza, 185–9, 197, 262, 264
identity, sexual, 211–14, 218, 222, 241
Infantado, Duke of, 129–31; *see also* Arteaga y Martin, Inigo
Ingrid, model, 99
intersex, classification as, 75–6, 212–13, 218, 227–31
Irving, Clifford, 188
Italy, 69–72, 160–74
Ivy Restaurant, 189, 239

Jacaranda, nightclub, 122, 125, 126, 128, 129, 131, 133, 147, 149
Jackson, Joseph, 209–10, 216, 217, 226
Jackson, Ray, 49
Jagger, Mick, 177
Jamaica, 16–18, 22, 30
Jamieson, Ada (later Cartmel), 2–8, 9, 31, 34–5, 183–4, 193, 194, 208–9
Jamieson, Freddie (brother), 3, 4, 6, 31
Jamieson, Frederick (father), 3, 4, 5, 7, 9, 67, 193–4
Jamieson, Ivor, 3, 10, 34–5
Jamieson, Marjorie, 3, 209
Jamieson, Roddy, 3, 4, 6
Jamieson, Theresa, 3, 12, 193, 209
Japan, 248–9
Jeanne, nurse, 85, 88, 90
Jean-Pierre, barman, 236–7, 256–7
Jersey, 37–40, 47–9, 156
Jicky, 43–4, 45
Joey, 38–40, 47, 49, 55, 58–61, 64, 75, 91, 92, 97–8, 100, 156–7, 219, 259, 266
John, Augustus, 145, 190
Johns Hopkins Medical School, 227, 230
Johnson, Cecilia, 154–5, 160, 170, 174, 180, 184, 185, 195
Jones, Brian, 180, 240
Jones, Dr Howard Jnr, 227
Jones, Salena, 78
Jorgensen, Christine, 64, 73, 227
J. Rowland Sales Ltd, 35–6
Juan-les-Pins, 61–5, 93, 120
Juarez, Bianca, 134
Juarez, Greg, 134
Ju-Ju, 253, 257
Jullian, Philippe, 191
Juste, Mme de, 245–7

Kaleidoscope, coffee bar, 36
Kaplan, Alan, 232
Keeler, Christine, 144
Kelly, Margaret, 66
Kendall, Kay, 58
Kennedy, Elaine, 239
Kensington, Juanita, 196
Kimfull, Donald, 143
King, Viva, 108, 145, 153, 189–92, 201–3, 205, 240, 261, 266, 275–6
King, Willie, 190
King's Road, Chelsea, 175–6, 254
Kingston, Jamaica, 16–18, 22, 30
Kinross, Patrick, Lord, 191
Klinefelter's syndrome, 212, 213, 218
Kyle, Tommy, 243–4, 246, 247–8, 267–8

Laine, Cleo, 240
Lambert, Kit, 232, 239, 253
Lancet, 227–8
La Rue, Danny, 34, 240
Lasquin, M., 50, 56, 57, 68, 69
Laubscher, Harry, 66
Lawrence of Arabia, 134–5
Laye, Evelyn, 240
Lear, Amanda, 69, 70, 120, 178–80, 196, 241–2, 268
Lear, Edward, 183
Lebroque, Sandra, 66, 80, 87
Lee, Les, 50, 54, 58, 60, 61, 63, 80–1, 87, 88, 91, 92, 112–13, 250
legal definition of sex, 207, 210, 211–14, 226–7
Legros, Fernand, 187, 188
Lennon, John, 177, 221–2
lesbianism, 246–7
Lessard, Real, 187
Leven, Gustav, 244, 268
Lewis, Leonard, 209
Lewis, Richard, 185
Lewis, Rosa, 120
Liberace, 240
Lichfield, Patrick, Earl of, 176
Lindsay, Eric, 49, 50
Little Gloria, 29, 34, 41, 42, 46–7
Liverpool, 2–11, 27–32, 274
Lloyd, Jeremy, 175
Lloyd, Sue, 99
Lobo, painter, 171, 176

Locke, Evelyn, 126, 148
Lockwood, Julia ('Toots'), 63, 80, 87, 88, 90–2, 94–5, 96, 97, 98, 114, 122, 250
Lockwood, Margaret, 63, 91
London: early days in, 33–7, 41–7; 1960s, 175–85, 189–99; restaurant venture, 226, 236–44, 249–52, 256–60, 273
Long Beach, 18, 24–5
Lopez, Carol, 155, 162–3, 166, 174
Lopez, Pepe, 155, 162–3, 173, 174
Louise, transvestite, 114–15
Ludwig II, 199, 200
Lulu, 268
Lundy, Edna, 8–10, 11, 12, 27
Lundy, John, 8–10, 11, 12, 27
Lyon's Corner House, 33

McBey, Marguerite, 143
McCarty, Billy, 243
McClory, Kevin, 133–4, 140
McDermott, Brian, 140
Macdonald, Bo's'n, 13, 15, 21, 22, 23
McDowell, Roddy, 261
McGee, Hetty, 143
McKuen, Rod, 51
MacLaine, Shirley, 140, 167
MacNamara family, 178
MacNamara, Terry, 178, 242–3
Madok, Edward, 194, 196–9, 203–4, 208, 249, 251, 252, 267
Madok, Jack, 198–9, 251
Madok, Julia, 198, 251
Madrid, 123–4, 130, 131, 146, 147
Magnani, Anna, 71, 167
Majorca, 184
make-up, 234–5
Malta, 201–3
Mancini, Al, 155, 166
Marais, Jean, 66
Marbella, 122, 124–37, 144–5, 146–9
Marcel, M., 50, 53, 54, 55, 79, 92, 95, 122
Margaret, H.R.H. Princess, 178, 233–4
Marie, matron, 85, 89
marriage, 147–50, 151, 153, 183, 229
Marshall, Cherry, 98–9
Mason, Jessica, 159, 160, 161, 162
Massimo, 168–9, 174
Maugham, Robin, Viscount, 187–9, 194, 197, 198, 239, 249
Maugham, W. Somerset, 188, 194, 240
Medinaceli, Doña Maria, Duchess of, 131, 135
Meirs, Nicolette, 148
Melvin, Duncan, 35, 104, 107–8, 110, 134, 272
Menchu, 128, 133, 138–9
Mersey, River, 29–30
Messel, Oliver, 192, 259
Mexico City, World Congress of Sexology in, 1979, 230
Michael X, 163
Milan, 69–70, 71–2, 76, 168
Miles, Sarah, 102–3
Milford Haven, Marquess of, 104
Mills, Baudouin, 114
Mills, Professor Ivor, 207, 208, 213, 214, 216, 228
Minnelli, Liza, 193
Mirabelle, 110
Mishima, Yukio, 248
modelling, 98–105, 119, 121–2, 131, 146, 157
Moncreiffe of that Ilk, Sir Iain, 120
Monique, *see* Coccinelle
Montagu of Beaulieu, Lord and Lady, 104
Moon, Keith, 239
Moore, Bobby, 240
Moore, Pauline, 104, 119, 140–1
Morgan, Desmond ('Dizzy'), 232, 236–7, 259
Morocco, 80–92
Morris, Brian, 176
Mount, Connie, 108, 191, 192
Moustique, Kiki, 70, 71, 72, 79
Mullen, Allison, 237, 251
Mullen, Micky, 197, 237, 251–2
Mun, Comte de, 186
Munich, 199–200
Munro-Kerr, Simon, 146, 147
Myer, Dr Jon, 230

Naples, 72, 159–60
Nemon, Oscar, 195
Nevern Square, 41–7, 121
Newall, Martin, 189
Newman, Nanette, 252
News of the World, 136, 137, 175, 183
Newton, Robert, 239
New York Seaman's Mission, 25
Niccolo, gigolo, 159–60, 166–7

nightclubs, *see individual names*
Nina and Frederick, *see* van Pallandt
Norman, Frank, 108
Norris Green, Liverpool, 2, 7, 274
North, Hon. John, 186, 252
North, Hon. Wendy, 252
Northern Sporting Club, Manchester, 139
Novak, Kim, 176
Nureyev, Rudolf, 240, 244

Obolensky family, 200
O'Connor, Des, 137
oestrogen injections, 53, 75
office work, 35–6
Oliver, Vic, 94
Ono, Yoko, 221–2
operation, sex-change, *see* surgery
Ormrod, Sir Roger, 210, 214, 215, 227, 228, 231, 275
Ormsby-Gore, Hon. Jane, 176
Ormskirk Mental Hospital, 30–1, 127
Osborne, John, 104, 239
Osborne, Sir Peter, 154–5
Osborne, Tommy, 34
O'Toole, Peter, 134–6, 144–5
Oxford, 204–5, 219–20, 225–6, 264

Pacific Fortune, S.S., 12, 13–25
Pakenham, Katie, 205
Pallenberg, Anita, 176
Palmer, Sir Mark, 175
Pamplona, 147
Paper, Doris, 4
Paradi, Enrico, 70–1
Paris, 49–50, 51–61, 65–9, 78–80, 92–6
Parlade, Jamie, 126
parliare, 45–6
Parton, Terry, 263
passport problems, 76–7, 96
Patterson, Vincent, 6–7
Paul, Gloria, 80, 87
Paul, Sandra, 99–100
Peki d'Oslo, *see* Lear, Amanda
Pembroke, Henry, Earl of, 233
People, 121, 273
Pepe, caretaker, 125, 127, 150
Pepe, cook at AD8, 233, 237
Perón, Eva, 252
Perry, Captain, 15
Perth, Nancy, Countess of, 111
Petit, Mme, 61, 65, 80, 92
Pettifer, Julian, 163
Phillips, Sian, 144
Piaf, Edith, 63
Picasso, Pablo, 93, 241
Pitt Street, Liverpool, 2
Plugge, Captain Lenny, 163–4, 261
Plumley, Geoffrey, 197, 198, 208
Pollock, Ellen, 145, 158
Pomfret, Mr, 48
Pope-Hennessy, James, 191
Positano, 158–60
Pratt, Sandy, 186, 187
Pratt, Sue, 104, 140–2
prejudice, 121–2, 157, 216, 223, 224–5, 271–2
Presley, Elvis, 67
prison, in Rome, 172–3
Proby, P. J., 176
Proctor, Kim, 144
Profumo scandal, 144, 165
Proops, Marjorie, 115
Proudfoot, James, 145
psychiatric treatment, 30–2
psychological sex, 212, 213–14
Pugh, Bronwen, 99–100, 101
Purdom, Edmund, 177
Pussy, 43, 44, 48

Radbrook College, Shrewsbury, 268–70
Rainey, Michael, 108, 176
Rampling, Charlotte, 175
Randell, Dr John, 104, 208, 214, 216
Rango fashion shows, 131, 146
Raphael, Clive, 180–5
Reed, Oliver, 154
Renée, Ricky, 178–9
Renoir, Rita, 66
restaurant venture, 226, 232–3, 236–44, 249–52, 256–60, 273
Rhyl, 32
Rice-Davies, Mandy, 165
Richard, Cliff, 138
Rigg, Diana, 186
Road to Hong Kong, The, 102–4, 122
Robbins, Harold, 268
Robby, seaman, 14, 15, 18–19
Roberts, Dawn, 44, 47
Rogelia, housekeeper, 125, 127, 150
Rogers, Ginger, 58
Rolling Stones, the, 177
Rome, 160–74
Ronay, Edina, 158

Rose, Sir Francis, 241
Ross, Geoffrey Aquilina, 164, 168, 169
Rossiter, Mr, of Cunard, 11
Roter Models, 104–5, 119, 122
Roth, Sir Martin, 207, 208, 214, 229
Rowallan, Lord, 116, 117, 132, 147, 165–6
Roxy, 27–8, 29, 33, 46
Ruby, of Le Carrousel, 53
Rumbold, Felicity, Lady, 192

St Amant, Jill, 161
St Asaph, 32
St Bartholomew's Hospital, 40
St Hélier, Jersey, 37–40
St John's Market, 8–10, 27, 28, 32
St Stephen's Hospital, 257
St Theresa's Primary School, 5
St Tropez, 93, 245, 251, 268
Sambrook, Harvey, 196–7
San Francisco, 18–19, 261
San Pedro, California, 18, 22, 25
Santa Marinella, 167–8
Sartre, Jean-Paul, 52, 61
Schiaparelli, Elsa, 58
Schmidt, Klaus, 186, 199–200
schooldays, 5–8
Schroter, Mr, 104, 105
Schroter, Mrs, 104, 105, 122
Schwarz, George, 252
sea: cadet training, 11–12; life at, 13–25
Searle, Alan, 188–9
Seaside Memorial Hospital, Long Beach, 24
'Secret of the World, The', 248
Seville, 129, 130, 135, 146
sex, definition of, 207, 210, 211–14, 226–31
sex-change, *see* surgery
Seymour-Smith, Candy, 66
Sharif, Omar, 134–6, 144–5
Shaw, Sandie, 176
Shawfield St, Chelsea, 154, 178, 181, 185
Sheherazade, 42–3, 44, 47, 255
Shepherd, Ariane, 64, 250–1
Shepherd, Sam, 250–1
Sherman, Robert, 230
Shipley, Colin, 12, 13, 15, 17, 20, 22, 23
Shivarg, Joan, 175, 197, 199
Shivarg, Shura, 175, 199
Short, John Fulton, 135
Shrewsbury, 268–70
Shrimpton, Jean, 175
Signon, model agent, 99, 100, 101, 105, 121, 146
Sigrist, Bobo, 133–4
silicone injections, 53, 77, 78
Simmonds, Maggie, 100, 157
Simon Dee Show, 221–2
Simpson, Charles, 273–4, 277, 278
Sinclair, Major Teddy, 185–6
singing engagements, 137–40
Singleton, Tony, 158, 197
Sirikrit, of Thailand, Queen, 192
Sitwell, Guy, 221
Skinner, Sarah, 126
Skippy, 78, 81, 93–4, 95
slang, 45–6
snobbery, 216
Snowdon, Earl of, 108, 176, 189
Society, entering, 106–14, 180–1
Soho, 34
Sondes, Earl, 148
Spain, 122, 123–7, 144–5, 146–9
Spence, Ivor, 186
Stamp, Chris, 176, 252
Stamp, Terence, 176
Stein, Gertrude, 241
Stocker, Caroline, 145, 149, 272
Stocker, Michael, 145, 149
Stone, Colin, 265, 267
Stork Club, 109–10
Stork Hotel, Liverpool, 28, 32
Strachey, Rosemary, 126, 138
Strasbourg, Court of Human Rights at, 277
suicide attempts, 23–4, 29–30, 272–3
Sunday Mirror, 226, 232
surgery, 73, 77, 79–92, 153, 230
Sutherland, Graham, 195
Sybilla's, 176
Sykes, Christopher, 108
Sykes, Jeremy, 233

Tallulah, 44–6, 47–9
Tangier, 142–3
Tannock, Anne, 164, 170
Tannock, Bob, 164, 170
Tapp, Alain, *see* Lear, Amanda
Tarquin, M., 56, 57
Taylor, Gerry, 267
Taylor, Vera, 267

television, 231–2, 248; commercials, 101–2
Tennant, Hon. Catherine, 175
Tennant, Hon. David, 112
Tennant, Hon. Pauline, 112
Terman-Miles Test, 212, 213–14, 228
Terry-Thomas, 186
tests, medical, 207–8, 212, 213–14, 216, 227, 228
Teynham Crescent, Norris Green, 2, 21
Thomas, Noyes, 136, 144, 175
Thring, Joan ('Mrs Ting-a-Ling'), 244, 268
Thynne, Lord Christopher, 233
Thyssen, Baron Heinrich von, 100
Tokyo, 248–9
Tom, 93
'Toni April', 56, 76, 219
Tour, Baron de la, 159–60
Townend, Peter, 127–8, 133, 138–9, 141, 147
Tramp, nightclub, 193, 257
transsexualism, 73–6, 211, 213, 214, 217, 218, 221, 227–31
transvestism, 211
Tree, Iris, 191
Two Eyes coffee bar, 36
Tynan, Kenneth, 254–6

underwear, modelling, 101
United States, 18–19, 22–5

Vaillant, Dr, 31, 217
Valois, Lil, Marquise de, 246, 247
Vane-Tempest-Stewart, Lady Jane, 107, 108
van Pallandt, Baron Frederick, 187
van Pallandt, Baroness Nina, 187, 251
Vassall, William, 97
Vic, homosexual, 32, 34
Vindicatrix, S.S., 11–12
Vitti, Monica, 170–1
Vogue, 101, 233
voice, timbre of, 111–12

Waitrose, grocer's, 40
Wallace, Aubrey, 180, 181–2
Wallace, Dicky, 204
Wallace, Marcel, 59, 60–1, 62, 219
Wallace, Rita, 36, 38, 39, 55–6, 58–60, 62, 98, 218–19, 242, 253, 258–9, 261, 266, 276
Wallace, Rosemary, 179, 180, 181–2, 183
Walton Hospital, 31–2, 74, 83, 213, 217, 218
Walton, Terry, 206, 208, 209, 211, 214, 219, 226
Wantage, Billy, 166, 168
Warhol, Andy, 253
Warlock, Peter, 190
Warner, David, 186
Warren, Rex, 203
Webber-Douglas Academy of Dramatic Art, 145, 249, 251
Welles, Orson, 188
Wellington, Gerald, 7th Duke of, 191
Westgate Terrace, 33
White, Michael, 110
Who, the, 232, 252
Wigington, Pat, 267
Williams, Mrs, landlady, 269, 270
Willoughby, Lady Jane, 114, 143, 144
Willoughby de Eresby, Lord Timothy, 108–14, 117, 142–4, 155
Wilson, Sir Angus, 191
Winforton Court, 267
Winn, Lord Justice, 232
Wips, nightclub, 110, 155, 176
World of Paul Slickey, The, 104
Wright, Richard, 51
Wyndham, Violet, 191

Young, Della, 107, 121
Young Vic Theatre, 252

Zamoyski, Count Adam, 204, 205

ARENA

TEN YEARS IN AN OPEN NECKED SHIRT

John Cooper Clarke

'In a vain attempt at bourgeois credibility, Lenny changed his name to John Cooper Clarke and under this title embarked on a polysyllabic excursion through Thrillsville, UK. Yes, it was be there or be square as, clad in the slum chic of the hipster, he issued the slang anthems of the zip age in the desperate esperanto of the bop. John Cooper Clarke: the name behind the hairstyle, the words walk in the grooves hacking through the hi-fi paradise of true luxury...'

This is the collected poetry of John Cooper Clarke – rock poet, story-teller and humorist – and publication is planned to tie in with the Channel 4 series of the same name. The book is brilliantly illustrated by Steve Maguire.

ARENA

SACRED SUMMITS

Peter Boardman

This is the story of a year in the life of a climber: three expeditions, each very different from one another in mood and style, to sacred mountains around the world. Tragically, the last book that the brilliant young mountaineer Peter Boardman was to write, *Sacred Summits* is a dramatic and moving testament to one man's will not to conquer but to understand.

'Much more than a climbing book ... as much an adventure of romantic discovery as one of physical challenge'

CHRIS BONINGTON

'Poignant, vivid ... he gets closer to the strange mystique of mountaineering than many more pretentious writers' *Observer*

ARENA

BACK TO THE ROOTS

Richard Mabey and Francesca Greenoak

Have you resigned yourself to a world where all herbs look pretty much the same and come in glass bottles – or do you sometimes think that it would be nice to have your own herbal garden, if only you knew how to go about it?

Are you happy in a world with only a few standard varieties of vegetables and fruits – or do you wish the day of the Up-to-date Onion, the English Wonder Pea and the Soldier Bean would return?

Richard Mabey, author of FOOD FOR FREE, and Francesca Greenoak have written a unique guide to every type of domestic plant – from herbs and vegetables to flowers and trees – which will initiate even the most city-bred among us in the traditional skills, methods and benefits of British plantcraft.